"Focusing on what he calls 'the canonical John'—the Gospel, the three epistles, and Revelation—Reeves keys in on a major Johannine theme: abiding. What does it mean, or better yet, what does it *look like* to abide in Christ? With the skill of a storyteller and a sensitivity to the narrative and cultural dynamics of the text, Reeves unveils what an authentic Johannine discipleship might look like. An engaging and creative book!"

Christopher W. Skinner, professor of New Testament and early Christianity at Loyola University Chicago

"Studies about the writings of the apostle John have been abundant throughout church history. *Spirituality According to John* represents this extensive literature responsibly, sifts it, and then offers its best insights for practical use. The book's value lies in its easy accessibility, its insights, and its wisdom designed for students, teachers, and pastors. Reeves is doing exactly what John was doing for his own churches: bringing the deepest insights about Jesus into the church. *Spirituality According to John* succeeds in every respect."

Gary M. Burge, dean of the faculty and visiting professor of New Testament at Calvin Theological Seminary

"What might we gain by taking seriously the witness of all the Johannine literature— the Gospel, the epistles, and the Apocalypse? We gain a witness incapable of being bound by one genre. We receive symbols, metaphors, imagery, and stories that point beyond the text to a living Word that still inspires, still amazes, and still beckons us to follow. In this volume, Rodney Reeves captures our imaginations by pointing to the myriad of ways the Johannine literature invites us to rethink all we thought we knew about God and God's work in the world. 'Come and see.'"

Carla Swafford Works, professor of New Testament at Wesley Theological Seminary, Washington, DC

"The Gospel of John traps us. We open it, we read it, we get lost in it; we learn its vocabulary and themes and movements and sudden bursts of claims; we meet characters we've never met before, and we hear conversations up close and personal, and we get lost in this Gospel's time and place—and we are trapped. In a good way. Never to be the same again. When we look up from this Gospel's pages to see the world around us, it's a little like the Pevensie children finding themselves again in the wardrobe, tumbling back on the floor of reality. As they wanted to return to Narnia, so we want to return to John's world. He first trapped me in 1974, and I've not been the same since. Rodney Reeves leads us to the door of the wardrobe, he opens the door, and he guides us long enough to get lost in the Gospel itself. What a wonderful book!"

Scot McKnight, professor of New Testament at Northern Seminary

"John shows how imperfect disciples like Peter can still follow Jesus. Although Peter doesn't become a 'rock' during John's Gospel, Reeves shows how John expects his readers to know that Peter eventually does. John's Jesus fires our imagination by inviting us to 'come and see' where he is going and what he is up to. Although well conversant in the scholarly discussions on John, Reeves is a deft guide through the tricky landscape of Johannine scholarship. Like his mentor John, Reeves teaches through metaphors, images, and stories, leading us down a delightful path toward discipleship. An easy-reading but thoughtful romp through John's writings. Come and see."

E. Randolph Richards, provost and chief academic officer at Palm Beach Atlantic University

"Combining solid scholarship, on-point personal reminiscence, and an informed literary imagination, Rodney Reeves offers a beautiful and exciting reading of the Johannine books for our moment in time. He reads John's stories through ours, and ours through John's, in his own prophetic voice. I want all my students to read this book."

Leslie Baynes, associate professor of New Testament and Second Temple Judaism at Missouri State University

"*Spirituality According to John* is an invitation to dwell with Christ—a life of faith moved by storytelling that imagines and reimagines lived experiences of God in community rather than by privatized systematic regurgitations of theologically correct abstract doctrines. Dr. Rodney Reeves offers theologically and socially engaged ministers and laypersons invaluable insights into Johannine spirituality foregrounded in the multivalent locution: 'abide.' It enshrines a Christian journey of faith that manifests itself in terms of seeing and believing, confessing sin, denying worldliness, keeping commandments, exercising mutual love, worshiping, and learning to hear Christ in Johannine words. This is an exceptional resource for spiritual formation that clergy, seminarians, and lay ministers will find indispensable for Christian ubuntu."

Aliou Cissé Niang, associate professor of New Testament at Union Theological Seminary

"The prologue to the fourth Gospel declares that the preexistent, incarnate Word is life and light, grace and truth. In *Spirituality According to John*, New Testament scholar, seasoned pastor, and skilled communicator Rodney Reeves probes the Gospel, letters, and Apocalypse of John to help Christ followers know better how to hear, confess, incarnate, and abide in the glorious Word and Son of God. Those who (would) long to follow, commune, and remain in the Word would be wise and would do well to read and reflect on Reeves's valuable volume. This is a rich resource for those who are willing to ponder and to practice the abundant life Jesus lived and gives."

Todd D. Still, Charles J. and Eleanor McLerran DeLancey Dean and William M. Hinson Professor of Christian Scriptures at Truett Seminary, Baylor University

SPIRITUALITY
According to JOHN

Abiding in Christ
in the Johannine Writings

RODNEY REEVES

Academic
An imprint of InterVarsity Press
Downers Grove, Illinois

InterVarsity Press
P.O. Box 1400, Downers Grove, IL 60515-1426
ivpress.com
email@ivpress.com

*InterVarsity Press® is the book-publishing division of InterVarsity Christian Fellowship/USA®, a movement of
students and faculty active on campus at hundreds of universities, colleges, and schools of nursing in the United
States of America, and a member movement of the International Fellowship of Evangelical Students. For
information about local and regional activities, visit intervarsity.org.*

All Scripture quotations, unless otherwise indicated, are the author's translation.

Cover design and image composite: Cindy Kiple
Interior design: Daniel van Loon
Images: pottery jug: © Nehru Sulejmanovski / EyeEm / Getty Images
   blue water splash: © proxyminder / E+ / Getty Images

ISBN 978-0-8308-5348-9 (print)
ISBN 978-0-8308-5349-6 (digital)

Printed in the United States of America ⊗

*InterVarsity Press is committed to ecological stewardship and to the conservation of natural resources in all our
operations. This book was printed using sustainably sourced paper.*

Library of Congress Cataloging-in-Publication Data
Names: Reeves, Rodney, 1957- author.
Title: Spirituality according to John : abiding in Christ in the Johannine writings / Rodney Reeves.
Description: Downers Grove, IL : IVP Academic, [2021] | Includes bibliographical references and index.
*Identifiers: LCCN 2021030786 (print) | LCCN 2021030787 (ebook) | ISBN 9780830853489 (paperback) |
   ISBN 9780830853496 (ebook)*
*Subjects: LCSH: Bible. John—Criticism, interpretation, etc. | Bible.
   Epistles of John—Criticism, interpretation, etc. | Bible.
   Revelation—Criticism, interpretation, etc. | Spirituality—Biblical
   teaching. | Word (Theology)*
Classification: LCC BS2601 .R44 2021 (print) | LCC BS2601 (ebook) | DDC 226.5/06--dc23
LC record available at https://lccn.loc.gov/2021030786
LC ebook record available at https://lccn.loc.gov/2021030787

P	23	22	21	20	19	18	17	16	15	14	13	12	11	10	9	8	7	6	5	4	3	2	1
Y	41	40	39	38	37	36	35	34	33	32	31	30	29	28	27	26	25	24	23	22	21		

For my wife, Sheri,

Who embodies every day the first verse I memorized as a child:

"Beloved, let us love one another, for love is from God"

CONTENTS

ACKNOWLEDGMENTS

First, I'd like to thank Dan Reid for not only reading the first draft and making several very helpful suggestions but also encouraging this project from the beginning. After *Spirituality According to Paul* was published, Dan wondered whether I had thought about working on a follow-up volume. Even though I've spent more time in Paul's letters, considering the spirituality of canonical John—seeing how story, prose, and apocalyptic literature affect our spiritual formation—was especially intriguing to me. Even though there are significant scholarly debates about the authorship of these works, I decided to take a canonical approach to John's spirituality, since most Christians read them as a Johannine corpus.

Second, although it is apparent how much I have relied on Johannine scholarship, I wanted to mention a few works that have had a huge impact on me. The influence of these scholarly works cannot be overstated, especially for my spiritual development. That may sound foreign to some—that academic works could be so determinative for my faith. But these scholars have helped me (and thousands of others) read the Scriptures well. Alan Culpepper's seminal work *Anatomy of the Fourth Gospel* opened up the literary design and beauty of John's narrative world, inspiring me to teach, preach, and hopefully embody what I see in the Gospel according to John. Raymond Brown's magnificent commentary on the Johannine epistles continues to be a feast for my soul. And, although there are many, many scholarly works on the Apocalypse that have helped me try to sort out the strange world of the Revelation of

John, three books made the last book of the New Testament seem more like home: Leonard Thompson's *The Book of Revelation: Apocalypse and Empire*, Richard Bauckham's *The Theology of the Book of Revelation*, and David deSilva's *Seeing Things John's Way*. When visiting a foreign land, it's always good to have such reliable guides.

Third, thanks to Anna Gissing for her help in bringing this manuscript to publication when a worldwide pandemic brought challenges and delays that frustrated us all. During the uncertainty of those days, the frightening world of John's Apocalypse was strangely reassuring.

Finally, thanks to Katya Covrett for letting me tell part of her redemption story. In the resurrection, I imagine we'll all gather around to hear the story of our lives—how Christ redeemed every single one of us for his glory. Since we all love hearing good news, it will take an eternity to take in the fullness of the gospel, a binge-worthy series that will keep us on the edge of our seats, always wanting to hear more about *him*.

INTRODUCTION

The Art of Christian Living

THERE ARE TWO KINDS OF CHRISTIANS: list makers and story-tellers. Answering one question reveals the difference: "What does it take to be a Christian?" List makers will talk about doctrines you must believe or commandments you must keep. As long as you believe the right things or do the right things, that's what makes you a Christian. Storytellers, on the other hand, will say: "Let me tell you about my grandmother. . . ." That's when I lean in, because I find the art of Christian living far more compelling than a theological argument. It didn't used to be that way, though. When I was a young man, I relished the opportunity to jump into the middle of doctrinal scrums over Christian beliefs. But these days, I'd rather hear about an embodied faith—a story that must be imagined to be believed.

It takes a lot of imagination to be a Christian, which explains why I've been imagining things for over fifty years. What Jesus looked like. What will happen when I die. What kind of disciple I would have been in Jesus' day. What heaven will be like. What it would feel like to see a miracle, to experience true love in the church, to witness the return of Christ. I used to think daydreaming about all these things was foolish, a waste of time. That I should concentrate more on what we're certain about, refining my doctrinal beliefs, nailing down my doubts. But for several years now, I've come to realize how much I have relied on my imagination for spiritual formation. The more I think about Christ—especially when I read the Gospels—the more I imagine what it means to be his disciple. And that's what the Scriptures are supposed to do: fire our imaginations. In fact, we can't read the Bible without creating an imaginary world in our heads, reading between the lines of words printed on a page. The literary artistry of the gospel writers compels us to envision not only what life was like back then but also what life could be like today. That's when I recall the stories I've heard about faithful grandmothers and godly grandfathers, connecting the dots between life in the Gospel and a gospel life, freely exploring the artistry of the Christian life—a faith that has to be imagined to be lived.

More than any New Testament writer, John counted on the imagination of his readers, taking an artistic approach to Christian spirituality.[1] Rather than telling his readers exactly what disciples are supposed to do, John relies heavily on their imaginations to help them see what it takes to *become* disciples of Jesus Christ. In John's Gospel, Jesus doesn't give specific instructions on how to follow him (sell your possessions, turn the other cheek, deny yourself). Instead, he uses metaphors to inspire followers to abide in him ("I am the vine, you are the branches," Jn 15:5).[2] Although Paul's letters are filled with specific instructions (do this, don't do that), John reminds his people that abiding in Christ means to "walk as that man walked" (1 Jn 2:6), leaving it to them to sort out the details of what it means to love one another. In his letters, Peter gives several reasons why believers have to suffer persecution. But John relies on visions of heaven coming to earth to encourage believers to "follow the Lamb wherever he goes" (Rev 14:4), sacrificing their lives for the kingdom come. For John, being a Christian is all about abiding in words.[3] That's why the Gospel of John, 1 John, and the Apocalypse—three completely different kinds of literature—begin with references to the importance of the word, both the Word incarnate and written words (Jn 1:1; 1 Jn 1:1; Rev 1:2-3). Indeed, John is the only New Testament author to rely on more than one genre to help believers imagine what it looks like to abide in Christ.

---

[1]The Johannine authorship of the Gospel, letters, and Revelation is highly debated among scholars. But, for the purposes of this study, I'm referring to "canonical John," seeing how the works attributed to him function as a resource for spiritual formation.

[2]Unless indicated otherwise, all translations of the Scriptures are mine.

[3]"Abide" (*menō*) is one of John's favorite words, appearing more than sixty times in the Johannine literature.

Matthew relied exclusively on narrative; we have no letters from him. Paul wrote only letters; evidently he didn't feel the need to write a Gospel (some might say, "Paul didn't know the historical Jesus. How could he write a Gospel?" But that didn't stop Luke). John, however, relied on three different genres to help his people abide in the words of Christ the Word. So, why did he do it? You would think his Gospel should have been enough: What better way to learn how to abide in the words of Christ than to hear the Gospel according to John? For, according to the Word, we abide in Christ when his words abide in us (Jn 15:7). So, when John's people gathered to listen to words of the Word—words written on paper, read by a literate member, heard by illiterate people, treasured by the faithful—what more would they need to abide in Christ? Evidently a lot more; not only three letters and the Apocalypse, they also needed a Gospel with more than red letters. For John's Gospel is a story about what the Word said *and did*. The Gospel isn't about just words spoken but words incarnated—a crucial distinction John makes from the very beginning (Jn 1:1, 14).

According to his stated purpose, John tells the whole story of Jesus Christ—both words and deeds—so that we might "see and believe" in him and have eternal life (Jn 20:30-31). But is that all there is to abiding in Christ? That would mean John's Gospel was written only for nonbelievers, and once it had its desired effect—converting nonbelievers—there would be no reason to keep hearing it. But we know that can't be true because of the Farewell Discourse (Jn 13:31–17:26), where Jesus prepares the Twelve for his departure—what they're supposed to do after he's gone. In other words, it's quite apparent John wrote his Gospel for believers as well as nonbelievers. John's Gospel shows us not only how "the Word became flesh and dwelt among us" but also how his words are fleshed out in his disciples. And yet, that doesn't happen in John's Gospel. We never get to see the words of Christ abide in the twelve disciples; they don't "bear much fruit" or "bear witness" of Christ or become "outcasts from the synagogue" or even keep the new commandment to "love one another as I have loved you" (Jn 13:34; 15:5, 27; 16:2). So, if John's Gospel was written to teach readers how to abide in the Word, but the twelve disciples don't show us what that looks like, how are we supposed to know what it means to abide in the Word? Are there other models of discipleship in the Gospel according to John?

Most of Jesus' interactions with people in John's Gospel are one-on-one conversations. Jesus doesn't "make disciples" like he does in Matthew's Gospel, where he climbs a mountain and delivers a sermon on discipleship to the masses, calling on them to "enter the narrow gate" and follow him. In John's Gospel, R. Alan Culpepper notices that "entry into the kingdom is individual, not corporate."[4] Furthermore, in John's Gospel Jesus never chooses twelve disciples from a crowd of people who have been following him. Rather than develop an ensemble cast of characters, John shows how different individuals responded to Jesus. No two characters are alike; they seem to come from every walk of life: from an anonymous Samaritan woman to a ruling Pharisee named Nicodemus.[5]

Scholars puzzle over why John featured all of these different kinds of people when telling the story of Christ. Does each character represent the wide spectrum of possible responses to Jesus, perhaps even functioning as a representative of a certain group of people in John's day?[6] Or do they simply serve the plot of the narrative, conversation partners whom John used to reveal the true identity of Jesus?[7] In other words, do the different characters in John's Gospel function as mirrors, simply reflecting who Jesus is? Or do some of these characters serve as windows on discipleship, helping us see what it looks like to abide in Christ? Does the Samaritan woman help reveal who Jesus is or who we're supposed to be?

It takes a lot of imagination for a writer to create a story and a reader to enjoy it. As is commonly known, writers rely on two devices to help

---

[4]R. Alan Culpepper, "Nicodemus: The Travail of New Birth," in *Character Studies in the Fourth Gospel: Narrative Approaches to Seventy Figures in John*, ed. Steven A. Hunt, D. Francois Tolmie, and Ruben Zimmerman (Tübingen: Mohr Siebeck, 2013), 255.

[5]Craig R. Koester, *Symbolism in the Fourth Gospel: Meaning, Mystery, Community*, 2nd ed. (Minneapolis: Augsburg Books, 2003), 35.

[6]Koester, *Symbolism in the Fourth Gospel*, 33.

[7]Hunt, Tolmie, and Zimmerman distinguish four approaches: characters as artifacts (historical), as fiction (rhetorical), as symbols (representative), and as symptoms (illocutionary; see *Character Studies*, 8).

readers follow their story: showing and telling. Showing invites the reader to discover the narrative plot on their own, puzzling over bits of information that help them weave the fabric of the point of the story. Sometimes readers need help making sense of the narrative world (Why did he do that? Where does she come from? How does that fit into the story?), so there are moments when either the narrator or one of the characters of the story tells the reader what's going on. Striking the balance is up to the writer. Does the writer prefer showing over telling, relying on the imagination of the reader to see what can only be inferred by puzzling over the story? Or does the writer take a more direct approach, offering lengthy discourses that explain specifically why this or that happened? So, regarding the Fourth Gospel, we can't help but wonder: Does John prefer showing or telling, especially when it comes to discipleship? That is to say, do we learn more about how to abide in Christ by reading the discourses in John's Gospel (telling) or by reflecting on different characters as they encounter Jesus (showing)?

To be sure, we can mine the didactic sections of John's Gospel for gold nuggets when Jesus tells his disciples what they are supposed to do: keep the new love commandment, bear witness of Christ, ask the Father for anything, find peace in the midst of persecution, and be "perfected in unity" (Jn 13:34; 15:27; 16:23, 33; 17:18, 21).[8] Plus, there are two times in John's Gospel when Jesus explains how his disciples are supposed to model his behavior (showing and telling): the lengthy episode of washing their feet (Jn 13:1-17) and the brief commissioning of the eleven disciples, "As the Father has sent me, I also send you" (Jn 20:21). And yet, other than the footwashing example, these teachings don't leap out at the reader. They are buried in the lengthy Farewell Discourse, when Jesus is more concerned about preparing his disciples for his brief absence (Jn 16:16-22) than giving directives for future disciples. Consequently, scholars pore over the entire Gospel looking for other teachings on discipleship, either seeing how Jesus' words sprinkled throughout the narrative can be

---

[8]Craig R. Koester, *The Word of Life: A Theology of John's Gospel* (Grand Rapids, MI: Eerdmans, 2008), 188-96.

synthesized into a set of instructions on genuine discipleship (telling) or considering how John expects his readers to mimic Jesus as the model of discipleship (showing).[9]

If Jesus is supposed to be *our* model of discipleship, why don't we see the twelve disciples imitate Jesus in John's Gospel? That's what happens in the Synoptic Gospels. Like Jesus, the Twelve cast out demons (Lk 10:17). Like Jesus, they travel to villages to preach the gospel (Mt 10:5-8). Like Jesus, the disciples perform miracles (Mt 10:1). In Matthew, Mark, and Luke we see how Jesus turned men into disciples, actually doing what Jesus claimed for his disciples in John's Gospel: "The one who believes in me will do the works that I do" (Jn 14:12). But that's not what happens in John's Gospel.[10] The only one who performs signs is Jesus. There are no exorcisms in the Fourth Gospel. And the only time the disciples left Jesus was to buy food (Jn 4:8). The only thing the Twelve actually do is abide with Jesus, going wherever he goes. But we never see the words of Christ abide in them. Since abiding is the essence of Johannine discipleship, you would think John would *show* us what that looks like.[11] Perhaps he does. We get to see how Jesus' words abide in several characters in John's Gospel who have responded to the quintessential invitation to becoming a disciple: "Come and you will see" (Jn 1:39).

Since none of the characters in John's Gospel fully embody the words of Christ—they are "imperfect believers," according to Susan Hylen—they don't function individually as models of discipleship.[12] We are not

---

[9]Cornelis Bennema, *Encountering Jesus: Character Studies in the Gospel of John*, 2nd ed. (Minneapolis: Fortress, 2014), 83-114. According to Michael J. Gorman, "missional discipleship" involves hearing, seeing, perceiving, knowing, remembering, believing, following, abiding, and bearing witness. See Gorman, *Abide and Go: Missional Theosis in the Gospel of John* (Eugene, OR: Cascade Books, 2018), 78-79.

[10]Since the disciples' "greater works" lie outside the narrative, the Twelve function as an "eschatological character," according to Jerome H. Neyrey, *The Gospel of John*, New Cambridge Bible Commentary (Cambridge: Cambridge University Press, 2006), 72-73.

[11]Rekha M. Chennattu writes, "Abiding in the word of Jesus that perfects the Mosaic law is the hallmark of Johannine discipleship: 'If you abide (*meinate*) in my word, you will truly be my disciples' (8:31)." See Chennattu, *Johannine Discipleship as Covenant Relationship* (Peabody, MA: Hendrickson, 2006), 113.

[12]Susan E. Hylen, *Imperfect Believers: Ambiguous Characters in the Gospel of John* (Louisville, KY: Westminster John Knox, 2009).

led to believe, for example, that the Samaritan woman or the man born blind shows us everything a disciple is supposed to be. Rather, they represent the full spectrum of different responses to Jesus.[13] More than that, together they reveal what it takes to be a disciple of Jesus—a story that begins with hearing the Word, then confessing the Word, incarnating the Word, and finally abiding in the Word. John's Gospel shows us what it looks like to abide in Christ individually.

Because of the different ways these characters respond to Jesus, we see that it takes all kinds of people to follow Christ—a collection of imperfect believers who abide in Christ. That may come as surprise given the dualism of John's Gospel. In the binary world of John's narrative (light versus darkness, truth versus deceit, life versus death, love versus hate), we might expect to find ideal disciples versus false disciples. But that's not what happens in John's story; not even the "beloved one" is an ideal disciple (he never confesses that Jesus is the Christ, the Son of God, per Jn 20:31). Rather, after hearing the story of the Fourth Gospel—seeing how the word of Christ abides in all of these different characters—John expects hearers to become disciples of Jesus as the word of the Gospel abides in them. Edward Klink writes,

> In this gospel, the characters in the gospel become the first of a kind of audience, both receiving and passing along a witness that started with the original disciples. That is, the implied reader of John becomes a real reader in that the implied reader can be used as a functional category for a "mode of reading," through which the gospel itself explains and constructs the kind of reader it not only assumes but also desires. John uses his audience like a character in the narrative who, after receiving this text-based witness, is beckoned to respond in faith.[14]

We can't help but identify with different characters in John's Gospel, wanting to be a bold witness like the Samaritan woman or a faithful

---

[13]Koester, *Symbolism in the Fourth Gospel*, 33; Richard Bauckham, *Gospel of Glory: Major Themes in Johannine Theology* (Grand Rapids, MI: Baker Academic, 2015), 16-17.
[14]Edward W. Klink III, "Audience," in *How John Works: Storytelling in the Fourth Gospel*, ed. Douglas Estes and Ruth Sheridan (Atlanta: SBL Press, 2016), 256.

follower like the beloved disciple. Consequently, anyone who has ears to hear the Gospel of John can imagine what it looks like to be a disciple of Jesus, then and now.

That's what John expected, that believers would gather together to hear his Gospel read to them (1 Jn 1:1-4). Yet, even that wouldn't happen unless members depended on each other: illiterate members can't hear unless literate members read. But some in John's churches decided they would be better off without John or the rest of the members. They *left* the church, thinking they could still be disciples of Jesus. So John sent letters to his people to teach them that disciples must abide in the word *together* as a community of faith. John knew we couldn't be disciples by ourselves. Believers need a fellowship—holding on to what we have in common—with John and with one another in order to have fellowship with the Father and the Son. According to John, you can't be a Christian without the church. That's why his letters emphasize the corporate reality of our discipleship. Those who remain in the fellowship, walking in the light of John's Gospel, confess their sins (1 Jn 1:5-10). Those who confess the truth—about themselves and about Jesus Christ—refuse to "go out into the world" (1 Jn 2:15-19). Members know that keeping the new commandment, "loving one another," can only happen in community (1 Jn 3:23-24). That's when the love of God is perfected in us (1 Jn 4:7-12): "By this we know that we abide in him and he in us" (1 Jn 4:13). It takes a church to love one another like Christ.

James Resseguie claims, "John generally prefers to show rather than tell."[15] That is especially evident when we read the Apocalypse—a book that requires a lot of imagination to see what it means to abide in Christ at the end of the world. Today, many of us are put off by the strange world of the Revelation, leaving it to television preachers to interpret the message. But John counted on worshipers gathering on the Lord's Day to hear the word in order to see the kingdom of God coming to earth. It may look like evil empires are running the place. But John pulls back the veil and shows us what's really happening behind the scenes—a vision that

---

[15]James L. Resseguie, *The Revelation of John: A Narrative Commentary* (Grand Rapids, MI: Baker Academic, 2009), 39.

can only be seen when we worship God. For every time the church gathers to worship our King, we deny the idolatrous rulers of the world. We can see their pretentious claims to power, acting like they deserve our loyalty and devotion. But we know better. God reigns. And the way he rules the world now is through the sacrifice of the slaughtered Lamb. Since we've been purchased as slaves of the Lamb by his blood, we follow the Lamb wherever he goes by offering ourselves in worshipful devotion to him. Indeed, worship is an act of war in the Revelation of John; our weapon against the fallen powers of this world is the sacrifice of our lives. We know Satan has been cast out of heaven, exiled on earth, trying to muck up the place that God has made, inciting the world to hate us. But John would have us envision the day when God will say, "It is done." Babylon will fall. Christ will defeat his enemies with his word. The evil one and all of his minions will be destroyed. Heaven will come to earth. We will live together with him forever—a vision that must be heard to be seen.

This is what John would have us see. The purpose of the church is to bear witness to Christ. Only those who abide in the Word reveal the light of Christ. There is no other testimony to the truth. In fact, John's evangelistic strategy is based on the singularity of the Word incarnated in the church: for children of the light will be drawn to the light, and children of darkness will be repelled by the light. The disciples' witness to Christ as the Lamb of God—a living sacrifice—is embodied in the church. As a result, since we follow the Lamb wherever he goes, giving our lives for Christ as he gave his life for us, disciples bear witness to two things at once: the world is passing away, and we have eternal life. Therefore, we are the final revelation of the end of the world in Christ. Once Christ returns and heaven invades the earth, it will be all over. Until then, we need ears to hear the Gospel, the letters, and the Revelation of John in order to see how the kingdom of God comes to earth: when his word abides in us, we abide in Christ the Word.

For John, abiding in words is the art of Christian living. So it takes a lot of imagination to follow Christ.

Come and you will see.

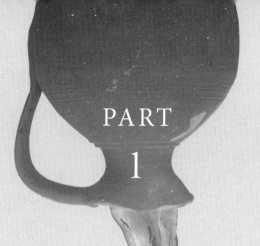

PART

1

JOHN'S GOSPEL

Following the Word Home

THE GREEK WORD FOR "ABIDE" (*menō*) refers to both a place and an attitude: to stay at home and to be at home. To abide with someone means you are staying with them, taking up residence with them, moving into their home. But to abide with someone can also mean that you're remaining with them, going wherever they go, finding a home with them. So, to abide means to live somewhere. But it also means to persist, to keep going, to remain, to last. When we say, "I can't abide by that," we're doing more than claiming we don't agree on some theoretical issue. We're saying, "That doesn't sit well with me," meaning that something personal is at stake—that there is an embodied reality to what we find objectionable.

Abide serves John's incarnational spirituality very well. He tells the story of how disciples abide with Jesus—going wherever he goes—but also how his Word abides in us—taking up residence in our lives. To abide in Christ means not only to stay with him no matter what (persistence), but also to find shelter in his words (home). Indeed, to remain in the Word is to live by words: heard, confessed, incarnated, and abided. The Word has come to prepare a room for his disciples in his father's house, teaching us how to abide in the Word, who is our way home (Jn 14:1-6). This is the Gospel story of John's spirituality.

1

COME AND SEE

Hearing the Word

IMAGINE THAT. It all started with a few simple words. A question, a request, and an invitation (Jn 1:38-39):

"What are you looking for?"
"Rabbi, where do you abide?"
"Come and you will see."

When we consider Jesus' encounter with these, his first disciples, we often skip over his question and rush straight to their request and his invitation—partly because we hear poetry in their words, a timeless appeal. Like the disciples, we want to know where Jesus abides so that we can be with him. This is because, no matter what happens in our lives— even if it gets really bad, as hard as carrying a cross—all we need to know is that he's with us. Jesus' invitation still rings true for us today. When he says, "Come and you will see," it sounds as if he is speaking to us too. Those who follow him have learned that, if we come to him, we will see *everything* . . . him, our world, ourselves, God. The rhythm of the disciples' request and his invitation strikes a chord with us, encouraging us to hear their conversation as if it were a paradigm for *our* discipleship:[1]

"Lord, where are you?"
"Follow me and you will see."

---

[1]"Come and see" is the beginning of discipleship. See Richard Bauckham, *Gospel of Glory: Major Themes in Johannine Theology* (Grand Rapids, MI: Baker Academic, 2015), 147.

But that's not how it began, with the disciples' query and Jesus' open-ended appeal. Rather, their first encounter started with Jesus asking *them* a question—one I think needs to be asked today, even of those who follow him: "What are you looking for?" When it comes to following Jesus, many of us are looking for many different things—hero, friend, personal assistant, teacher—just like the first disciples.

Notice that Jesus asks the question of those who have already begun to follow him (Jn 1:37). They are following Jesus because their mentor, John the Baptizer, pointed him out as the "Lamb of God who takes away the sin of the world" (Jn 1:29, 36). John told them he had seen the Spirit of God light on Jesus like a dove. As far as the "water-Baptizer" was concerned, that made Jesus the "Son of God," because he was empowered to be the "Spirit-Baptizer" (Jn 1:30-34)—one can only give what has been given. After John points out Jesus a second time to his disciples, Andrew and an unnamed disciple start to follow Jesus, which causes the Nazarene to take notice of them (Jn 1:38). That must have been an awkward moment. All of the sudden two men are following Jesus, causing him to stop, turn around, and *stare* at them (how long? We don't know).[2] Obviously, this was the first time anyone had shown this kind of interest in him. Then, eventually breaking the silence, Jesus asks them: "What are you looking for?"—a question he never asks again of any other follower in John's Gospel.

Now, what they should have said in light of the common Jewish hope for national restoration was "The Messiah"—especially since the Baptizer had indicated as much. John's ministry had been so successful, exciting messianic hopes among the people, that leaders from Jerusalem had sent an envoy to the desert to check out the latest fad and report back: "Who do you think you are? Elijah? *The* Prophet?" (Jn 1:19-22). According to Jewish historian Josephus, John and Jesus weren't the first holy men to show up in Israel and excite messianic hopes—and they wouldn't be the last.[3] But John makes it clear he isn't the Messiah (Jn 1:20). Furthermore,

---

[2]*Stare* is from the Greek verb *theaomai* (the English word *theater* derives from the noun).
[3]Josephus, *Antiquities of the Jews* 17.10.4-10; 18.1.1; 18.5.2; 20.5.1.

he denies that he is the reincarnation of the two great prophets Israel expected to show up just before the end of the world—neither Moses (Deut 18:18) nor Elijah (Mal 4:5-6). He is just a voice crying in the desert, trying to prepare Israel for the day God will visit his people, just as Isaiah predicted (Is 40:3; Jn 1:22-23).

When the man whom the Baptizer calls the Son of God asks these two former disciples of John, "What are you looking for?" they should have impulsively replied, "You! We've been looking for you! Aren't you the Messiah, the long-awaited hope of Israel's deliverance?" But that's not what they say (even though they *were* looking for him, Jn 1:41). Rather, somewhat surprisingly, Andrew and the anonymous disciple simply want to know where Jesus is staying, which makes me wonder what Jesus was doing there in the first place.

SIMON, THE CONVERT

John had been baptizing in Bethany "beyond the Jordan" (obviously not the same village where Lazarus, Martha, and Mary lived, Jn 11:1), which means Jesus had traveled some distance from Nazareth to be baptized by John (Jn 1:45). Evidently, after his baptism, Jesus had decided to remain in the area for quite a while—John describes the baptism of Jesus as something that happened several days before (Jn 1:29-34). So, why didn't Jesus return home to Nazareth after his baptism? Why did he hang around the crowd surrounding John? Was he simply taking in the spectacle, relishing the sight of such a huge crowd of Jews submitting to John's baptism? Or was Jesus hoping to find his first disciples there? Certainly, those who repented of their sin, looking for the justice of God's kingdom, would be ideal candidates for his ministry. But, as John's Gospel is careful to point out, Jesus doesn't "find" his very first disciples. Rather, they find him, encouraged by the Baptizer to "Behold the Lamb of God" (Jn 1:36). It is John's witness and their desire to abide with Jesus that gets the whole thing started. After they remain with Jesus that first night (where was Jesus staying in Bethany beyond the Jordan? A friend's house? In the open air? We don't know), the dominoes of Jesus' messianic mission started falling. First, they find other disciples (Jn 1:40-42); then Jesus does the same (Jn 1:43-51).

It doesn't take much for Andrew to become a disciple of Jesus. The Baptizer's witness coupled with "abiding" with Jesus for one night convinces Andrew: "We have found the Messiah" (Jn 1:41). That's what he tells his brother, Simon, who must be part of the crowd in Bethany since Andrew is able to lead him directly to Jesus (Jn 1:42). He offers no explanation, makes no arguments. Andrew simply claims that Jesus is the Messiah, and that is enough for Peter to "come and see." Simon doesn't hear anything more and doesn't say anything at all. All he does is walk up to the "new Messiah" only to hear Jesus say, "You will be called 'Cephas' [the Aramaic word for 'rock']," which is translated "Peter" [the Greek word for "rock"]). That's it. No persuasion. No confession. No problem.

It may have taken Andrew a day and a night to become Jesus' disciple. It only takes Simon Peter a brief moment, one encounter with Jesus, and he is "converted." Or is he? That's the assumption we make, because we know how the story ends. Just as Jesus predicted, Simon became known by his nickname, Peter—a rock-steady disciple who led the early church. But we also know that Simon didn't become Peter overnight. Indeed, it could be said that while it took Andrew only three verses to become a disciple of Jesus, Simon's conversion required twenty-two chapters.[4]

I used to assume that Simon became a disciple the very moment Jesus changed his name. Now I'm not so sure. First, Simon doesn't say a thing, which seems odd compared to the others. The Baptizer says the right things about Jesus. Andrew, Philip, and Nathaniel say the right things about Jesus. Simon never says a word. Peter makes no confession of faith like the others. His silence, therefore, is conspicuous to me. It's not that I question Jesus' prophecy. Throughout John's Gospel, the narrator refers to Simon as Peter. But *Jesus* never calls him Peter. Why? Maybe it's because Simon never seems to live up to his nickname—at least in a positive way. Indeed, when it comes to following Jesus in John's narrative

---

[4]Of course, John's Gospel has only twenty-one chapters. And so, I'm pointing to the end of Peter's story (Jn 21:18)—which happens long after the last verse of John's Gospel.

world, Peter seems to be more hardheaded and hardhearted than rock solid. Even though Simon was one of the first followers to come and see Jesus, it seems to have taken Peter a much longer time to *hear* the word.

And yet, eventually Simon says the right thing. In fact, it's the only time in John's Gospel where Peter comes off looking good (Jn 6:66-69). Of course, by this time Simon and the rest of the Twelve have already come and seen a lot: Jesus turning water into wine, promising the nobleman, healing the lame man, feeding five thousand, and walking on water. Yet, at this point the Twelve hadn't heard a lot. That is to say, most of the didactic material about Jesus comes while the disciples are absent (the Baptizer, the Samaritan woman) or comes across as a private conversation between Jesus and another person (Nicodemus). In other words, even though Simon (and the Twelve) have been following Jesus for quite a while, they aren't privy to most of what Jesus says or what others say about him. They don't hear "For God so loved the world, that he gave his only Son," or "He who believes in the Son has eternal life," or "Whoever drinks of the water that I shall give him shall never thirst," or "Yesterday at the seventh hour the fever left him." Therefore, when Jesus began to say strange things about "eating his flesh" and "drinking his blood" (Jn 6:53), the Twelve must have thought, "He doesn't say much, but when he does it sure sounds bizarre." Of course, we hear echoes of the Eucharist in the words of Jesus. But, the disciples couldn't. Therefore, it's not surprising that the disciples were shocked and offended by his strange words (Jn 6:60-66). But Simon wasn't. That's a bit surprising to me.

When it comes to words, the less Simon says, the better. Indeed, as we will come to find out, the converse is true: the more Peter talks, the more he gets into trouble. So, it's not surprising that Peter has nothing to say when he first meets Jesus. Then, for six chapters of John's Gospel, Simon is mute. When he finally speaks up, Peter's confession is not all that spectacular. Simon says what even demons confess about Jesus: "You are the Holy One of God" (Jn 6:69; Mk 1:24; Lk 4:34). But that's not all. After many of Jesus' disciples walk away, no longer following him because they are so offended by his words (Jn 6:66), Jesus asks the Twelve: "Do you

want to leave me too?" To which Simon Peter replies (pitifully? faithfully?): "Where else would we go, Lord? You have words of eternal life"
(Jn 6:68). Here, Peter simply repeats what Jesus has just told them: "The
words that I have spoken to you are spirit and life" (Jn 6:63).[5] So, it's hard
to tell whether Peter's remark about having nowhere else to go is evidence of insightful devotion ("Wherever he leads I'll go") or pitiful res-
ignation ("What else are we going to do?"). Nevertheless, even though it
takes him six chapters, Peter finally ends up saying the right thing about
Jesus. Yet, from this point forward, even though Simon talks like he's the
spokesperson for the Twelve, it's his words that will get him in trouble.

The next time Simon Peter speaks up (and nearly every time afterward),
he contradicts what Jesus has just said—the opposite of what happened
in John 6. It's almost as if, for whatever reason (pride? arrogance? stub-
bornness? ignorance?), Peter is out to prove Jesus wrong. The pattern is
so predictable that Peter's penchant for disagreeing with Jesus becomes
wearisomely laughable:

Jesus: "What I'm doing you won't understand now, but you will un-
         derstand later."
Peter: [acting like he understands now] "You will never wash my feet."
Jesus: "If I don't wash your feet, you'll have no part with me."
Peter: [acting like he understands now] "Then wash my hands and
         head too!"
Jesus: "Where I am going you cannot come."
Peter: "Lord, where are you going?"
Jesus: "Where I am going, you cannot follow me now; but you will
         follow me later."
Peter: [acting like he's going to follow him now] "Lord, why can't I
         follow you now? I will lay down my life for you."
Jesus: "You will lay down your life for me? [laughs] I'm telling you

---

[5]Labahn thinks Peter's confession is the "right answer" to the question asked by Jesus at the beginning of this entire episode: "Where are we to buy enough bread for everyone to eat?" (Jn 6:5).
See Michael Labahn, "Simon Peter: An Ambiguous Character and His Narrative Career," in
Character Studies in the Fourth Gospel, ed. Steven A. Hunt, Francois Tolmie, and Ruben Zimmermann (Tübingen: Mohr Siebeck, 2013), 155.

Jesus:	the truth: before the cock crows you will deny me three times."
Jesus:	[later that evening] "I told you that I am he; if I'm the one you're looking for, let my disciples go." [Peter acts like he's not going anywhere, draws his sword and attacks the high priest's slave]
Jesus:	"Put the sword up; shall I not drink from the cup the Father has given to me?"
Servants:	[Persisting in following Jesus now, Simon is confronted by servants of the high priest] "You are one of his disciples!"
Peter:	"I am not."

This is the story of how Simon reveals that he is Peter—but not in the best sense of the word. Peter is petulant. Hardheaded, Simon Peter refuses to take Jesus at his word. "You don't understand." "Yes, I do." "You can't follow me now." "Yes, I can." "You need to leave now." "No, I don't." "You will deny me three times." Yes he does, and without even a whimper of regret. Unlike the Synoptic Gospels, where Peter walks away weeping bitterly with great remorse, in John's narrative world, hardhearted Peter denies that he is a disciple of Jesus and walks away like a cold-blooded traitor. No tears, no regrets. So much for the disciple who claimed he would die for Jesus.

In the Synoptic Gospels, Peter denies that he *knows* Jesus. But in John's Gospel, Simon denies three times that he is a *disciple* of Jesus (Jn 18:15-18, 25-27).[6] Truer words were never spoken. For even though the narrator describes Simon Peter as "following Jesus" (Jn 18:15), we soon realize that Simon meant what he said, living up to his reputation as the petulant disciple: "You are one of his disciples." "No, I'm not." The juxtaposition of the interrogation of Jesus and of Simon is breathtaking. Jesus is on trial for his life, his enemies questioning him about *his disciples* and what he has taught them. Tragically, at that very moment, as Peter is denying that he is a disciple, Jesus says confidently to the chief priests, "Ask those *who heard me* what I taught them" (Jn 18:21). Given Simon's disclaimer, it's

---

[6]James Resseguie, *The Strange Gospel: Narrative Design and Point of View in John* (Leiden: Brill, 2001), 153.

quite apparent that Peter wasn't one of those *who truly heard Jesus.* It's not only evident in his denial in word, but also in deed—getting at the heart of why Simon denied Jesus in the first place. We typically don't ponder that question too much. The answer seems rather obvious: Simon was afraid for his life. He didn't want to die. But hadn't Simon already promised to die for Jesus (Jn 13:37)? Why did he back out now?

Perhaps it's because Simon was willing to die for *his hero*—the kind of Messiah he wanted to follow.[7] But when Jesus turned out to be the kind of Messiah he no longer wanted to follow, one who was willing to die for his enemies (rather than slay them), hardhearted Peter said, "No thanks. I won't follow a Messiah like that." How do we know Simon was looking for a take-no-prisoners-and-slay-your-enemies-with-a-sword Messiah? Malchus, the slave of the high priest could tell us—or rather *show* us, by holding up his bloody ear (Jn 18:10). Simon didn't want to give up without a fight. Therefore, he was probably shocked to hear Jesus rebuke him for his reckless behavior (Jn 18:11). At that moment, it was probably painfully obvious to Simon that he would no longer call himself a disciple—for the *way* Jesus established the kingdom of God on earth was not the way for Peter. That's why, I think, Simon walked away without any regrets. What he said was true. He may have been following Jesus from a distance, but he was no longer a disciple of the way.

It's no wonder, then, that John seems to have tacked on the episode of Jesus confronting Peter.[8] Simon wasn't sorry at all for denying Jesus. So, according to John's Gospel, Jesus had to take care of some unfinished business between him and his hardheaded, hardhearted disciple. After all, Jesus had predicted that one day Simon would be called Peter, marking a genuine conversion. As everyone knows, conversion doesn't happen without repentance, a genuine sorrow for sin, truly regretting what we've done. So, how do we make someone feel sorry for their sin? Sit them

---

[7]I owe this insight to my wife, Sheri.

[8]To many scholars, John 20:24-31 is the perfect ending to the story "come and see." John 21 looks like an addendum to the Gospel; see the discussion in Marianne Meye Thompson, *John: A Commentary*, New Testament Library (Louisville, KY: Westminster John Knox, 2015), 431-34. Thompson argues for the unity of John's Gospel.

down like a parent scolding a child and put them in time-out? My mom used to make me stand in the corner of the living room, nose pressed up against the wall, undistracted, so that I would have plenty of time to "think about what you've done." Regret often came within minutes. Is that what Jesus should have done, put Simon in time-out to make him think about what he had done—especially since he approached Jesus that day on the seashore like nothing had happened? Indeed, we wouldn't blame Jesus if he had wagged his finger at Simon and said, "I'm disappointed in you." But that's not what he did. Instead, he asks Simon three times, "Do you love me?"—the question that leads to true repentance.

It must have bothered Simon that Jesus didn't call him Peter. Instead, Jesus used the same name as when they first met (Jn 1:42)—seemingly going along with Simon, acting like nothing had changed. "Simon, son of John, do you love me?" (Jn 21:15-17). By his response, Simon sounds like he hasn't learned his lesson, counting on his words to prove his faithfulness: "Yes, Lord. You know that I love you." What I find compelling is that, of the seven disciples gathered around Jesus that early morning, Simon would have been the *only one* to have understood why Jesus had to ask the same question *three* times. If Simon had repented of his sin (or at least showed some remorse that he denied Jesus *three* times), then perhaps this whole exchange could have been avoided. It wasn't his sin that grieved him; it was that Jesus asked him the same question three times (Jn 21:17). By giving the same answer ("you know that I love you"), Simon tried to act like nothing had changed. And that's why, I think, Jesus wouldn't call him by his nickname. Peter was still just "Simon, son of John." But one day, just as Jesus predicted, Simon would become Peter, when he fed Jesus' lambs and followed him all the way to the cross (Jn 21:18-19). Repentance is revealed by what we do more than what we say.

A few times in his Gospel, John points the reader to things that transpired after John 21 (Jn 2:22; 10:16; 12:16; 14:26; 15:26-27; 16:2-4, 8-14; 20:29). But of all of these post-Gospel events, the death of Simon is the most peculiar. That the Holy Spirit would come and guide the disciples "in all truth," helping them to remember Jesus' teaching, that Jesus would have "other sheep" he would bring into the fold, that the disciples would make sense of what Jesus said and did after the resurrection—all of these post-Gospel events make sense to us because we have Acts and the Epistles. But Jesus' enigmatic reference to the eventual martyrdom of Simon Peter sounds odd by comparison (Jn 21:18). Indeed, given his reaction to Jesus' prophecy, Simon also acts like it is an odd thing for Jesus to say. Pointing out the beloved one, Simon wants to know: "Lord, and what about this man?" (Jn 21:21). Simon sounds like he believes Jesus is picking on him. "If I'm going to die a horrible death, what about him?" And yet, the beloved one had already followed Jesus all the way to the cross. Peter hadn't. So Simon may have interpreted Jesus' prediction about his eventual martyrdom as punishment for his unfaithfulness, especially since Jesus threw in the line that someone would take Simon "where you do not wish to go" (Jn 21:18)—as if Jesus knew that Peter would be a reluctant martyr. It's as if Jesus were saying, "One day, *Simon*, you will learn to follow me all the way to the cross. *Then* you will finally keep your promise. *Then* you will lay down your life for me. *Then* my prophecy will come true. *Then* everyone will know what I have known all along: you are Peter."

According to an apocryphal story, Jesus' prophecy regarding Peter's martyrdom did come true. Peter was crucified in Rome, impaled on a cross upside down at his request—intended to be a symbolic picture of both the depravity of humanity and the subversive work of Christ's cross.[9] Did John's readers know about how Peter died? Perhaps. They certainly knew about the fate of the beloved one (Jn 21:23). And, since the narrator interprets Jesus' vague prophecy as "signifying by what kind of death [Peter] will glorify God" (Jn 21:19), he seems to presume readers would know how Peter died.[10] Therefore, the literary effect of the way

---

[9]Acts of Peter 37. Peter declares from the cross, "For the first man, whose image I bear, in falling head downward showed a manner of birth which did not formerly exist, for it was dead, having no motion. . . . Concerning this the Lord says in a mystery, 'Unless you make the right as the left and the left as the right, and the top as the bottom and the front as the back, you shall not know the Kingdom.'" See Acts of Peter 38, in *The Apocryphal New Testament*, ed. J. K. Elliott (Oxford: Clarendon, 1993), 425.

[10]Being led to a place where Peter doesn't want to go could mean any number of things—prison,

John has framed the discipleship of Simon—from Jesus' first prophecy to his last—is that Jesus is the Lord of Simon's life. His words will come true. Simon will be called Peter. One day Peter will be crucified.

By pointing to a post-Gospel event, then, John signals that Peter will eventually do what Jesus required of him, "follow me" (Jn 21:19)—all the way to the cross, glorifying God even in his death. In other words, *it would take a story beyond what was written to reveal the conversion of Simon to Peter*: how a hardheaded, hardhearted man became a rock-solid disciple who followed Jesus to the end.[11] Consequently, John's literary technique sounds like an apt description of our discipleship too. For, it will take a story beyond what has been written to reveal our conversion, from the beginning to the end.

BECOMING A CHRISTIAN TAKES TIME

I grew up in a church that talked about conversion as a singular moment, a one-time transformational experience. Our pastor emphasized the importance of "getting saved," the event when a lost person was converted to our Christian faith. Stories of dramatic conversions were often held up as the model; whether through personal testimonies or biblical examples, we were told over and over again about the power of the gospel to change a sinner's life *immediately*. "Once I was blind but now I see" was our mantra. Weeklong revival services were held twice a year to harvest souls for the Lord. Then, once someone was "saved," we would teach them how to be good members of our church. The evidence of conversion, the proof that a new disciple really meant it when they prayed the sinner's prayer, was measured by their participation in church activities. The church even issued handy offering envelopes for members (our names printed on the front), with a checklist on the bottom so that we could report whether we were 100 percent Christians that week:

---

exile, persecution, a transitory life, being homeless—not just martyrdom.

[11]According to Bauckham, true discipleship (following Jesus) can only happen *after* the resurrection (*Gospel of Glory*, 145-46). So also Resseguie (per Simon Peter): "Only in the *afterward* of Jesus' death will Peter be able to follow" (*Strange Gospel*, 153, emphasis original).

worship attendance (30 percent), Sunday school attendance (20 percent), on time (10 percent), studied lesson (10 percent), tithing (10 percent), daily Bible reading (10 percent), visitation (10 percent). Most Sundays, I was only a 70 percent Christian, rarely measuring up to what the church said it meant to be truly dedicated to Christ. Yet, even though I wasn't a 100 percent Christian, I had no doubts that I was "saved." My conversion was never in question, as evidenced by my willingness to share my personal testimony during Sunday evening services, recounting the details of when I became a Christian.

Then I went away to a Baptist college and heard my philosophy professor, Dr. Dan Cochran, talk about how none of us really are Christian, especially since the word *Christian* means "Christlike." Rather than claim, "I'm a Christian," we should all admit that we are actually *becoming* Christian—that we won't truly be Christlike until the last day, at the resurrection. He wanted us to realize that our conversion to Christ didn't happen all at once. It would take a lifetime to become Christian, being "transformed" daily by the "renewing of our mind"—something Paul emphasizes (Rom 12:1-2).

That same year, we had a guest speaker (I don't remember his name) give a series of talks during chapel, "The Criteria for Evaluating Spiritual Growth." Much to my surprise, he never mentioned the checklist that appeared on the bottom of our offering envelopes. Instead, he spoke about the fruit of the Spirit, virtue ethics, and the importance of character formation. For the first time in my life, I began to reconsider my conversion to Christ—that it didn't happen overnight. Being a Christian takes time, a statement that came as a relief. No wonder I never measured up. Slowly, daily, Christ converts his disciples to his way of thinking, his way of living, his priorities, his kingdom—just like he did for Simon Peter, a lesson his young disciple would learn when he got old (Jn 21:18).

It doesn't surprise me, then, that old Simon Peter wrote about conversion as something that takes time, that salvation is a growth process for all of us (1 Pet 2:2). Christ is gathering stones to build the temple of the living God—each rock fitted for his divine purpose—even a man named Peter (1 Pet 2:4-6). Some might see all of us as rejects. But God loves to take what "the builders rejected" and use it as the cornerstone—Christ Jesus proves it (1 Pet 2:7-8). That's why old Peter keeps reminding his young converts of who they are in Christ. Over and over again he writes, "You are this" and "You are that"—the mother lode appearing in 1 Peter 2:9: "You are A CHOSEN PEOPLE, A ROYAL PRIESTHOOD, A HOLY NATION, A PEOPLE FOR *GOD'S* OWN POSSESSION" (NASB). This is what *God has said* about us (Peter quotes Moses and Isaiah). We may not look like choice people, act like royalty, or seem very holy. But, since Christ's prediction about Simon came true—"you will be called Peter"—we believe these prophecies will come true for us too. Just like Peter, it will take the story of our lives built together—beyond what has been written—to reveal our conversion in the end. Until then, we look for signs that God is at work among us.

NICODEMUS, THE SEEKER

Miracles are signs of God's presence. When we witness the miraculous, however we may try to explain it, we are seeing God at work. Of course, the handiwork of God is seen in the everyday happenings of life too—what could be called daily signs of divine presence. The sun rises; the sun sets. Rain falls from heaven; trees rise from the earth. The grass dies; the flower blooms. Those who have eyes to see God at work among us—his faithful gifts are so reliable that it's easy to take him for granted—recognize God's presence among us. "The heavens tell the glory of God," writes the psalmist. "And their expanse declares the work of His hands. Day to day pours forth speech" (Ps 19:1-2 NASB). When creation talks, we listen to God. When things happen, we see God. Therefore, it's not surprising that whenever believers witness the unusual, hear of the miraculous, we see God. For we are convinced that every good gift—whether ordinary or extraordinary—comes from God. Since he rains his gifts on the just and the unjust, we know that God is with all of us. It just takes eyes to see the signs.

So, when Nicodemus surmised, "Rabbi, we know that you are a teacher who has come from God because no one can do the signs that you do unless God is with him" (Jn 3:2), it sounds like something we would say. As a matter of fact, compared to the *only* confession of faith made by Simon Peter (Jn 6:68), Nicodemus's confession sounds just as meaningful. "God is with him" is nearly the same as saying "God is with us." Furthermore, Peter says the same thing to Cornelius about Jesus: "God was with him" (Acts 10:38). Since John wrote his Gospel so that his readers would be able to see miracles as signs of God's work and therefore "believe that Jesus is the Christ, the Son of God" (Jn 20:31), Nicodemus seems to personify the desired result of John's Gospel story. Those who see the signs recognize God in Jesus. Yet, most readers are suspicious of Nicodemus—and with good reason.

First, the narrator has just informed us that simply because someone sees the signs and is drawn to Jesus doesn't necessarily mean that someone is a "believer" to be trusted. This is because Jesus didn't trust such people (Jn 2:23-25). Second, the narrator uses several negative images to introduce Nicodemus: he's a Pharisee, he's a ruler of the Judeans, and he came to Jesus under cover of night (Jn 3:1-2). In light of the prologue, we already know that Jesus will be rejected by "his own," that the world will not listen to the Baptizer because he bore witness to the Light, and that those who live in darkness will be repelled by the Light (Jn 1:5-11). That sounds like a sneak preview of Jesus' encounter with Nicodemus. Finally, and perhaps most tellingly, Nicodemus *never* confesses Jesus as "the Christ, the Son of God" (the goal of John's Gospel). Therefore, it's easy to dismiss Nicodemus as an unqualified disciple, questioning whether he ever showed any signs of being a true believer. Nicodemus may see signs of the kingdom, but does he ever see the King?

Then again, the same question could be asked of Simon. Does Peter ever display any signs of being a true believer *within the pages of John's Gospel*? Yes, no, maybe? That's why some think Nicodemus deserves a second look. While it's true that Nicodemus comes to Jesus at night, at least he's drawn to the Light.[12] While it's true that Nicodemus is a Pharisee

---

[12]"In so doing, John foreshadows Nicodemus's ultimate discipleship in 19:39-42." See Craig S. Keener, *The Gospel of John: A Commentary* (Grand Rapids, MI: Baker Academic, 2010), 1:536.

(one of the groups that opposed Jesus), nevertheless, Jesus treated him like a dialogue partner, expecting him to understand Jesus' teaching (Jn 3:10, 12).[13] And while it's true that Nicodemus was puzzled by Jesus' teaching, nowhere does the narrator say that he rejected what Jesus said.

John has created a gap in the narrative, forcing the reader to wonder whether Nicodemus will eventually become an opponent of Jesus. Or will he continue to be Jesus-friendly, believing that "God is with him" because he sees the signs? When times get tough, will he betray Jesus like Judas or deny him like Simon Peter? Or will Nicodemus come through in the end—someone who shows his true colors when the world turns black and white? Due to John's literary technique, then, the next time Nicodemus reappears in John's Gospel (Jn 7:50-52), readers are inclined to lean in and take notes: "What's going to happen here?" It's also why, when Nicodemus raises his voice in protest (in the midst of Jesus' enemies!), we can't help but begin to develop a favorable opinion of this particular Pharisee. He seems to be the *only* insider to stick up for Jesus.

What tripped up the insiders about Jesus was that he was from Galilee (Jn 7:52). Of course, by this time, the things Jesus said and did had already troubled "the Jews" (Jn 2:18-20; 5:16-18; 7:1-32). But when some of the people began to wonder out loud whether Jesus was the Christ (Jn 7:26, 31, 41), the rebuttal by those who opposed Jesus was based on where he came from: "But the Christ doesn't come from Galilee, does he? Do not the Scriptures say that the Christ comes from the seed of David and from Bethlehem, the village where David was from?" (Jn 7:41-42). The last king of Israel, the one who would claim David's throne and bring about God's everlasting reign on earth, had to share David's nativity (Ps 89:3-4; Mic 5:2)—everyone knew that. But in John's narrative world, Jesus' heavenly origin was far more important than any earthly nativity. John didn't need to tell the story of Jesus' birth because "He was in the beginning with God" (Jn 1:2). Those who believe in him are not born of

---

[13]J. Ramsey Michaels, *The Gospel of John*, New International Commentary on the New Testament (Grand Rapids, MI: Eerdmans, 2010), 179-80; Francis J. Moloney, *Belief in the Word, Reading the Fourth Gospel: John 1-4* (Minneapolis: Fortress, 1993), 109-15.

blood or of the flesh but of God (Jn 1:13). That's what Jesus tried to teach
Nicodemus regarding the kingdom of God. What is born of the flesh is
earthly; what is born of the Spirit is heavenly. Therefore, only those who
have eyes to see the exalted King will enter the kingdom of God (Jn 3:3-
13). Indeed, it will take heavenly eyes to see the King when he comes into
his kingdom.[14]

Nicodemus may see the signs of God's reign on earth. But will he see
the kingdom when Jesus is lifted up as king of Israel and the whole world?
Of course, that will be a difficult thing even for Jesus' disciples to see: *how*
Jesus is exalted as the last king of Israel isn't what anyone was expecting,
not even a teacher of the law. One has to be "born again" and "born from
above" to see it. "Just as it is *impossible* to do what Jesus has been doing
unless 'God is with him,' so it is *impossible* 'to see the kingdom of God'
unless one is 'born from above,'" says J. Ramsey Michaels.[15] Jesus says he
will look more like a serpent on a pole lifted up in the wilderness than a
royal son of David exalted to his heaven-ordained throne in Jerusalem
(Jn 3:14). When that happened, when Jesus was lifted up on the cross, the
scandal of the Christ having come from Galilee paled in comparison.

Jesus wasn't reticent to use negative imagery to reveal how he pictured
himself and his mission. You would think he would do just the opposite,
relying exclusively on flattering images to convince everyone that he was
God's Messiah. He certainly does that a lot in John's Gospel—more than
any other Gospel. Even though Jesus spends most of his time in the
Synoptic Gospels teaching about the kingdom of God, he prefers to talk
about himself in John's Gospel. He claims he is the light of the world, the
living water, the bread of life, the good shepherd, the resurrection and
the life, and perhaps most famously, he says he is the way, the truth, and
the life. To be sure, the revelation of Jesus as the Christ, the Son of God,
is John's purpose—in word and in deed. Even the miracles are supposed

---

[14]"Jesus speaks of a rebirth that enables the one reborn *to see* the kingdom of God. However familiar the reader is with a Jewish notion of God as King, something different is being introduced
by these words of Jesus to Nicodemus" (Moloney, *Belief in the Word*, 110, emphasis original).

[15]Michaels, *Gospel of John*, 179, emphasis original.

to be signs of Jesus' identity. But some of those signs make Jesus look bad (Jn 5:1-18; 9:1-34). And much of what Jesus says about himself—even the positive imagery of being the bread of life—has a negative effect ("How is this man able to give us his flesh to eat?" [Jn 6:52]). Mixing in a few blatantly offensive images only makes things worse, especially for a Pharisee like Nicodemus.

As Nicodemus is already confused by Jesus, it certainly doesn't help when Jesus compares himself to the serpent that God used to punish Israel for its rebellion (Jn 3:14-15)—a strange story from the Hebrew Scriptures that seems to contradict the very lesson God tried to teach Israel regarding the perils of idolatry (the bronze serpent was eventually idolized by Israel; see 2 Kings 18:4). In order to stay God's punishment, Moses was instructed to make a "graven image," requiring Israel to "look at the serpent of bronze and live" (Num 21:9 NRSV). To compare yourself to an idol—a serpent, no less—and say, "You need to see me like that" seems to invite unmerciful scrutiny. So, when Nicodemus appears to stick up for Jesus before the Sanhedrin, claiming, "Our law doesn't judge a man without listening to him" (Jn 7:51), it should take us by surprise. What he should have said was, "Since our law doesn't judge a man unless we've heard from him first, let me report that I've talked to the man. He compared himself to an idol. That those who believe *in him*—not in the LORD!—will live forever. This man is dangerous. He's a false prophet. Yes, his signs come true. But, just as Moses warned us, even false prophets can perform signs, trying to convince us to worship other gods (Deut 13:1-5). And so we must 'purge the evil from among us.'"

But that's not what Nicodemus says, and I wonder why? Yet, what intrigues me more is what this Pharisee *does* after Jesus is "lifted up like a serpent."

Nicodemus makes three appearances in John's Gospel: extensively at the beginning (Jn 3:1-15), briefly near the middle (Jn 7:50-52), and toward the end, when he helps Joseph of Arimathea inter the body of the crucified Jesus (Jn 19:39-42). Since Nicodemus was a member of the Sanhedrin, he probably saw everything that happened to Jesus. He heard

Caiaphas condemn Jesus to death (Jn 11:49-50). He probably saw Jesus welcomed into Jerusalem with shouts of messianic praise, "Blessed is he who comes in the name of the Lord, even the King of Israel" (Jn 12:13). He heard Jesus respond to the high priest's interrogation, "Why do you question me? Ask those who heard what I said to them. They know what I said" (Jn 18:21)—including Nicodemus. He saw the abuse, the hatred. He heard the cries, the mockery. He was probably there when Pilate asked, "Shall I crucify your king?" and the crowd responded, "We have no king but Caesar" (Jn 19:15). He read the sign, "Jesus the Nazarene, the King of the Jews" (Jn 19:19). He heard Jesus say, "It is finished" (Jn 19:30). He probably saw Jesus die. Indeed, it's very likely Nicodemus saw the whole thing because he's the man who brought a hundred pounds of burial spices to inter the body of Jesus (Jn 19:39). I picture with my mind's eye the arrangement between Joseph and Nicodemus, "I'll get his body; you get the spices." So, as the man who first came to him at night gathered what was necessary for Jesus' burial—in light of the strange turn of events that no one saw coming except Jesus (and perhaps his enemies)—I wonder whether this Pharisee was troubled by the same question he asked at the beginning: "How can these things be?" (Jn 3:9).

There's a lot of king talk in John's version of the trial and execution of Jesus: "Are you the king of the Jews?" (Jn 18:33); "My kingdom is not of this world" (Jn 18:36); "So you are a king?" (Jn 18:37); "You say I am a king" (Jn 18:37); "Shall I release to you the king of the Jews?" (Jn 18:39); "Hail, king of the Jews" (Jn 19:3); "Shall I crucify your king?" (Jn 19:15); "We have no king but Caesar" (Jn 19:15); "Jesus the Nazarene, the king of the Jews" (Jn 19:19); "Do not write, 'the king of the Jews'; but that he said, 'I am king of the Jews'" (Jn 19:21). Yet, despite all of the talk of king and kingdoms, the crucifixion seemed to confirm two undeniable realities: (1) Rome ruled Jerusalem, and (2) Jesus looked more like a serpent lifted up on a pole than a king. Even though Jesus claimed, "Whenever I am lifted up from the earth, I will draw all people to me" (Jn 12:32), the only people drawn to him at that time who were calling him "king" were his enemies. There were no disciples at the cross lifting up Jesus as their

Messiah. Instead, in John's Gospel, talk of a king and a kingdom around a cross is foolish nonsense (Jn 19:21).

That's why I think Nicodemus comes off looking like a disciple in the end.[16] In light of the cross, it's not what he said but what he did that reveals his faith. It has to do with the amount of burial spices he brought to prepare the body of Jesus. Usually, a pound of spices—worth quite a bit of money—would suffice (Jn 12:3-7). Nicodemus brought a *hundred pounds* (Jn 19:39). Why? Kings were interred with large quantities of aloes and myrrh. According to Josephus, it took five hundred servants to carry the burial spices for Herod the Great's funeral.[17] The olfactory effect would be obvious: one could smell the burial of a king for miles. So it looks like Joseph and Nicodemus orchestrated a royal burial for Jesus. Raymond Brown writes, "The idea that Jesus was accorded a burial fit for a king would correspond well to the solemn proclamation that on the cross he was truly 'the King of the Jews.'"[18] All who lived in Jerusalem, both the rulers responsible for Jesus' death and the pilgrims attending the holy city during Passover, would have caught the scent that a king was buried in the city of David that day.

Nicodemus may have never offered the proper confession, "Jesus is the Christ, the Son of God." But his actions spoke volumes. Even though nearly all of Jesus' disciples abandoned him, there was one man who despised the shame and buried Jesus like a king. And I wonder, as the wind carried the royal scent for miles, whether Jesus' words echoed in Nicodemus's ears, bringing a grin to his solemn face: "Don't be surprised that I said to you, 'It is necessary for you all to be born from above.' The *pneuma* blows wherever it wants, and you hear its voice, but you do not know where it comes from or where it is going: so also is everyone who

---

[16]So also Susan E. Hylen, *Imperfect Believers: Ambiguous Characters in the Gospel of John* (Louisville, KY: Westminster John Knox, 2009), 37; Rudolf Schnackenburg, *The Gospel According to St. John*, trans. David Smith and G. A. Kon (New York: Crossroad, 1990), 3:296-97; and Keener, who sees Nicodemus as a model for Jewish "secret" disciples to "go public with their confession of faith in Jesus" (*Gospel of John*, 2:1162).

[17]Josephus, *Jewish War* 1.33.9.

[18]Raymond E. Brown, *The Death of the Messiah* (New York: Doubleday, 1993), 2:1261; also Michaels, *Gospel of John*, 981-83; Thompson, *John*, 406.

has been born by the *pneuma*" (Jn 3:7-8). Indeed, one has to be born with spiritual eyes to see the kingdom of a crucified Christ.

WHAT ARE YOU LOOKING FOR?

I've often wondered what kind of disciple I would have been if I had lived in Jesus' day. Would I have been like Nicodemus, an educated man who came to Jesus with more questions than answers? Or would I look more like Simon, a guy from the working-class world who had a long stubborn streak? Since I was a college professor, I often identify with Nicodemus— perhaps that's why I'm willing to give him the benefit of the doubt. Asking questions that deserve good answers was my livelihood. Then again, I come from blue-collar stock—a carpet installer's son who is too proud to admit it when he's claimed too much. Is that why I'm so hard on Simon for not measuring up to his nickname?

Indeed, there tends to be a reflective quality to John's work. What we see is who we are. That's why I wonder what I would have done if I were one of the first disciples of Jesus. When I had just begun to follow Jesus, if he had turned to me and asked, "What are you looking for?" I wonder what I would have said. "Heaven when I die"? Or "the promise of a better life"? Or "no more fear of hell"? Or even "forgiveness of my sins"? Given what I think are the reasons I first began to follow Jesus, there's no telling what I would have said. Nevertheless, for a man who's been trying to follow him for over fifty years, I know exactly what I would say today.

Jesus: "What are you looking for?"

Me: "I'm looking for *you*, in a world filled with hate and violence, war and hunger. I'm looking for *you*, in a world of sorrow and pain, abuse and suffering. I'm looking for *you*, when a child dies of disease, when a teenager is killed in a car wreck, when a young mother is taken from her children due to Covid. I'm looking for *you*, when my mother died, when members of my family no longer believe, when my colleague has to retire early because she's dying of cancer. I'm looking for *you*, when Egyptian Christians are murdered. I'm looking for *you*, when earthquakes level entire cities. I'm looking for *you*, when a little boy sits in shock with a bloody face, covered in ashes, taken from a pile of rubble after a bomb destroyed his whole world. I'm looking for *you*—and I'm not the only one."

In Elie Wiesel's Nobel Prize–winning book, *Night*, he tells the horror story of how he survived the Holocaust. Riddled with survivor's guilt, Wiesel tries to make sense of the inexplicable evil he saw with his own eyes, endured in his own body: the persecution and execution of his people, family, and friends, carried out by the hardheaded, hardhearted Nazis. It all happened so fast, the escalation of violence: from being stripped of their possessions, ghettoized in their own hometown (Sighet, Transylvania), crammed into cattle cars and transported to concentration camps (first Birkenau, then Auschwitz, and finally Buchenwald), to enduring severe persecution—beaten, starved, tortured, executed, cremated—their numbers dwindled by the hundreds every day.

Throughout the ordeal, as Wiesel recounts his descent into what he called the "Kingdom of Night," he lays bare his struggle to believe in God.[19] At first, Elie and his family looked for any signs of God's presence, good news that they were not forgotten. They found reasons to celebrate small graces: hope in each other, a chance to sleep, thickened soup, and mud that cloaked coveted shoes: "I had new shoes myself. But as they were covered with a thick coat of mud, they had not been noticed. I thanked God, in an improvised prayer, for having created mud in His infinite and wondrous universe."[20] But eventually night overwhelmed them when the Secret Service executed a young boy along with two men, forcing the prisoners to watch the hanging:

> "Where is the merciful God, where is He?" someone behind me was asking. At the signal, the three chairs were tipped over. Total silence in the camp. On the horizon, the sun was setting. "Caps off!" screamed the *Lageraelteste*. His voice quivered. As for the rest of us, we were weeping. "Cover your heads!" Then came the march past the victims. The two men were no longer alive. Their tongues were hanging out, swollen and bluish. But the third rope was still moving: the child, too light, was still breathing. . . . And

[19]Elie Wiesel, *Night*, trans. Marion Wiesel (New York: Hill and Wang, 2006), 118.
[20]Wiesel, *Night*, 38.

so he remained for more than a half hour, lingering between life and death, writing before our eyes. And we were forced to look at him at close range. He was still alive when I passed him. His tongue was still red, his eyes not yet extinguished. Behind me, I heard the same man asking: "For God's sake, where is God?" And from within me, I heard a voice answer: "Where He is? This is where—hanging here from this gallows."[21]

That was the turning point. Wiesel no longer praised God or asked for his help. The holy days meant nothing to him; observing Yom Kippur, asking God to forgive him of his sins, seemed useless. He even refused to recite Kaddish, the prayer for the dead. It was because, to him, in the darkness of night, God died with that little boy.

Elie is short for *Eliezer*, which means, "God helps him"—the last word Elie heard his father whisper just before he died. Elie feared that his father's fragile condition would make him an ideal candidate for "selection," when the weak and the lame would be culled from the group and sent to the incinerators. His father said he was ready to die. But Elie wouldn't hear of it, doing everything in his power to protect him. Suffering from an acute fever that left him delirious, his father began to cry out his son's name in the middle of the night. A guard warned him to shut up, but Elie's father persisted, "Eliezer, Eliezer." The officer beat him with a club, striking a death blow to his head. Always before, Elie would try to shield his father from such punishment. Not this time. He remained silent, listening to his father die as he breathed his last word, "Eliezer"—a betrayal Elie regretted for the rest of his life.[22]

Perhaps that's why he prefers to go by the name *Elie* (which means, ironically, "My God"—an echo of Jesus' cry from the cross). *Eliezer* is too painful, too sorrowful, too many bad memories. Yet, I hear a prayer in his name. That one word, *Eliezer*, could be heard as a dying man's desperate cry for redemption, "God, help him." And God did. Because, in the end, Elie not only survived the atrocities of the death camps of the Nazis, but he also embodied the hope of his father's last wish: that God

[21]Wiesel, *Night*, 64-65.
[22]Wiesel, *Night*, 110-12.

would help his son. "I express to you my deepest gratitude as one who has emerged from the Kingdom of Night. We know that every moment is a moment of grace, every hour an offering; not to share them would mean to betray them. Our lives no longer belong to us alone; they belong to all those who need us desperately."[23]

When I read Elie's story with resurrection eyes, I can't help but think about another innocent Jew who was viciously murdered on the day we call Good Friday—the day when God died. For his sacrifice teaches us that God shows up in the darkest of places, leading us out of the kingdom of night.

Staring at the death of the innocent one, someone behind us asks, "Where is God?" We say, pointing to the crucified King, "Where is he? This is where—hanging from the cross."

---

[23]Wiesel, *Night*, 120.

2

SEE AND BELIEVE

Confessing the Word

As I write these words, I lost my mother to cancer nine months ago. Even though, as a pastor, I have walked with many church members through the valley of the shadow of death, hearing them talk about death as loss, I didn't know what that meant. In fact, I used to think *loss* was a polite way to talk about death to ease the pain of grief. We were even taught in seminary that to speak bluntly about death was harsh and insensitive. To spare the feelings of the bereaved, one should never ask, "When did your mother *die*?" Rather, we were to say, "When did you lose your mother?" But, after I had performed dozens of funerals, I began to rebel against my education, believing that death didn't deserve such niceties. Death made me angry. So I spoke openly about death, calling out our enemy who tries to hide in the shadows of propriety. Since death is our ugly reality, there was no need to pretend otherwise. One has to speak truth to power. Expressions such as "passing away," "no longer with us," and "loss" would no longer do. Besides, those who died in Christ weren't lost. Believers know exactly where they are.

But minutes after my mother died, I was surprised by loss. I thought there would be relief, knowing she wouldn't hurt anymore. I thought there would be comfort, believing that death wouldn't have the last word. I thought there would be hope, confident we would see each other again in the resurrection. But I felt none of that. No relief. No comfort. No hope. All I felt was a deep and abiding sense of loss, an emptiness that stayed with me for days, reflected in my remarks during her funeral: "How can I describe the significance of my mother in a few words? Why would I even try? Death seems too strong for words. The measure of her life can't be summed up with words. This moment, this sorrow, this aching loss is too much for words. Words fail me when it seems I need them the most."

Of course, we read from the Scriptures, hoping to "comfort one another with these words," as Paul claims (1 Thess 4:18). But I'm ashamed to say divine words seemed hollow to me during the funeral. I kept expecting my theology to kick in, correcting my feelings of loss. But nothing changed. Life moved on. I felt empty. In the months that followed, much to my surprise, I was compelled to visit my mother's grave several times. Staring at the headstone—her name etched in granite, as if I were trying to come to terms with the reality of death—I realized the gravity of my loss. It wasn't just the death of my mother that wounded me. I realized I was wrestling with the absence of Christ. I didn't blame him for my mother's death; we had been expecting it due to her poor prognosis. Yes, we prayed for her healing. But it didn't surprise me when she died. What surprised me was this deep emptiness, the loneliness of words, feeling like Christ had left me. I knew that couldn't be true in light of the promise that he would never leave or forsake us (Heb 13:5). But, when your mind says one thing (words!), and your heart says another (loss), what are you to do except grieve?

That's what I hear in the stories of Martha and Thomas: a profound sense of loss during the absence of Christ. In both episodes, grief dominates the narrative. In both cases, the absence of Christ made death hurt worse. In both situations, words were not enough to heal their broken heart; signs weren't necessary to see and believe. Rather, for Martha and Thomas, Jesus was the sign of their faith. They weren't looking for a miracle. What they really needed was for Jesus to be their Immanuel, God with us—especially in the face of death—something I needed too. Consequently, Martha and Thomas have taught me how to grieve in the absence of Christ.

MARTHA BELIEVES

By the time Jesus arrived, Lazarus (the Greek form of the Jewish name Eliezar) had been dead four days. Jesus had missed the funeral of his good friend, even though he was only about a day's trip from Bethany when he heard the news from Lazarus's sisters that "the one you love is sick" (Jn 11:3). At first, Jesus seemed to say that Lazarus's sickness wouldn't lead to death (Jn 11:4), so there was no need to rush over to Bethany (Jn 11:6). After a couple of days, Jesus decided it was time to go, to "wake up Lazarus" because he had "fallen asleep" (Jn 11:11)—which seemed really odd to the disciples because sleep was often interpreted as a good sign that the sick person would get better (Jn 11:12). Why would he want to wake him up? Then, for no apparent reason, Jesus appears to have changed his mind about Lazarus' condition. It was serious. In fact, Lazarus had already died (Jn 11:14). That's quite a swing in prophetic outcomes: from "His illness won't result in death" to "Lazarus is dead." It's no wonder the disciples were confused. They had been trying to talk Jesus out of going to that part of Judea because the rulers wanted to kill him (Jn 11:8). Now, even though it was too late to save Lazarus, Jesus was resigned to go. Why? He said it was for the sake of his disciples, that they would learn to believe (Jn 11:15). Who could stop him? No one, which explains why Thomas declared (courageously? fatalistically?), "Let's go so that we can die with him" (Jn 11:16).

Death hangs like a noose over this entire episode, from Jesus' prophecy (Jn 11:4) to Lazarus' rotting corpse (Jn 11:39) to the rulers' response to the seventh sign: "From that day, therefore, they decided that they would kill him" (Jn 11:53). According to John's Gospel, raising Lazarus from the dead was the last sign, the perfect sign, the sign to end all signs that Jesus was the Christ, the Son of God. If you didn't see the Messiah after this sign, you were blind; if you didn't believe in the Son of God after he conquered death, you were hardhearted (Jn 12:37-43). Only God had power over death. Why couldn't they see it? With the once-dead Lazarus walking among the living—a flesh-and-blood memorial of Jesus' power over death—wouldn't they have *had* to see the sign? Lazarus, the man whose name meant "God helps him," was the embodiment of the seventh sign.

Indeed, as long as he was around, the people would see the sign. That's why the rulers decided to kill Jesus *and* Lazarus (Jn 12:9-11). Lazarus was a mobile billboard of the messianic work of God in Christ. Ironically, both the perfect sign and the incarnation of life had to die so that people would no longer "see and believe." Yet, doubly ironic, it will be because of Jesus' death that many will believe in him, even though they "have not seen" (Jn 20:29).[1] They could kill the one whom God helped. But Jesus *is* the sign of God who lives forever because *he is* the resurrection and the life (Jn 11:25).

That's what Jesus told Martha when she confronted him for not being there when she needed him: "Lord, if you had been here my brother would not have died" (Jn 11:21)—the same thing Mary said to Jesus when she came to him (Jn 11:32). This is more than a statement of faith; Martha wanted Jesus to know that he had let her down. It had to do with the timing of Jesus' arrival. Martha knew Jesus was only a day away from Bethany when he received the news that Lazarus was deathly ill.[2] The messenger sent by the sisters would have returned to them after two days, not only indicating that he found Jesus ("Why didn't he come with you?") but also probably reporting what Jesus said about Lazarus: "This illness won't result in death but is for the glory of God so that the Son of God may be glorified through it" (Jn 11:4). So, when the messenger returned home after two days *without Jesus*—Lazarus already dead and buried—Martha must have been hurt and confused. By all appearances, Jesus was wrong (this sickness did result in death) and insensitive (he didn't come right away). That certainly didn't square with what she believed to be true: "Lord, the one whom you *love* is sick" (Jn 11:3). Jesus' actions didn't match her beliefs. Therefore I imagine that, having heard Jesus was near

---

[1]Craig S. Keener writes, "To the informed, repeated reader of this Gospel, the promise of Jesus' glorification through Lazarus's death constitutes a double entendre: Jesus is glorified because Lazarus's raising leads directly to Jesus' arrest and passion, by which he is 'glorified' (12:23-24)." See Keener, *The Gospel of John: A Commentary* (Grand Rapids, MI: Baker Academic, 2010), 2:839.
[2]So also Keener, *Gospel of John*, 2:839-90.

Bethany (Jn 11:20), Martha ran out to confront him, dressed in mourning clothes, hair disheveled, face covered with ashes, muttering to herself: "This is the way you treat those whom you love?"[3]

That's why Martha's response confuses me.[4] When she confronts Jesus ("Lord, if you would have been here, my brother would not have died," Jn 11:21), is she complaining ("Why didn't you come right away?"), or trying to mask disappointment ("You let me down, but I still believe in you"), or both? When she says, "Even now I know that whatever you might ask from God, God will give it to you" (Jn 11:22), is she suggesting that Jesus raise her brother from the dead? If that is the case, why does she protest when Jesus orders the tomb to be opened, objecting to the foul odor of Lazarus's four-day-old rotting corpse (Jn 11:39)?

Or could it be that, when she says essentially, "Even now I know God will answer your prayers," Martha is saying one thing ("I still believe in you") but Jesus hears something else ("Raise my brother from the dead")? That is to say, Martha wants Jesus to know that she still believes in the resurrection of the dead on the last day (Jn 11:24), "but she has not fully grasped just what that means," according to Marianne Meye Thompson.[5] That would be especially apropos for John's readers: like God, Jesus "is able to do far more abundantly beyond all that we ask or think" (Eph 3:20)—the seventh sign proved it. Martha models for us what faith looks like when we're faced with the death of our loved ones. We confess faith in Christ by affirming two things at once: sometimes Jesus does more than what we pray for (the miracle of giving life to the dead—resuscitation), and everyone who dies in Christ will be raised on the last day (the miracle of giving *eternal* life to the dead—resurrection).

The difficulty of sorting out Martha's response is compounded by the fact that she offers the picture-perfect confession of faith in Jesus (according to John's stated purpose, Jn 20:31). In fact, she's the *only* character

---

[3]Keener thinks Martha rushing to greet Jesus was a sign of respect (*Gospel of John*, 2:843).
[4]So also Marianne Meye Thompson: "It is difficult to explain her barely concealed reproach of Jesus (v. 21)." See Thompson, *John: A Commentary*, New Testament Library (Louisville, KY: Westminster John Knox, 2015), 245.
[5]Thompson, *John*, 245.

in John's Gospel who says exactly what a believer is supposed to confess: Jesus is the Christ, the Son of God (Jn 11:27). So, since she makes the proper confession, readers can't help but wonder: Why does she question Jesus, not only complaining to him about his absence but also questioning his decision to open Lazarus's grave? Martha seems to embody a mixed message: a believer who confesses her faith and questions the one she believes in. "You are faithful, but you let me down. You will never forsake us, but you left us hanging. You are good, but this is bad. You love us, but you weren't here to help us. You are life, but my brother is dead."

Even though Martha's behavior is a bit confusing to us, her response to Jesus should sound familiar to those who read the Psalms. It's because she speaks just like the psalmist who laments the absence of God in times of distress—a brilliant observation made by Gail O'Day in her character study of Martha. Martha didn't experience a lapse of faith, pangs of doubt spoiling her once-sterling confession of Christ. Martha hadn't lost hope when she complained to Jesus about him not being present in her hour of need. Rather, Martha was talking to Jesus like the psalmist who offers lamentation to the God of Israel. O'Day writes, "Martha's words move from complaint (v. 3) and petition (v. 21) to confidence (v. 24) and confession (v. 26). . . . Martha's words contain the basic elements of a prayer of lament. Just as the psalmist can simultaneously complain about God's absence and ask for God's rescue, here Martha does the same."[6] Indeed, it shouldn't surprise us that Martha sounds as if she's taken the psalmist's lamentation to heart, moving quickly from complaint to praise. For she had been grieving the death of her brother for four days, wailing lamentations, probably repeating lines from Psalms 6; 13; 35; 74; 79; 89— perhaps thinking of Jesus as she sang:

How long, LORD?
Will You hide Yourself forever?
Will Your wrath burn like fire?

---

[6]Gail R. O'Day, "Martha: Seeing the Glory of God," in *Character Studies in the Fourth Gospel: Narrative Approaches to Seventy Figures in John*, ed. Steven A. Hunt, D. Francois Tolmie, and Ruben Zimmermann (Tübingen: Mohr Siebeck, 2013), 498.

Remember what my lifespan is;

For what futility You have created all the sons of mankind!

What man can live and not see death?

Can he save his soul from the power of Sheol?

Where are Your former acts of favor, Lord? (Ps 89:46-49 NASB)

In other words, to put it bluntly, Martha talks to Jesus like Israel talked to God. O'Day says, "Her expressed faith is in Jesus as the Son of God. She moves from lament to praise not on the basis of a sign (which is still to come in this story), but on the basis of Jesus' self-revelation in vss. 25-26: 'I am the resurrection and the life.'"[7]

But what about Martha's protest when Jesus instructed the mourners to unseal the tomb of Lazarus (Jn 11:39)? Doesn't that reveal a deficiency in her faith that Jesus is the resurrection and the life? Not necessarily. O'Day suggests that Martha did the best she could given what she knew at the time.[8] She affirmed the resurrection of her brother on the last day but had to state the obvious dilemma: Lazarus was already decomposing, a "fact that is necessary to propel the storyline forward."[9] Martha's comment focuses the reader's attention on Jesus and his power over death and decay. Consequently, Martha's character serves a rhetorical purpose, helping the reader to see that one doesn't need a sign to believe in Jesus. Jesus is the sign—the resurrection and the life—the embodiment of his words, the object of our faith.

Others maintain Martha serves John's literary purpose but for different reasons. Some see her as the only one who can match the words of Jesus to the sign, seeing the glory of God in Jesus.[10] Or perhaps, as Keener says, she models a "deeper level of faith: if she believes, then she will see."[11] According to J. Ramsey Michaels, "Now [Jesus] tells her that because of her faith, what matters for her is not what she can smell—the

---

[7]O'Day, "Martha," 500.

[8]Also Andreas J. Köstenberger, *John*, Baker Exegetical Commentary on the New Testament (Grand Rapids, MI: Baker Academic, 2004), 343.

[9]O'Day, "Martha," 501.

[10]Thompson, *John*, 249-50.

[11]Keener, *Gospel of John*, 2:848.

foul odor of death—but what she is about to 'see'—the 'glory of God.'"[12]
But I wonder whether there's something more going on here. To take
O'Day's observation even further, perhaps Martha was rehearsing her
complaint—just like the psalmist—by pointing out that Lazarus had
been dead for *four days* (Jn 11:39). Since women were responsible for the
rituals associated with death, not only the details of the funeral but also
preparing the body for burial, then perhaps Martha was calling attention
to the consequences of Jesus' delay. Her attempts to cover the stench of
death—Jews didn't embalm bodies but covered corpses with aloes and
myrrh—would only last so long, about three days. It was the women's job
to protect their family's honor by covering the shame of death. Since the
period of mourning lasted at least a week, during which family and
friends would visit the grave, sealed tombs locked out offensive odors of
the unclean. Indeed, smelly bodies were shameful, which is why the
psalmist counts on God to protect his honor in the face of death:

> Therefore my heart is glad and my glory rejoices;
> *My flesh also will dwell securely.*
> For You will not abandon my soul to Sheol;
> You will not allow Your Holy One to undergo decay. (Ps 16:9-10 NASB)

Martha's concern was honorable. Opening Lazarus's tomb would have
shamed the family. Besides, the repugnant scent of Lazarus's rotten
corpse was another reminder that Jesus had disappointed Martha by not
coming right away. In fact, it could be said that Lazarus stunk because of
Jesus. It's one thing to grieve over death; it's something else to have
someone rub our noses in the reality of death's offensive presence. "Smell
this." That's why I think Martha says, "Lord, he already stinks. It's been
four days" (Jn 11:39). I hear a subtle complaint in her words, "It's been . . .
four . . . days"—her lamentation of death was also a protest of the absence
of Christ. Death stinks because Jesus wasn't there when Martha needed
him. Now, only God could help the one named "God helps him." Jesus
knew that better than anyone (Jn 11:41).

---

[12]J. Ramsey Michaels, *The Gospel of John*, New International Commentary on the New Testament
(Grand Rapids, MI: Eerdmans, 2010), 642.

Although Jesus was the only one who seemed to know what was going
on, all of us wonder why he did what he did—disciples then and now. We
puzzle over Jesus' behavior as well as Martha's. Why did he wait four days
to come to Bethany? To make sure Lazarus was good and dead? Is that
why he said to the Twelve that Lazarus' illness would reveal the "glory of
God, so that the Son of God would be glorified by it" (Jn 11:4)? If that
were the case, then Jesus let Lazarus die so that he could raise him from
the dead. Wasn't that being a little callous toward Martha's emotional
welfare? Or was Jesus trying to get Martha to move past her grief and
trust him completely—to see that faith in him not only meant believing
in the resurrection on the last day but also that he could bring Lazarus's
rotting corpse back to life?

But if Jesus knew from the beginning that he would raise Lazarus from
the dead, why did *he* weep (Jn 11:35)? What troubled Jesus so much that
he "was aggravated [*enebrimēsato*] in the spirit" when he saw the mourners
weeping (Jn 11:33)? Was he angry over their lack of faith (Jn 11:37): "I'm the
resurrection and the life. I'm here now. Why is everyone still grieving?" Or
did Jesus weep because he took to heart how much death wounds the
people he loves? Was he angry at death, knowing that he would face the
same enemy? Or was Jesus simply grieving the death of his friend (Jn
11:36)? Is that why he asked to see the tomb—he needed to grieve too?

There may be several reasons why Jesus did what he did. But, to me, the
simplest answer makes the most sense: Jesus wept because death hurts.

I'm glad Jesus wept. Even though Jesus knew he was their only hope—
the resurrection to Martha's grief, the life to Lazarus's death—he joined
the mourners in their lament. He was no coldhearted Messiah, standing
aloof as the Son of God, unable to relate to the heartache of humanity.
He suffered like we all suffer; he wept like we all weep. John wants to
make it plain—especially in the last sign—their bereavement didn't end
when Jesus showed up.[13] Indeed, even in the presence of Christ, there is
grieving over death. Even though we believe in the resurrection, we weep

---

[13]"The family's bereavement does not end, simply because Martha has confessed her faith in Jesus
as the Son of God" (O'Day, "Martha," 501).

at the graves of our loved ones. We may complain to the Lord. But we still confess he is faithful. We may lament his absence. But we still believe he loves us. We may be troubled by death's foul odor. But we still sing songs about the glory of God and his Christ.

DEATH IS A THIEF

My mom was the church organist. Music was around me constantly during all my growing-up years. Hymns enveloped our home, especially on Saturday nights, when she practiced the organ for Sunday services. I have fond memories of Mom practicing, Dad lying on the couch soaking up the music while my brothers and I prepared our Sunday go-to-meeting clothes—shirts ironed, matching ties, shoes shined. My mom worked hard at being a good musician. But it was a labor of love, especially evident when she played her favorites, songs such as, "Heaven Came Down and Glory Filled My Soul." Her head would tilt sideways, elbows mildly flapping, left leg pumping to and fro to reach the bass pedals. She was in heaven. I loved seeing her like that. No wonder we grew up music lovers. In fact, I can't imagine life without music. This simple gift brings healing to my soul like few other divine graces.

Yet, when my brother (the musician in the family) led us during the funeral to sing one of Mom's favorite songs, it hardly felt like "Heaven Came Down." The glory of God didn't fill my soul when the music played. Instead, a line from the Psalm 137 kept running through my head: "How can we sing the LORD's song in a foreign land?" (Ps 137:4 NASB). Indeed, this kind of loss was foreign to me; I hardly felt like singing praise to the Lord. What I needed was a song of lament. I wanted to complain to God about how much it hurt, how much it felt like he wasn't there, how much I needed him. The happy times of Mom playing the organ, the healing power of music, the joy of singing were gone. Death took them. What was supposed to help only hurt. What I needed to sing was the unsingable song—which is why, for the first time in my life, Psalm 137 came true for me. Captive Israel's words echoed in my ears when I had nothing to sing:

By the rivers of Babylon,
There we sat down and wept,
When we remembered Zion.
Upon the willows in the midst of it
We hung our harps.
For there our captors demanded of us songs,
And our tormentors, jubilation, *saying,*
"Sing for us one of the songs of Zion!"
How can we sing the LORD's song
In a foreign land? (Ps 137:1-4 NASB)

It was pouring rain that day when we buried my mom. Sheets of water fell on us, slowing our procession to a crawl as we made our way to a small cemetery in the country. I was strangely comforted by the heavy thunderstorm, the weather reflecting my heart. By the time we arrived, the ground was soaked—a muddy mess. The family quickly huddled under the tent to hear the Scriptures read, to sing a few more songs. After the final prayer, Dad broke down and wept inconsolably. We tried to comfort him and each other. Even though the brief graveside service was over, it didn't feel like the end. Nobody moved. We all just stood there: Dad wailing, the rain falling harder than ever, the casket before us covered in flowers. Nobody wanted to leave; none of us wanted to stay.

In the midst of the awkward, paralyzing silence, I asked us to sing one more song, another one of Mom's favorites: "Victory in Jesus." As we fumbled our way through the first verse, I noticed that some of our family members weren't singing. Respectfully, their heads were bowed as the rest of us tried to finish the song, singing the chorus like we meant it:

O Victory in Jesus, my Savior forever
He sought me and bought me
With His redeeming blood.
He loved me ere I knew him
And all my love is due him

He plunged me to victory
Beneath the cleansing flood.[14]

But this flood didn't bring cleansing. The hearse was stuck in the mud. The driver asked for our assistance. My mom's grandsons jumped in to help, pushing the back of the hearse while the driver gave it a little gas. Wheels dug deeper into the mud. Just about the time it looked like he was stuck there for good, the driver asked for one last push. He revved the engine, the wheels spinning fast, slowly edging out of the trench, flinging soggy soil everywhere, the hearse splattering funeral clothes with mud—one last, fitting tribute to the spoils of death.

When I visited my mother's grave several weeks later to see the new headstone, it was bright and sunny. In the light of day, I stared at the mound of dirt, flowers tossed haphazardly on top, ruts in the marred grass left by the hearse, the glimmering headstone, the last bit of fall colors dotting the landscape, and my mom's name etched in cold stone. Same place, different scenery. *How could such a horrible day end up looking like this?* Then, I remembered an old family picture of this very spot: a four-year-old version of my mom in her Sunday best standing beside the new grave of her grandfather—the plot next to my mom's grave. *She's come full circle*, I thought to myself. Then, my theology kicked in. *No. That's not right. She hasn't come full circle. This may be the place where she's buried. But this isn't the end.* Then I imagined the resurrection, the day when my mom and her grandparents will come forth from the grave—like Lazarus unbound by grave clothes—because Jesus will call their name. "This will be the first place they see in the resurrection," I muttered to myself. "Me too, if they bury me here. What a day that will be, when everything we have learned comes true." *Then* we will *see* what we *believe*: Jesus is the resurrection and the life, just like he said.

Oh, how I long to see the resurrection with my own eyes.

---

[14]Eugene M. Bartlett (1885–1941), "Victory in Jesus."

THOMAS SEES

Like most of the major characters of John's Gospel, Thomas is intriguing—
perhaps more than all the others. First, even though he barely shows up
in the Synoptic Gospels, Thomas is a major disciple in John's narrative
world (appearing four times, Jn 11:16; 14:5; 20:24-28; 21:2). Why does John
feature Thomas when Matthew, Mark, and Luke practically ignore him?
Second, *Thomas* (*Toma* in Aramaic, *Didymos* in Greek) means "twin."
Because of the way John constantly refers to him as "the one called
'Didymus'" (Jn 11:16; 20:24; 21:2), some have suggested that perhaps
Thomas was Jesus' doppelgänger—that he looked so much like Jesus that
the disciples referred to him as "the twin." (Due to Hollywood films, we
all know what Jesus looked like: long brown hair; sharp, handsome features; beard; twinkly eyes.)[15] Third, Thomas is the first disciple to recognize that following Jesus will cost him his life—the true meaning of
discipleship (Jn 11:16).

Fourth, since Thomas wasn't present the first time the resurrected
Jesus appeared to his disciples (Jn 20:24), one can't help but wonder:
(1) Did Thomas miss out on receiving the Holy Spirit, thereby lacking the
authority to forgive sins (Jn 20:22-23)? (2) Or did John intend to cast
Thomas in a positive light, since he was the only man who refused to live
in fear, hiding behind locked doors like the rest of the disciples (Jn 20:19)?
(3) Furthermore, did John intend to lead his readers to infer that Thomas
was the beloved disciple since he knew about the wound in Jesus' side (Jn
20:25)—something that only an eyewitness would know about (Jn
19:31-35) since the Synoptic Gospels don't include that detail in their accounts of the crucifixion of Jesus?

Fifth, was Thomas's desire for physical evidence of Jesus' resurrection
a good thing—he simply wanted the same experience as the other disciples? Or was it a bad thing since it earned him the nickname "doubting
Thomas" (we certainly don't call him "the twin")? Sixth, did Thomas

---

[15]See discussion on the "cinematic Jesus" in David B. Capes, Rodney Reeves, and E. Randolph
Richards, *Rediscovering Jesus: An Introduction to Biblical, Religious and Cultural Perspectives on
Christ* (Downers Grove, IL: IVP Academic, 2015), 240-53.

follow through with his demand, actually touching the wounds of Jesus? Or was seeing Jesus enough to believe? Finally, in light of Thomas's profession of faith (Jn 20:28)—the strongest confession of them all—does he play a positive role in confirming the corporal resurrection of Jesus (versus the Gnostics)?[16] Or does Thomas's need for visual confirmation (Jn 20:25) undermine the purpose of John's Gospel (readers don't need to see in order to believe), thereby prompting both Jesus' mild rebuke and his blessing for John's readers (Jn 20:29)?

Thomas is an ambiguous character in John's Gospel. We don't know whether to admire him or scoff at him. Are we supposed to see him as a model disciple, ready to die for Jesus, offering the most profound confession of faith in all of Scripture? Or has he justifiably invited our contempt, earning the moniker "doubting Thomas," a disciple who *demanded* physical proof of Jesus' resurrection before he would believe? Is he a good guy, or a bad guy, or someone in between? Once again, we find ourselves looking into the mirror of John's Gospel, trying to recognize our reflection. How we see Thomas may reveal our place in the story of abiding in Christ, even helping us to identify his "twin."[17]

Consider how the Twin says what disciples are supposed to say—things I'd like to think that I would say as a true follower of Jesus. When Thomas encourages his fellow disciples to follow Jesus "in order that we might die with him" (Jn 11:16), the Twin sounds like the kind of disciple Jesus is looking for in the Synoptic Gospels. Indeed, his call to "let us go and die with Jesus" takes the reader of John's Gospel by surprise. That's because in John's narrative world Jesus doesn't say things such as, "Whoever wants to follow me must deny himself and take up his cross daily and follow me" (Lk 9:23), or "Whoever wants to save his life must lose it; and whoever loses his life for me will find it" (Mt 16:25), or even

---

[16]The Gnostics were second-century heretics who denied the humanity of Christ because they believed the physical world was evil. Some claimed Christ was an angel who looked like a man (docetism), while others maintained a Christ-spirit inhabited the human Jew Jesus (adoptionism). Consequently, they denied the physical resurrection of Jesus Christ.

[17]For the possibilities, see Thomas Popp, "Thomas: Question Marks and Exclamation Marks," in Hunt, Tolmie, and Zimmermann, *Character Studies in the Fourth Gospel*, 525-28.

"Sell your possessions and give the money as alms to the poor" (Lk 12:33). In John's Gospel, Jesus doesn't require his disciples to sacrifice their lives for him. When it comes to following Jesus in John, it's more about what you get (eternal life) than what you give up. Indeed, the *only* challenge the disciples have to deal with is the absence of Christ; the only thing they have to give up is his presence. Due to his absence, they will endure the hatred of the world because the world hates Christ. Once he's gone, the world will hate Christ by hating his disciples. Consequently, Jesus spends a lot of time in John's Gospel trying to prepare his followers for his departure—the so-called Farewell Discourse (Jn 13:31–16:33). This seems to be the only requirement of discipleship in John: remaining faithful to Jesus in his absence.

So, when the Twin infers that following Jesus will mean losing his life, we should be a little mystified. Why would he say something like that—especially when we know that following Jesus in John's Gospel leads to *life*, not death? The seventh sign proves it. "But wait," the observant reader might say. "The Twin didn't know that. He made his inference *before* Jesus raised Lazarus from the dead! Besides, it wouldn't mean much at all to be prepared to 'die with Jesus' when the very man you are following can raise you from the dead! No big deal (is that why Jesus rebukes Peter in John 13:38?). But to be willing to die for Jesus *before* Christ revealed that *he is* the Resurrection and the Life—now that's something to admire. The Twin wanted to be with Jesus no matter what, even in death." But what does the Twin do when he has to face death *without* Jesus?

I think that's what the Twin is driving at when he asks the question, "Lord, we don't know where you are going. How are we able to know 'the way'?" (Jn 14:5). To the casual reader, it seems that Thomas has misunderstood Jesus' talk about his departure. His "going away to prepare a place" could be understood simply as Jesus informing the Twelve about his future travel plans. What makes them think he is referring to his death? Jesus simply says, "Where I am going you cannot follow me now, but you will later" (Jn 13:33, 36)—a rather vague statement that could mean several things. But Peter immediately takes Jesus' talk about going away as a reference to his death, prompting the disciple to promise to die for Jesus (Jn 13:37). Even though Jesus rebuffs Peter about his pledge, his assumptions are correct: Jesus is talking rather enigmatically about his death and return (Jn 14:1-3).

Furthermore, Jesus states plainly that his disciples should already know "where I am going" (Jn 14:4). What could that mean? That they should already know that Jesus is going to die? Certainly, the Twin already figured that out a long time ago (Jn 11:16). Yet, Jesus has never *explicitly* told the Twelve that he will die in Jerusalem (like he does several times in the Synoptic Gospels, where he practically gives his disciples a blow-by-blow account of what will happen to him and them: Mt 16:21; 17:22; 20:18-19; 26:31-32). Instead, Jesus says things such as, "If I am lifted up from the earth, I will draw everyone to me" (Jn 12:32), and "For a little while longer the light is among you" (Jn 12:35)—vague expressions that can hardly be characterized as "speaking plainly" about his upcoming death (Jn 16:29).

It's no wonder, then, that both Peter and the Twin don't know where Jesus was going (Jn 13:36; 14:5). He's talking about his departure like they should already know "the way." But they don't have a clue. In John's Gospel, Jesus doesn't prepare his disciples for the way of the cross like he does in the Synoptic Gospels. Therefore, it must have come as a relief to them when Jesus answered the Twin's question with the simple claim: "I am the way" (Jn 14:6). For they were very familiar with *that* path; it was one they had taken for three years. Wherever Jesus goes, disciples abide with him.

So, at the precipitous moment when Jesus was arrested, saying to his captors, "Let these *men* go on their way" (Jn 18:8 NASB), I wonder whether it confused the disciples or whether they thought, "We knew this would happen." Notice that the disciples are not described as abandoning Jesus in his hour of need like we read in the Synoptic Gospels. There's no story of the Twelve falling asleep in Gethsemane—Jesus having to wake them up, reminding them to watch and pray. There's no surprise visit in the middle of the night, the disciples waking up confused and disoriented. Judas doesn't point out Jesus to his captors. There's not even a kiss of betrayal. None of these things make it into John's account. Instead, everything happens according to Jesus' plan. *Jesus* asks the mob, "Whom do you seek?" *Jesus* identifies himself as the man they came to arrest, "I am he." *Jesus* gives the disciples permission to leave him when he says to the soldiers, "Let these men go." Everything happens according to Jesus' plan—he prepared his disciples for this moment, his departure: "You cannot follow me now but you will later" (Jn 13:36).

So, in John's narrative world, the disciples do exactly what they were supposed to do. They don't abandon Jesus. We don't read lines such as, "And they all left him and fled" (Mk 14:50) or "Then all the disciples abandoned him and ran away" (Mt 26:56). Rather, the Twelve fulfill Jesus' prophecy (Jn 13:33, 36) and take their cue from him that it is time to exit the scene (Jn 18:8)—even though Peter is unwilling to go without a fight (Peter *still* thinks he's going to lay down his life for Jesus; Jn 18:10). All of this happens according to the divine plan, "in order that the word might be fulfilled when he said, 'I didn't lose a single disciple that you gave to me'" (Jn 18:9). The only challenge the Twelve will face, the only cost of discipleship according to John's Gospel—the absence of Jesus— has finally begun. Now it is time to see how they will handle it (Jn 14:19, 28-29; 16:4-7, 16-24), whether his words will abide in them in the meantime (Jn 14:23–15:8).

When Jesus gave advice to his disciples on how to handle his absence, it was based on the assumption that he had given his "peace to them" (Jn 14:27). The evidence of peace in his absence would be that (1) they would not lose faith (Jn 14:29), (2) they would keep his commandments/his word (love each other as he loved them; Jn 13:34; 15:12-14, 17), (3) they would have joy in the midst of sorrow (Jn 15:11; 16:5-6, 19-24), (4) they would be courageous (Jn 16:31-33), and (5) they would ask anything in his name (Jn 14:13-14; 15:16; 16:23-27). Eventually, things would get better, when Jesus returned to them and gifted them with his "Helper" (Jn 14:3, 16-20, 26; 15:26; 16:7-16). But during the interim—that perilous time without his presence, when the world hated them like it hated Christ (Jn 15:18–16:3)—the disciples had to go at it alone, abiding in his words to find peace. By remembering his words, they could abide in his words, which could keep his disciples "from stumbling" until he returned to them (Jn 15:20; 16:1).

We don't get to see in John's Gospel whether the Twelve exhibited the peace of Christ while he was gone. We're not told what they did, what they thought—how they handled the absence of Christ. Of course, John does feature a few individual disciples during the interim: Peter, the "other disciple," and the beloved one. Apparently, Simon didn't bear witness to the peace of Christ because he denied that he was a disciple of Jesus (Jn 18:15-27). Perhaps it could be said that a few disciples—the beloved one and the three Marys—exhibited the peace of Christ to some degree. At least they followed Jesus to the cross. But what about the rest of the Twelve? By all appearances, because they were hiding in a locked room "for fear of the Jews" (Jn 20:19), the disciples were not abiding in the words, "Don't let your heart be troubled or fearful" (Jn 14:27). They all seem to be troubled and fearful, except one: the Twin (Jn 20:24).

Why wasn't Thomas among the disciples who were hiding in fear? Maybe the Twin wasn't afraid—the one disciple who lived up to Jesus' expectations, not having a troubled and fearful heart. Perhaps John intended for Thomas's absence to be conspicuous to the reader, demonstrating that he was the *only* disciple bearing witness to the peace of Christ. While the rest of the disciples were acting like cowards, the Twin went about his business in Jerusalem like he had nothing to hide. That would make sense; he had already decided that he was willing to die with Jesus (Jn 11:16). What a powerful image, the Twin in full public view after the crucifixion! In my mind's eye I see the citizens of Jerusalem musing over the spectacle: "Who is that guy? Is that Jesus walking around the city? That can't be right. He's dead and gone. Wait a minute. That's the Twin. Ha! He looks like a dead man walking!"

If Thomas were the only courageous disciple, it would also explain why Jesus needed to appear to his fearful disciples first: they needed to see

Jesus and receive the Helper before they could bear witness to the peace of Christ. In fact, they were so fearful, Jesus had to say it *twice*, "Peace be with you" (Jn 20:19, 21). So, when the once-cowering-but-no-longer-troubled disciples reported to the Twin that they've seen Jesus, it's no wonder Thomas wanted to see the Lord for himself (Jn 20:25). The Twin may have been courageous, but he was still troubled by the *way* Jesus died.

In John's narrative world Jesus never talked about the cross. Of course, we are able to read between the lines in hindsight—just like the narrator—and see veiled references to the crucifixion (Jn 3:14; 8:28; 12:32-33; 18:31-32). But the disciples didn't see it coming. In fact, in John's narrative world, since Jesus never told them explicitly that he would be executed—much less how it would happen or who would do it—it must have come as quite a shock to see Jesus crucified. That's a completely different scenario from what we read in the Synoptic Gospels, where Jesus speaks openly about who, what, when, where, and why he will be crucified. But the way John tells the story, the Twelve would only understand Jesus' talk of being "lifted up" as a reference to the cross ex post facto. "So, that's what he meant when he said, 'lifted up'—he wasn't talking about being lifted up in honor. He was talking about a cross." That's why, I think, the Twin emphasized the traumatic details of Jesus' death, wanting to see the scars of crucifixion (Jn 20:25). He already anticipated that Jesus was going to die; he was trying to make sense of why Jesus had to die *like that*.

When the Twin heard the disciples say, "We have seen the Lord" (Jn 20:25), we might have expected doubting Thomas to ask, "Are you sure it was he?"[18] We also wouldn't be surprised if he demanded the *same* treatment: "I won't believe unless I see him too." And yet, the Twin said he wouldn't believe unless he handled the *wounds* of the crucified one. That's an odd request, needing to see the wounds of crucifixion to believe in the resurrection. It would have made better sense if the Twin had demanded to see the body of the resurrected Christ *without* the wounds of death. After all, since Jesus is the resurrection (Jn 11:25), shouldn't he

---

[18]Popp, "Thomas," 516.

embody life without any trace of death? But, for some reason, the Twin didn't say, "I won't believe until I can touch his resurrected body." Instead, rather ironically, Thomas claimed he needed to handle the marks of death in order to believe in the resurrection of Jesus. Jesus obliged. One week later, the resurrected Messiah appeared before the same group (plus Thomas) and encouraged the Twin to touch the scars left by the cross (Jn 20:26-27). Then Jesus said, "Don't be an unbeliever [*apistos*]; rather, be a believer [*pistos*]"—a line that could also be translated, "Don't be unfaithful; rather, be faithful" (Jn 20:27)—provoking an immediate confession of faith from the Twin: "My Lord and My God" (Jn 20:28).

Should we give Thomas the benefit of the doubt? Strangely enough, it depends on how we read the last line (Jn 20:29), whether Jesus asks a question or makes a statement. Did Jesus chide the Twin for needing to see him in order to believe? Those who think so tend to hear Jesus asking a rhetorical question: "Because you have seen me, have you *now* believed? Blessed *are* they who did not see, and *yet* believed" (NASB).[19] Then the narrator rushes in with a reminder to his readers: "That's why I wrote this Gospel, so that you would believe and be blessed with eternal life even though you didn't see with your own eyes the signs Jesus performed" (my paraphrase of Jn 20:30-31). By offering his blessing to John's readers, then, Jesus is rebuking Thomas for needing empirical proof of the resurrection. In this light, the Twin is an example of inferior faith, unable to believe what he hears.[20] Others think Jesus has affirmed Thomas for moving from "unbelief" to "belief," evidenced by his confession of faith (Jn 20:28).[21] So, Jesus was offering his confirmation of the Twin, "Because you have seen me, you have believed" (NIV), which was also true of the Twelve (Jn 20:19-25). Then Jesus speaks directly to John's readers—believers who can only rely on words—and pronounces a special beatitude for them, "Blessed are those who have not seen but still

---

[19]Ben Witherington III, *John's Wisdom: A Commentary on the Fourth Gospel* (Louisville, KY: Westminster John Knox, 1995), 341, 343-44.

[20]James Resseguie, *The Strange Gospel: Narrative Design and Point of View in John* (Leiden: Brill, 2001), 163-64.

[21]Keener, *Gospel of John*, 2:1211; Popp, "Thomas," 525.

believed."[22] Faith in Jesus requires both apostolic testimony (those who
have seen) and those who believe it (those who have heard).[23]

"DO YOU BELIEVE THIS?"

I don't blame the Twin for needing to see Jesus, to touch the wounds of
the crucified one, in order to believe Christ conquered death—especially
a death like that. The cross was a horrible way to die. Even though John's
version of the death of Jesus sounds triumphant compared to the Synoptic Gospels—the victorious declaration, "It is finished!" (Jn 19:30) replaces the despondent cry, "My God, my God, why have you forsaken
me?" (Mt 27:46)—his account of the crucifixion is still hard to read. The
execution of Jesus was so vicious, so inhumane, so cruel, so shameful, so
pitiful, so shocking. If I were in Thomas's sandals, I would have been
shaking my head in disbelief, "We knew he was going to die—he said so.
But, why did he have to die *like that*? He said he was the way, the truth,
and the life. Is this what he meant? Is the cross truly the way to life?"
Thompson writes, "Jesus' death threatens to end Thomas' faith because
Thomas cannot accept the reports that Jesus has risen; he cannot believe
on the basis of the testimony of others; and faith cannot be directed
toward a dead man."[24]

More than that, I think Thomas was so offended by the cross—apparently obsessing over the gruesome details—that he reveals why "faith
cannot be directed toward a [crucified] man." The Twin may have lived
up to Jesus' warning about not being fearful. But by all appearances he
was offended by the cross of Jesus Christ. Nobody saw that coming, an
astonishingly tragic event that would *only* make sense in the hindsight
of resurrection. Ironically for the Twin, the proof of a resurrected
Messiah would be revealed by the wounds of the cross. The stumbling
block to faith (Jn 16:1) became the reason to believe. Indeed, once he saw

---

[22]Edward W. Klink III, "Audience," in *How John Works: Storytelling in the Fourth Gospel*, ed.
Douglas Estes and Ruth Sheridan (Atlanta: SBL Press, 2016), 255.
[23]Popp, "Thomas," 522-23.
[24]Thompson, *John*, 425.

the wounds of death, the Twin believed that Jesus was the Lord of the resurrection and the God of life (Jn 20:28).

Death is ugly. Even though we know it's coming, it's still shocking. Despite the fact that we accept death as a part of life, it can be so disorienting when it happens. Even though some deaths are far worse than others—adults murdered, teenagers killed in car wrecks, children dying of cancer—the loss of life is always devastating. Death is permanent. Death never stops. Death spoils life. Death intrudes. Death stinks. Death hurts. You would think, therefore, that a mighty God would keep death from ruining his good work of life. But, rather than keep death at bay, God lets death have its way. Instead of protecting his creation from the ruins of death, God entered the ruin of creation to take in death and all of its torturous ways. Jesus knew he was the resurrection and the life because he was destined to be the crucified and the sacrifice—an ugly death swallowed up by a beautiful life, a pungent stench overwhelmed by a sweet bouquet, a harsh reality transformed by a new hope, a wicked reign overpowered by a good king. Lazarus's tomb may cast a foul odor, and the wounds of the cross may scar the work of God. But, praise be to God, death doesn't have the last word. The scent of death may linger, and a violent death may cause even the faithful to stumble, but those who see Jesus—the resurrection and the life—abide in his peace. This is our confession: Jesus is the Christ, the Son of God, who gives eternal life to those who believe. And because of this, we say defiantly to death: "Jesus has already given *us* the last word. 'Blessed are those who have not seen and still believe.'"

That's the hard part, believing what we can't see. We see suffering. We see disease. We see death. No faith is required to see such things. But what I really want to see is what the Twin saw: the death of death. I want to see the glory of God. I want to see the Word incarnate. I want to see resurrection *with my own eyes*. We believe that will happen one day, when we see what Martha and Thomas saw. Until then, however, all we have are words—words heard, words lived. And, for those of us who believe in the Word incarnate, words should be enough—at least, that's what I tried to say at the end of my remarks during my mother's funeral:

I've learned many things from my mom. Her love of music, her love of Christ, her love of the church, how she reveled in family get-togethers, cherished a delicious meal, loved to read, and, most of all, how she cared for us. The same qualities I see in my sweet wife, my children, my family. It's the word becoming flesh and dwelling among us. The Word incarnate I need to see when words fail me.

For the love of Christ, until the resurrection, all we have are words, the Spirit of God, and each other. And, because of Christ, that is more than enough.

3

BELIEVE AND SEE

Incarnating the Word

"LET ME SHARE WITH YOU A PARABLE." In the film *Jackie*, a priest is walking with Jackie Kennedy, trying to console her as she questions the senselessness of a God-ordained world filled with suffering. She wonders out loud whether she should have chosen a more austere life—one without risk—settling for the more predictable world of a shop girl or stenographer, having married an "ordinary, lazy, ugly man." After a long, pensive pause, the priest says, "Let me share with you a parable," and proceeds to give a brief version of when Jesus healed the man born blind (Jn 9:1-7). The disciples' question, "Rabbi, who sinned, this man or his parents, that he should be born blind?" (Jn 9:2), not only sets up the story in John's Gospel, it also serves the priest's purpose very well. After repeating Jesus' answer ("Neither this man sinned nor his parents, but in order that the work of God might be revealed in him," Jn 9:3), the priest connects the dots for Jackie: "Right now you are blind. Not because you've sinned. But because you've been chosen—so that the works of God may be revealed in you."[1] In the rough-and-tumble world of cause and effect—why did this happen to me?—the parable is supposed to break through the blinding pain of Jackie's suffering to help her see the purposes of God.

The film puts many issues on display, not only rehearsing the tragic death of John F. Kennedy through the eyes of the first lady but also

---

[1] *Jackie*, directed by Pablo Larrain (Los Angeles: Fox Searchlight Pictures, 2016).

juxtaposing the attempts by those closest to her to make sense of a world gone crazy. Of course, as a minister I was intrigued by the role of the priest, especially how he listens patiently to her as she lashes out at God. When he decided to use a parable to answer the question of theodicy (how can a good, powerful God allow such horrendous evil?), I leaned in and wondered which parable of Jesus he would recite. The wheat and the tares? (God allows the evil one to muck up things presently, but evil will be destroyed in the end.) The sheep and the goats? (Ours is not to know why bad things happen to good people; we should keep our eyes open to help the least of these.) Or maybe he would tell the most famous parable of all, the good Samaritan (a fleshed-out version of Jesus' teaching "Love your enemies"). And so, when the priest says, "Let me share with you a parable" and tells the Gospel story about the healing of the blind man, I immediately thought, "That's not a parable! Ignorant screenplay writers. They can't tell the difference between fiction and reality. Besides, everyone knows there are no parables in John's Gospel."

That brings up a good question: *Why* are there no parables in John's Gospel, especially when Jesus relied on them so much in the Synoptic Gospels to teach the people about the kingdom of God? Jesus tells parables to help his disciples envision the reign of God on earth, to get them to see how the kingdom of heaven comes to earth. That's why he starts a series of parables with "Behold!" which is a more antiquated way of saying, "Look at it like this!" (Mt 13:3; Mk 4:3). If the people could *hear* what Jesus was saying, then they would be able to *see* the kingdom come on earth as it is in heaven. To see the kingdom of God (*the* King reigning on earth), one must embody the words of Jesus (Mt 7:24-27)—something Jesus emphasizes in John's Gospel too (Jn 5:24; 6:63, 68; 8:31-32, 38, 43, 47; 12:47-50; 14:23-24; 15:7). Indeed, John relied on his Gospel in the same way Jesus counted on parables: to help us see the King and his kingdom through the incarnation of his word. Perhaps the priest was right. Not just the story of Jesus healing the blind man, but John's *entire* Gospel works like a parable when the word of Jesus is fleshed out right before our eyes and we are invited to abide in the narrative as if it were our story too.

"Go! Your Son Lives"

When God speaks, things happen. "Let there be light," and it was so. "Let there be life," and it was so. In the beginning, God used words to create everything. Whenever he speaks, *even now* his words work, eternally echoing everywhere, through all time, sustaining all creation, accomplishing his intended purpose. That's how John sets up his Gospel, predicating the work of God on the Word of God (Jn 1:3-4). When God speaks, there is light and life. That's why, when the "true light came into the world and lit up every person" (Jn 1:9), people were either drawn to the light or repelled by it. Those who were drawn to the Light were given life, becoming "children of God" (Jn 1:10-13). That's also why the Word of God "was fleshed out among us"—so that all who have eyes to see the Light would be able to gaze on the theater of God's glorious presence (Jn 1:14).[2] As far as John is concerned, the glory of God enlightens every person. Once you've seen it—the glorious Word of God fleshed out—you realize what grace and truth really are because the incarnated Word has explained God better than anyone or anything (Jn 1:14-18).

It comes as no surprise, then, that when Jesus speaks things happen. As the Word of God, Jesus says nothing except what God has told him to say (Jn 12:49). His words are God's word. Consequently, whenever Jesus speaks, there is light and life. He says, "Get up. Pick up your mat and walk" (Jn 5:8), and the lame man walks. He says, "Lazarus, come out!" (Jn 11:43), and the dead man walks. In fact, in five of the seven signs, Jesus' words make things happen (Jn 2:7-8; 4:50; 5:8; 9:7; 11:43)—the five miracles unique to John's Gospel. Yet, when it comes to all seven signs, faith shows up only in two: the healing of the nobleman's son (at the beginning) and sight to the man born blind (at the end).[3] In other words, faith doesn't seem to play any role for those who needed the miracle in the other five signs: not the head waiter, the lame man, the hungry multitude, the boated disciples, or Lazarus. None of these needy people

---

[2]The word John uses, *etheasametha*, "we beheld his glory," is where we get the English word *theater*.
[3]Of course, the first sign resulted in the faith of the disciples (Jn 2:11); but they were not the ones who needed the miracle.

needed to believe to receive their miracle. But, when it came to a sick boy and a blind man, faith mattered.

An official within Herod Antipas's administration (or perhaps a member of Herod's family) believed that Jesus was his only hope to save his son from death (Jn 4:46-47, 52).[4] Not trusting his slaves to fetch Jesus (Jn 4:51), the VIP traveled to Cana hoping to find Jesus and have him "come down and heal his son" (Jn 4:47). He had heard that Jesus was in Cana—about a day away—but how reliable was the information? Even if it was true, there was no guarantee that Jesus would still be there once the desperate father arrived. Since a crowd tended to follow Jesus wherever he went (Jn 4:45), imagine the relief the nobleman felt when he saw the large mob in the little village at such a late hour (around 7 p.m.; Jn 4:52).[5] Wasting no time, the father took royal privilege—probably barging through the crowd—went straight up to Jesus and explained his desperate situation (Jn 4:47).

At this point, Jesus should have said, "I will come and heal him" (see Mt 8:7). After all, Jesus had already performed several signs, indicating his desire to help many people (Jn 2:23; 4:45). But, that's not what Jesus says. Instead, he seems bothered by the man's request, offering a rather terse reply: "There's no way you people will believe unless you all see signs and wonders" (Jn 4:48). Honestly, given Jesus' reputation and the father's pitiful situation, that doesn't sound like Jesus at all. In fact, it's a little disappointing to hear Jesus respond so callously to what is obviously a life-and-death situation. What's going on here?

Perhaps Jesus was trying to put the privileged man in his place.[6] A man of such nobility (great power or great birth) was probably used to getting his way.[7] Plus, in John's Gospel, Jesus has already shown a resistance to

---

[4]The word, *basilikos*, "royal," is an adjective, "royal law" (Jas 2:8), "royal robe" (Acts 12:21); but here it is a substantival adjective, meaning "royal man."

[5]John seems to have used Roman time, i.e., the "seventh hour" = 7 a.m./p.m. (see Jn 19:14, where Jesus was interrogated by Pilate "about the sixth hour" = 6 a.m.).

[6]James Resseguie, *The Strange Gospel: Narrative Design and Point of View in John* (Leiden: Brill, 2001), 134.

[7]Keener suggests that John's audience would be suspicious of this man, questioning his "ortho-doxy" since he belonged to Herod's household, notorious for being marginal Jews. See Craig S. Keener, *The Gospel of John: A Commentary* (Grand Rapids, MI: Baker Academic, 2010), 1:630-31.

comply with "command performances"—even from his mother (Jn 2:4).[8] Others see significance in the plural pronoun "you all."[9] The narrator has just told us the reason so many Galileans had gathered around Jesus: they were attracted to the signs he performed (Jn 4:45)—a problem that shows up later (Jn 6:14-15, 22-40). These people were following Jesus for the free food and the sideshow. Consequently, Jesus' rebuke was intended for the Galilean sign-seekers as much as for the nobleman: "There's no way *you people* will believe unless *you all* see signs and wonders" (Jn 4:48). Even though Jesus performed signs to reveal his identity so that they would believe *in him*, the miracles ended up frustrating his purpose. The Galileans were more interested in the signs than in the one to whom the signs pointed.[10]

If the nobleman had approached Jesus with a sense of entitlement, then he surely would have been offended by Jesus' mini-sermon about everyone wanting to see signs. After all, the narrator makes it plain that Jesus directed his snide remark *to him* (Jn 4:48). But rather than offer a rebuttal ("Look, I didn't come for a sermon. I'm not here to see the circus. I heard you were merciful—that you will heal anyone. I thought you would help me. I guess I was wrong"), the desperate father simply repeats his plea: "Lord, please come down before my child dies" (Jn 4:49). Now we see why Jesus directed his comment to the father about all of these thrill seekers hoping to see a sign. It had to do with what the nobleman expected. Notice that he said he wanted Jesus to "come down" to Capernaum, meaning he wanted Jesus to return home with him (with the Galilean mob in tow!) to heal his son. Perhaps he expected Jesus to use the typical methods of Jewish holy men: laying hands on the boy and

---

[8]Marianne Meye Thompson, *John: A Commentary*, New Testament Library (Louisville, KY: Westminster John Knox, 2015), 113-14; Resseguie, *Strange Gospel*, 132.

[9]For example, see Andreas J. Köstenberger, *John*, Baker Exegetical Commentary on the New Testament (Grand Rapids, MI: Baker Academic, 2004), 170; Ben Witherington III, *John's Wisdom: A Commentary on the Fourth Gospel* (Louisville, KY: Westminster John Knox Press, 1995), 128.

[10]The same problem shows up in Matthew's Gospel, where Jesus expected the Galileans to repent when they saw the miracles he and his disciples performed (Mt 11:20-24). See Rodney Reeves, *Matthew*, Story of God Bible Commentary (Grand Rapids, MI: Zondervan, 2017), 229-31.

praying to God.[11] If Jesus complied, the father and the Galileans would see signs and wonders, having witnessed the miraculous healing of his son. In that respect, the nobleman would be just like the Galileans, which is why, I think, Jesus refused to "go down" to Capernaum immediately. Instead, Jesus simply says to the father, "Go! Your son lives" (Jn 4:50)— which brings us to the point of the story: to see whether the man was willing to believe the word in order to see the sign. Indeed, he was: "The man believed the word that Jesus said to him and walked away" (Jn 4:50). How do we know he "believed the word"? The desperate father returned home *without* Jesus.

A day away from home, the nobleman didn't know that Jesus' word worked immediately: "Your son lives," and it was so (Jn 4:52). Even though the narrator doesn't explore the interim, I can't help but wonder what the father thought about as he traveled back to Capernaum. If I were in his sandals, all kinds of thoughts (fear, wonder, anxiety, hope) would have been buzzing through my head. In my mind's eye, I see him bedded down for the night—somewhere between Cana and Capernaum— rehearsing the day's events:

> What just happened? I came all this way hoping I would find Jesus, and I did! What a relief. All I had to do was convince him to come home with me to heal my son. [I wonder how my boy is doing? Is he all right?] Then Jesus gives a little speech about people needing to see signs and wonders to believe. Why did he say that to me? I could care less whether I see a miracle. I just want my son to live. [Oh God! I love my son. It would kill me if he died.] I begged Jesus to come with me. Then he simply said, "Go home. Your son is alive." That's it. That's all he said. And, for some strange reason, I believed him. Could it be true? Is that all it took, for Jesus to give the word? Did he heal my son? When I get home tomorrow, will I see him alive and well? What if he's not? What if he's still sick? Should I have tried harder to convince Jesus to come with me? What am I going to say to my wife when she sees me *without* Jesus? Do I tell her the whole story? Why did I leave without

---

[11]Geza Vermes, *Jesus the Jew: A Historian's Reading of the Gospels* (Philadelphia: Fortress, 1981), 65-78.

him? [Oh Lord! I'm such a fool.] But, what if it's true? What if Jesus was right? What if my son is better? What if he began to feel better soon after I left? How would I know? By the time I get home, it will have been two days. Maybe Jesus knew it. My son is better. That's what Jesus was trying to say. The fever broke and my son is well. So, I've wasted a trip, coming all this way only to turn right around and go back home. I don't care. As long as my son is well, that's all that matters. [God in heaven, please let it be true.]

Of course, there is no way of knowing whether the nobleman puzzled over what Jesus said as he returned to Capernaum. Yet, when he finally made it home the next day and heard that his son was alive, the father couldn't help but ask exactly *when* his son got better (Jn 4:52). Imagine the look of wonder on the father's face when his slaves reported innocuously, "Yesterday, at the seventh hour, the fever left him" (Jn 4:52)—the very moment when Jesus said, "Your son lives" (Jn 4:53).

The only person who saw the sign was the one who needed it the most. The Galileans traveling with Jesus in Cana didn't get to see the sign. No one back home in Capernaum saw the sign—not the slaves, not the family, not even the boy who was sick with fever knew a miracle had occurred. Strangely enough, not even Jesus was there to see the sign come true. Instead, only one man saw the sign: the father. Yet, even he didn't get to see with his own eyes the miracle of his son getting better as soon as Jesus gave the word. In fact, the only way the father was able to see the sign (Jesus is the Word of life) was through believing the word: both from Jesus and from the slaves. This bears repeating: *only the father* was able to see the sign performed by Jesus, because he was the only one who could correlate Jesus' promise and the testimony of the slaves.

Now we know why Jesus said, "There's no way you people will believe unless you see signs *and wonders*" (Jn 4:48). The Galileans wanted to see a miracle. But that wasn't true of the nobleman from Capernaum. He didn't need to see signs *and wonders* to believe. He wasn't there to behold the wonder of Jesus' word coming true, the healing of his son. Instead, *all he needed was what he heard to see the sign and believe in Jesus*—a faith that led others to believe in Jesus too (Jn 4:53). First ears, then eyes.

Believing before seeing. "So, faith comes from hearing, and hearing comes through the word of Christ" (Rom 10:17)—something the nobleman from Capernaum knew better than anyone.

Have you ever noticed how often Jesus seems to defy expectations? It happens all the time, not only in John's Gospel but also in the Synoptic Gospels. Conventional wisdom says this; Jesus says something else. This is what should happen; Jesus does something else. The customary gives way to the extraordinary. Surprise replaces routine. In fact, it could be said that Jesus was predictably unpredictable—especially when it came to signs: (1) There's no wine. That's not my concern. I'll do it anyway. (2) Come down to my house. You people just want to see miracles. I'll do it anyway. (3) Do you want to carry the bed that carried you? It's the Sabbath. I'll do it anyway. (4) How can we feed all of these people? We only have this much food. I'll do it anyway. (5) These people are hankering for a miracle-working Messiah. The disciples face stiff winds boating across the sea. I'll do it anyway. (6) God made this man blind because of sin. It's the Sabbath. I'll do it anyway. (7) You didn't come in time. His body stinks. I'll do it anyway.

Time after time, sign after sign, Jesus did what nobody expected. Why? Why did he always seem to defy conventional wisdom? Was it because he considered himself a rebel? Did he get a kick out of going against the grain, defying the odds, constantly surprising *everyone*? Was that his modus operandi, purposely choosing to do the exact opposite of what was customary? *Let's see. What are they expecting? What do they think should happen? What would any normal person do? Well, that's not me. Time to shake things up. And now for something completely different.* Is that it? Was Jesus a petulant prophet trying to stir up trouble (see 1 Sam 16:4)? Or did he have grander designs when he performed signs?

It may appear to us that Jesus *always* behaved unconventionally, as if he were purposely trying to provoke us to see him differently—uniquely—as the "only begotten of God." "Look! I'm not who you think I am. I'm not going to conform to your expectations of what a messiah should be. I'm not that man. I'm more than that." To be sure, radical behavior is an effective way to defy conventional thinking. But Jesus was out to do more than prove he is God's Son. He came to earth to do more than perform signs. He came to change us, to reclaim us, to restore us, to re-create us by his word and through his word—his word becoming flesh *in us*. Not only so that we could *see* the glory of God among us, but that we might *be* the glory of God in the world. Indeed, John's Gospel shows us how we are meant to be the miraculous signs of God's work because God's Word is in us. We are signs pointing to Christ because his Word abides in us. Since we are signs of the incarnated Word, our very presence will be a provocation. That's what signs do: they provoke, they challenge conventional wisdom. They are the constant reminder that things are not the way they are supposed to be. Jesus flipped the wrong-side-down world right side up—a strange sight for those used to the way the world works. Therefore, Christ's word in us will be as strange as the signs he performed. Just ask the nobleman from Capernaum, who embodied the idea that we must believe the word to see the sign—even when Jesus defies our expectations.[12]

This is the hard part: taking God at his word when he fails to meet our expectations. Part of the problem is that God is so reliable, so generous, so good to us every day, that it's easy to expect good things. Think of how many things he does for us every day even though we don't ask for them. God gives life every day not because I hoped for it but because God is reliably generous. Of course, there are some people who prayed to God to see another day, and he answered their prayers. Indeed, sometimes we hear of God coming through for others when there is no hope. They needed a miracle. They turned to God as their only hope. And he did it. Inexplicably, undeniably God helped them, healed them, saved them. This is our God: he does ordinary and extraordinary things *all the time*.

When we find ourselves in trouble, needing our God to come through for us like he's done for many others, we can't help but expect him to help

---

[12]Craig R. Koester writes, "*Characters in the Gospel respond to the signs with genuine faith if they have already been brought to faith by what they have heard from or about Jesus. . . .* For them, the sign is not the beginning of a relationship with Jesus but something that occurs within an existing relationship." See Koester, *The Word of Life: A Theology of John's Gospel* (Grand Rapids, MI: Eerdmans, 2008), 164, emphasis original.

us too. After all, God is no respecter of persons. He doesn't play favorites. Whether we're a VIP or a beggar on the side of the road, Jesus has shown us very clearly that God loves us all the same. We should expect no less for those we love. And so, when we come to him in desperation and say, "Lord, come to my house before my son dies," the last thing we need to hear is a sermon about faith and miracles. We've heard enough. It's time for action, to see his promises come true. "Lord, come down to my house or else my son will die." But he doesn't move. He doesn't comply. He doesn't do what we ask. Instead, all he says is, "Go your way. Your son lives." That's it? The only thing he has to offer a desperate man looking for help for his son is a promise? Yes. Evidently, Jesus thinks that should be enough.

But I want to *see* the work of God. I want to *see* the word of God come true. Is that too much to ask? We were told, "Believe in God and he will supply all your needs." We were told, "Do the right thing and God will bless you." We were told, "God is good all the time." We were told, "God keeps his word." We were told, "Cast all your care upon him because he cares for you." We were told, "The prayers of a righteous man accomplish much." We were told, "God will do more than we can ask or think." Promise after promise, verse by verse, we were told that our God is the kind of God who makes promises and expects his children to believe his word. When we believe his word and things don't work out like we were told, like we expected, what do we do now? When we throw ourselves down before him in abject humility, begging him to do what only he can do, praying without ceasing, crying our eyes out, shouldn't we expect God to do *something*? This is life and death. This is the only thing that matters. "Lord, please come down to my house. I need you to do this one thing for me. You're my only hope. Please. Only you can make it happen. That's why I'm here. That's why I'm begging you in prayer. I believe in you. Where else can I go? What else can I do? I'm counting on you, that your word is true. I need to *see* your word come true. I have to see."

What does he offer me in my desperation? What does he do when he fails to meet my expectations of what God *should* do? He treats me like a VIP and sends me home with words. I keep walking, hoping, waiting, wondering, bedding down on the side of the road, staring at the stars at night, longing for the day when I see the sign come true. In the meantime, on this journey, all I have are words—promises I carry in my heart until the day when Jesus, the Word of life, says, "Let there be light," and the darkness will be no more.

"Go Wash in the Pool of Siloam"

Only a parent would understand. It's our greatest fear—doing something that damages our children forever. It's one thing to suffer the consequences of your own mistakes. It's quite something else to see your children have to deal with the aftermath of bad parenting. That's why many of us second-guess ourselves all the time: *Did I do right by him? Was I a good mother to her? Maybe I was too hard on them. Too easy on them? Why didn't I see that coming? How could I miss what was happening? Things haven't worked out like I thought they would. Is it my fault? Did I fail him? Did I drive her away? There are no perfect parents. I did the best I could. Why wasn't that good enough? Why did it have to turn out like this? It kills me to think they are suffering because of me. If I had known then what I know now. . . .* Mulling over the past in light of a seemingly hopeless future is a parent's worst nightmare.

Perhaps that's why the last performance I saw of Tennessee Williams's *The Glass Menagerie* had such a profound impact on me. It felt like I was a prophet peering into the future, anticipating worst-case scenarios. Our college-age daughter, Grace, was playing the part of Amanda, the middle-aged mother of a crippled recluse. Seeing a forty-something version of my twenty-one-year-old daughter pining away for her glory days as a young debutante was hard to watch. As Amanda is typically dismissed as a hardhearted, calculating sycophant, this version of her evoked in me a profound sense of empathy. Having been abandoned by the husband of her youth, Amanda was left with little resources to raise her son and invalid daughter during the Great Depression.

My wife and I were sitting on the front row, taking in the drama of Amanda trying to snag the affection of the one and only "gentleman caller" for her daughter. It was a pitiful sight, watching her soaking up the attention of this young man while trying to coax him into finding interest in her shy, socially inept, crippled daughter. As she relives her glory days, flitting about the apartment while reenacting how all the young men used to pursue her, reality hits her in the face, remembering the fateful moment when she fell for the charms of her wanderlusting husband. Then, it seems history repeats itself when her plan to match her daughter with the suitor falls apart. Amanda discovers that the young man, brought to the house under false pretenses, is already engaged. At that moment, Amanda wilts before our eyes, realizing her one and only shot to secure a future for her daughter has walked out the door, leaving her hopeless. Taking in the shock of it all, Amanda sits deathly still on the sofa, head bowed, shoulders slumped, and mutters to herself, "Things have a way of turning out so badly." That line—delivered by a middle-aged version of my daughter—sunk deep into my heart. To see my daughter give up hope, even though it was only an act, felt like grief to me. After the performance, Grace reported, "Dad. We heard you sigh. . . . It was loud." Embarrassed, I tried to explain why her performance hit me like a ton of bricks. But I only came off sounding like the typical proud parent.

If a daughter's theatrical performance of hopelessness could deliver pangs of grief to the heart of a proud father, imagine the tortured existence of parents who had to watch their son beg for alms every day because he was born blind. Since the God of Israel had warned idolaters that punishment for their sin could last up to four generations (Ex 20:5), it was assumed that a man was born blind because of sin—either his prenatal sin or his parents' sin (Jn 9:2).[13] Talk about a hopeless future! For, if God has it in for you, there's nothing you can do to make life better. No one would deny the curse of God was persistent; there were beggars everywhere—especially around the temple—proving the law of divine retribution. That would have been quite a sight: every time you go to worship God in his temple, you see the evidence of his curse just outside the doors.

---

[13]See Keener, *Gospel of John*, 2:777-79.

I imagine, therefore, the pangs of shame felt by the blind man's parents whenever they went to worship God. Seeing their son begging—he would have no idea they were there—his parents probably avoided any contact with him. After seeing him in his helpless state, did they reminisce about the good old days, rehearsing in their minds the day he was born? So much promise! Then, having to relive the horror of their eventual discovery. Their baby boy was blind. Such heartache, such despair. What every parent wants is to give their child a hopeful future. But they, because of their sin, had brought him nothing but misery. When you give birth to the curse of God, what else is there to do but mourn the day he was born? And so, when they heard that their son had been healed—he could see!—I wonder whether it seemed to them that the Pharisees were asking the wrong questions (Jn 9:19). "Is this your son, whom you say was born blind?" (We should know; we were there.) "Therefore, how does he now see?" (How should we know? We weren't there.) Instead, what the Pharisees should have asked was *the question*—the only one that parents of a cursed child would want answered: Why did God change his mind?

Throughout the story of the sixth sign, the man born blind is the center of attention, the object of curiosity. From beginning to end, he is a question mark—his presence a provocation. The disciples want to know, "Who sinned—this man or his parents—that he should be born blind?" (Jn 9:2). Neighbors want to know, "Is this not the man who used to sit and beg?" (Jn 9:8). The Pharisees want to know, "How did he open your eyes?" (Jn 9:26). Even Jesus wants to know, "Do you believe in the Son of Man?" (Jn 9:35)—a question the blind man was probably never asked because who cares what a cursed man thinks? In fact, that's what makes this story so appealing to me: we see how a marginalized man, forgotten by society, ignored by humanity—the invisible man—all of a sudden becomes visible because of Jesus Christ.

Ironically, as we watch the blind man enjoy his fifteen minutes of fame, the one who made it all happen is practically absent from the story. Jesus briefly appears at the beginning and the end of the sixth sign. Peculiar, isn't it? Even though the blind man has been brought to the center of attention, Jesus (although absent) is the main subject of the story. Indeed, the blind man embodies the sixth sign—the word of Jesus becoming flesh—that reveals the Light of the world to all who have eyes to see. But those who are blind can't see it.

Several times in his Gospel, John links the words and the works of Jesus. Readers can't miss the correlation. Who Jesus is, is what he does. Jesus says, "I am the resurrection and the life" (Jn 11:25) and raises Lazarus from the dead. What he does is who he is. Jesus feeds five thousand men and says, "I am the bread of life" (Jn 6:35). In John's Gospel, word and deed go hand in hand. Yet, in both of these examples, Jesus puts some distance between his claim and the miraculous sign. In other words, he doesn't say, "I'm the resurrection" while he raises Lazarus from the dead. He doesn't yell out, "I am the bread of life" while the masses chow down on miraculous manna.

But when it comes to healing the man born blind, Jesus collapses word and deed into one singular moment. As he paints the blind man's eyes with mud, Jesus says, "I am the light of the world" (Jn 9:5-6). Of course, the sign doesn't come true until the blind man washes the mud from his eyes at the pool of Siloam (Jn 9:7), located at the bottom of a steep hill, several hundred yards south of the temple. One wonders, why the delay? Why not spit in the man's eyes and heal him on the spot? That certainly would have added to the drama of the synchronous word and work of Jesus. The light of the world lights up the darkness of blind eyes! Who *sees* the kingdom of God? A blind man! A public-relations expert couldn't have planned it any better. But that's not what he does. Instead, Jesus does something highly unusual—even for rabbis who were known miracle workers. Jesus spits on the ground (uncouth?), makes a muddy paste, then applies it to the man's eyes (Jn 9:6). What a weird thing to do, especially for those of us who are sighted. I can see the disciples wincing as they took in the sight, "Dirt in his eyes? How is that going to help?"

Some interpreters hear echoes of Genesis 2:7, where God makes Adam out of a mud pie. If God used dirt to create man, how much more would his Son use dirt to finish what was left undone in the womb?[14] That's why Jesus says his blindness isn't due to sin but so that "the works of God might be revealed in him" (Jn 9:3)—both the hidden work of God in the womb and the public work of God via the sign. Others think the detail of Jesus mixing saliva and dirt sets up the problem of working on the Sabbath, since kneading was prohibited.[15] Finally, some hear an even more subversive purpose in Jesus' method of bringing healing to the blind man's eyes, since both saliva and dirt rendered people ceremonially unclean.[16] In other words, by pasting the blind man's eyes with mud, Jesus deconstructed the purity code: that which is unclean makes a cursed man clean.

Whatever the reason for Jesus' unusual method of healing the blind man, one thing is certain: it seems to trip up the Pharisees. They ask *three* times how the blind man was healed (Jn 9:13-15, 19, 26-27). The irony isn't lost on us. What brought sight for one blinded the other. Mud in the blind man's eyes obscured the vision of the Pharisees. They couldn't see how a man like Jesus could do the work of God even while looking on the very man whom Jesus said would reveal the work of God (Jn 9:3, 16-18, 24, 29). The one who was sent to the pool of Siloam (which means "sent") revealed the one who was sent by God so that all may see "while there's still daylight" (Jn 9:4-7). Indeed, like the sun that rules the day, the light of the world would have a double effect: he would bring light to the dark eyes of the blind and blind the eyes of those who said they could see in the dark (Jn 9:4, 39-41).

My favorite part of the story is when the blind man tries to enlighten the Pharisees on the Sabbath day. The Pharisees were used to teaching people the ways of God on the Sabbath, when Jews gathered to hear the law of Moses read to them and interpreted for them. But, on this

---

[14]An interpretation going all the way back to Irenaeus. See J. Ramsey Michaels, *The Gospel of John*, New International Commentary on the New Testament (Grand Rapids, MI: Eerdmans, 2010), 545-46.

[15]Rudolf Schnackenburg, *The Gospel According to St. John*, trans. Cecily Hastings, Francis Mc-Donagh, David Smith, and Richard Foley (New York: Crossroad, 1990), 2:242-43.

[16]Köstenberger, *John*, 283.

particular Sabbath, things are backward. This time a commoner is sent to the experts to teach them about the works of God, offering a tight, logical argument based on his own experience (Jn 9:24-33).[17] According to the newly sighted man, there are three undeniable realities facing all of them: (1) even though he was blind, now he sees (Jn 9:25); (2) God does not hear sinners, but he listens to anyone who fears him and does his will (Jn 9:31); and (3) this has never happened before, restoring the sight of a man born blind (Jn 9:32). In light of these absolute truths—the second one, I'm sure, he heard many, many times ("God will never heal you because you were born entirely in sins," Jn 9:34)—the commoner draws an *obvious* inference (a double negative in Greek for emphasis): "If this man were not from God, he could do nothing" (Jn 9:33).

I find it amusing that the simpleton relies on a double negative to make his point. Rather than coming out and saying it, "This man is from God," the once-blind-but-now-seeing man leaves it to the Pharisees to figure it out, musing over their blindness (I hear sarcasm in his voice): "Well, here is the amazing thing, that you do not know where He is from, and *yet* He opened my eyes" (Jn 9:30 NASB). It's as if the blind man were saying: "Look who's blind now! Maybe we can find the healer so that he can open your eyes too!" (my paraphrase of Jn 9:27). But the Pharisees object: "You are *that* man's disciple; *we* are disciples of Moses" (Jn 9:28; again, the Greek is emphatic). The Pharisees may have eyes to read Moses (something the blind man has never done). But they are blind to the work of God—even though he's standing right there, staring them in the face.

When the Pharisees accused the blind man of being a disciple of Jesus (Jn 9:28), it was probably the nicest thing anyone ever said to him. I wonder whether he relished the compliment, giving him courage to teach the disciples of Moses about the Christ. For even the blind man grew in his understanding of Jesus. First, the one who opened his eyes is simply "a man called Jesus" (Jn 9:11). Then, the blind man claims Jesus is a prophet

---

[17]Andy M. Reimer, "The Man Born Blind: True Disciple of Jesus," in *Character Studies in the Fourth Gospel: Narrative Approaches to Seventy Figures in John*, ed. Steven A. Hunt, D. Francois Tolmie, and Ruben Zimmermann (Tübingen: Mohr Siebeck, 2013), 432.

(Jn 9:17). (The irony is rich here: since Jesus opened his eyes, the Pharisees want to know what *the blind man sees* about the man they're convinced is *not from God*; Jn 9:16-17. Indeed, only Jesus can open the eyes of the blind.) Finally, the man with restored sight is convinced Jesus is from God because he performed the never-before-seen sign (Jn 9:30-33).

What did the Pharisees do when confronted with the testimony of the blind man—the incarnation of the sixth sign that Jesus is the light of the world? Like anyone else who has become accustomed to seeing in the dark—"somebody douse the light, it's hurting my eyes!"—they put out the bright light. That a man "born entirely in sins" is teaching them on the Sabbath is too much to take: "They threw him outside" (Jn 9:34). The man who used to beg, the outsider who became an insider for a brief moment, the invisible man who was *the object* of curiosity on the Sabbath, the sinner who acted like he had something to say to the teachers—this man is returned to his previous station in life, outside the temple. But that doesn't matter, for outsiders are the very people Jesus is looking for (Jn 9:35).

"THE MAN BELIEVED THE WORD"

"Do you believe the parable?" Strangely enough, when it comes to Jesus, that's a question we never ask. Some wonder whether we should believe in miracles—either that Jesus performed miracles or that miracles can happen today.[18] Others question whether we have the actual words of Jesus. Scholars debate whether Jesus actually taught this or that parable.[19] But I've never heard anyone ask, "Should we believe the parable?" In other words, we never question whether a parable of Jesus is *true*. Rather, we simply accept the parables of the prodigal son and the good Samaritan—that they are telling the truth about us, about the world, about the way things are supposed to be.

---

[18]See Craig S. Keener, *Miracles: The Credibility of the New Testament Accounts*, 2 vols. (Grand Rapids, MI: Baker Academic, 2011).

[19]Charles W. Hedrick, *Many Things in Parables: Jesus and His Modern Critics* (Louisville, KY: Westminster John Knox, 2004), 23-26.

Given that Jesus told parables to *challenge* conventional wisdom of how the world works, it's a little surprising that we unquestioningly accept them. It's not that we don't recognize the offensive parts of the story, the places where Jesus holds up a mirror and basically says to his generation, "Is this wrong?" The Samaritan is a hero? The foolish father gives in to the selfish request of his prodigal son? These things are not supposed to happen in the real world. But in Jesus' story world, where he's trying to get his listeners to envision the reign of God on earth, people love their enemies and fools reveal the grace of God. It's almost as if Jesus were playing with our sense of reality, opening our eyes to the impossible. Since all things are possible with God, these parables work, helping those of us who have a hard time seeing that these things could happen (really? loving enemies? being foolishly wasteful with God's grace?). Indeed, through his parables Jesus helps the blind see the glorious work of God.

In the same way Jesus invited his listeners to envision the reign of God through parables, John wrote his Gospel to help readers to see the signs of God's work in Jesus *and in themselves*.[20] Just as the parables force us to find our place in the kingdom of God—they have a reflective quality that maps the world and our location, "you are here"—so also John's Gospel mirrors back to us who we are in the light of who Jesus is. How we respond to him reveals our identity. It happens without effort: we see ourselves in the stories of Jesus' encounter with different people, as if what happened to them has happened to us. Even though Jesus didn't heal our blind eyes like he did for the man born that way, we take the newly sighted man's confession as our own: "once I was blind, but now I see" (Jn 9:25). We read his story of progressive revelation—a journey of faith—as an apt description of our spiritual formation. In other words, we treat the story of Jesus healing the man born blind as if it were a parable *for us*. That's not to say that we take it as fiction. Scholars may debate the historicity of the miracle or the historical words of Jesus. But

---

[20]Cornelis Bennema, *Encountering Jesus: Character Studies in the Gospel of John*, 2nd ed. (Minneapolis: Fortress, 2014), 371.

these things don't have to be proven to us for the story to be true. In fact, even though most of us don't know what it's like to be born blind, we still read the sixth sign as if it were *our* story *because it is true.*

That's why, when we hear the disciples ask Jesus, "Rabbi, who sinned— this man or his parents—that he should be born blind?" (Jn 9:2), his response sounds like a strong critique of *our* cause-and-effect world. Like the presumption behind the disciples' question (someone is to blame for this undesirable outcome), we tend to make the same judgments about the suffering of others. As long as there's someone to blame, we can all feel better about our chances of avoiding such horrors. For example, I heard my childhood pastor blame the serial tragedies of the Kennedy family on the patriarch, Joe Kennedy. Every time the Kennedys suffered another devastating loss (assassination, death by cancer, death by plane crash), we would hear a sermon about how "God will not be mocked. Whatever we sow we will reap" (Gal 6:7). Since Joe Kennedy was known to be a "bootlegger" (we never questioned whether that was the case), then God was punishing the Catholic patriarch for his sins—a divine judgment that would last for three to four generations.

At the same time, I've wondered whether such cause-and-effect thinking has convinced some Christians that *they* are the ones cursed by God. Like Amanda from *The Glass Menagerie*, they believe that "things have a way of turning out so badly." They can never catch a break. Therefore, when they face a tragedy that eventually lands on *all of us* (sickness, disease, disaster, death), they chalk it up to an "act of God." He's out to get them, rubbing their noses in the disappointment of their pain. It's a pitiful sight, seeing a parent care for her disabled daughter as if it were a prison sentence. It's hard to convince them that they're not being punished for their past. Then again, who can blame them? Haven't we all heard the preacher say over and over again, "The wages of sin is death"?

HERE'S MUD IN YOUR EYE

He had an exasperated look on his face when he entered my office. Since I was his pastor, he came to me for advice. He wanted to know whether he should tell his wife about the one-night stand he had with her sister several months ago. As he related the circumstances of his impulsive behavior, I couldn't tell whether he was trying to spin an excuse to save face in front of his pastor or making a clumsy attempt at repentance. When I asked him, "Why are you coming to me now?" I expected him to explain how he was tortured by regret for having broken his marital vows. But there was more to it than that. Tears welled in his eyes as he told me their family secret. His wife had miscarried during the first trimester of her pregnancy with what was supposed to be their firstborn child. No one knew they were expecting. His wife was devastated. He felt helpless, unable to comfort her because he was convinced that God had punished him for his sin. He asked me: "What if I tell her it's my fault? Will that help her, knowing it's not her fault but mine? I want to man up and accept responsibility for my behavior. But, I'm afraid she'll never forgive me for what I've done. She's been depressed for a long time. Nothing seems to help. I can't stand to see her suffer because of me. I can't take it anymore. What should I do?"

I wish I could say that I thought like a Catholic priest at that moment, telling the story of Jesus healing the man born blind, hoping to bring relief in the midst of such tragedy. But that didn't come to mind. Instead, I turned to what Jesus said to the Galileans who assumed that God had punished some Jews, evidenced by the fact that they were executed by Pilate, and other Jews because they died due to an accident at a construction site at Siloam (Lk 13:1-2, 4). Jesus' response seems apropos: "Do you suppose that these Galileans were greater sinners than all other Galileans, because they suffered this fate? I tell you, no, but unless you repent, you will all likewise perish" (Lk 13:2-3). I thought it would help; Jesus said it plainly. Bad things don't happen to some of us because we are "greater sinners." God doesn't work that way. Yes, repentance matters for the future. But God doesn't give us what we think we deserve for the past.

It didn't help. My words—I was hoping they would wash him clean— seemed to roll off him like water on a duck's back. I was trying to deconstruct his cause-and-effect worldview, washing his eyes with Scripture.

But Jesus' words seemed to obscure his vision like mud. All this tortured man wanted to know was whether he should tell his deep, dark secret to his grieving wife (a question I refused to answer). Did I do the right thing? I still don't know. But after he left, I remembered the story of Jesus' healing the man born blind. As I reread the passage, Jesus' words leaped out at me: "Neither this man sinned nor his parents, but in order that the works of God may be revealed in him" (Jn 9:3). At that point, I began to have an argument with God: "But Lord, this man *did* sin. He broke his vow. And yet, I still don't believe his child died because of him. Even in the midst of this tragedy, your work can still be revealed in him. I wish I would have told him that too. We tend to dwell over what has been. But you, Lord, inspire us to envision what will be. It's true. If Jesus can heal a man born blind, then even an unfaithful husband, convinced that God is punishing him for his sin, can be the very place where the glorious work of God is revealed."

That's why we bask in the sun of Jesus' words. While the cause-and-effect world tends to look backward—tracing a bad situation back to our mistake—Jesus prefers to look ahead and talk about what will be. The world says, "You're getting what you deserved." Jesus says, "God is on your side." The world says, "You've made your bed; now lie in it." Jesus says, "Take up your bed and walk." The world says, "You're cursed by God." Jesus says, "You are the work of God." The world says, "There's nothing to see." Jesus says, "I am the light of the world." The world says, "It's a dark world." Jesus says, "There's still some daylight." The world says, "There's mud in your eye." Jesus says, "Go wash in the pool that is sent by God." The world sees what was—a beggar (Jn 9:8). Jesus sees what will be—the glory of God . . . and "the darkness did not grasp it" (Jn 1:5 NASB). Indeed, the night-and-day difference is revealed when "the man believed the word that Jesus spoke to him" (Jn 4:50; 9:38). We must take Jesus' words to heart, especially in the dark. The word becoming flesh makes all the difference in the world.

4

SEE AND COME

Abiding in the Word

IT'S SOMEWHAT PREDICTABLE that John was our favorite Gospel. I came of age in a fundamentalist Southern Baptist church. John 3:16 was our mantra. Being born again was our gospel call. Believing in Jesus was the essence of our faith. Not living like the world was our ethical standard. Our pastor seemed to follow an unofficial lectionary that inspired a threefold rotation of sermons: (1) how to get saved (repent of sin and believe in Jesus), (2) why Christians should avoid the ways of the world (being worldly ruins our witness), and our favorite (3) when Jesus is coming back to rapture believers and turn loose the powers of hell on earth (could happen any moment). In certain respects, John's Gospel was tailor-made for our evangelical preferences. Jesus talks a lot about believing in him, receiving eternal life, and overcoming the world in John's Gospel. Even better, Jesus sounds more like God in John ("I am," Jn 8:58). The cross looks more like a victory in John ("It is finished," Jn 19:30). And the resurrection seems more real in John ("Reach here your finger," Jn 20:27). No wonder new converts were encouraged to read the Fourth Gospel first. John seemed to be the perfect Gospel for our evangelical purposes, especially when it came to challenging a "watered-down version of the gospel," what our pastor referred to derisively as "the social gospel."

In John's narrative world, Jesus appears to be completely unconcerned about the poor. Nowhere in John's Gospel does Jesus say things such as, "Feed the poor" or "Clothe the naked." Instead, he seems resigned to their plight, "The poor you will always have with you, but you do not always have me" (Jn 12:8)—a passage our pastor loved to quote when he questioned the social gospel. The question isn't whether a man has food in his stomach. It is whether he has Jesus in his heart. For even Jesus mocks the crowd hankering for daily bread (Jn 6:26-40). He says they should hunger for the only food that matters—the eternal bread that comes down from heaven (Jn 6:38). "Feed a man for a day," our pastor loved to say, "and he'll be hungry tomorrow. Give people the bread of life, and they'll live forever." Nonbelievers, on the other hand, die in their sins (Jn 8:24).

Besides believing in him, the only other thing Jesus requires of his disciples in John's Gospel is to "love one another"—a commandment he repeats several times and demonstrates through footwashing (Jn 13:14-17, 34-35; 15:12-13, 17). That's completely different from what we read in the Synoptic Gospels, where Jesus not only gives specific instructions to the masses during his Sermon on the Mount (do this; don't do that; Mt 5:17–7:12) but also tells his disciples what to do in certain situations (for example, how to deal with an unrepentant brother; Mt 18:15-22). What makes Jesus' approach to discipleship in John's Gospel even more peculiar is that several times during the Farewell Discourse he encourages his followers to "keep my commandments" (Jn 14:15, 21; 15:10-14, 17). Yet, Jesus gave them only *one* commandment—what he called a "new commandment"—to love one another as he loved them (Jn 13:34). To be sure, during these "last words" to his disciples, Jesus offers a few imperatives to help his disciples deal with his departure: "Don't let your heart be troubled/fearful" (Jn 14:1, 27); "Abide in me/my words/my love," "Keep my words" (Jn 14:23; 15:4-5, 7, 9-10, 20); "Ask anything in my name" (Jn 14:13-14; 15:7, 16; 16:23). But here Jesus sounds more like he's offering pastoral encouragement than giving specific instructions on how to be a disciple. In other words, ethical requirements for following Jesus are practically nonexistent in John's Gospel.[1] Jesus doesn't tell us exactly *what*

---

[1]Recently, Johannine scholars have pushed back against this observation. See Sherri Brown and Christopher W. Skinner, eds., *Johannine Ethics: The Moral World of the Gospel and the Epistles of John* (Minneapolis: Fortress, 2017); also Jan G. van der Watt and Ruben Zimmermann, eds., *Rethinking the Ethics of John: "Implicit Ethics" in the Johannine Writings* (Tübingen: Mohr Siebeck, 2012).

to do in John's Gospel. Rather, all we get are vague expressions ("Abide in me") and one commandment ("Love one another"). According to John's Jesus, that should be enough. Here's why.

John operates with the presumption that disciples should know what to do without being told because that's how Jesus discipled the Twelve. When John's Jesus encourages his disciples to "abide in his word," he acts like they need no further explanation—other than the simple analogy of vine and branches (Jn 15:1-10). The reason Jesus is convinced his disciples don't need further instructions on "how to" abide in him/his word is that he gave them the words of God (Jn 17:8). He has told them everything they needed to know. He gave them every word God had given him—no more, no less. What else is there to say? The Word of God became flesh and dwelt among them. Now, it is their turn for the Word of God in Christ to be fleshed out in their lives—the fruit of their abiding in him (Jn 15:16). Jesus expects his words to keep them connected to the vine and therefore produce grapes.

Yet, as readers of John's Gospel, we never get to see that happen. The Twelve will learn how to abide in Jesus after remembering what he said—words that would become Scripture to them after the resurrection (Jn 2:22; 12:16; 20:9). But within John's narrative world, the Twelve never produce grapes. Instead, they appear as learners, watching others abide in Jesus' word and seeing them produce fruit: a Samaritan woman, Mary of Bethany, and the unnamed beloved disciple. These three disciples do what is right without being told and therefore bear fruit by leading others to Jesus. Because they abide in his word, others see and come—not only the people of Sychar and the citizens of Jerusalem, but even people like us who have eyes to read the Gospel according to John.

THE EVANGELIST

The Twelve missed their chance. They had just returned from a Samaritan village, having secured provisions for their trip to Galilee, when they found Jesus talking to a woman at the well where they left him (Jn 4:27, 31-33). Two things confused them. First, they wondered why Jesus was talking to her (Jn 4:27). Second, they questioned whether someone (the woman?) had already given Jesus something to eat, since he refused the food they brought from Sychar (Jn 4:31-33). Of course, as readers of John's Gospel we know the answer to both questions. Jesus was talking to the woman because he started a conversation with her (Jn 4:7). We also know that no one had given Jesus anything to eat while the Twelve were gone. In fact, even though he asked the woman for water, we're never told whether Jesus was given anything to drink. As far as we know, Jesus was both hungry and thirsty when the Twelve returned to him at the well. And yet, Jesus claimed he was satiated: "I have food to eat that you know nothing about"—food that nourished his soul by doing what God sent him to do (Jn 4:32, 34). But the Twelve didn't know about such food, evident by the fact that Jesus had sent them into the village to get food "that you didn't work for" (Jn 4:38)—a reference *not* to the food they brought from Sychar but to the villagers who were coming to Jesus because of the witness of the Samaritan woman.

At this point Jesus sounds like he's chastising the Twelve for their ineptitude. He expected *them* to do what the Samaritan woman had done: bring a harvest of people to Christ, "gathering fruit for eternal life" (Jn 4:30, 34-38). But they didn't. So he made them look at the people coming to him as he talked about planting and harvesting. Even though the disciples had come from the same town, these people were coming to Jesus *because of her* (Jn 4:35). It's almost as if Jesus were saying, "Look! Someone else is doing your work."

It all happened so fast it even took Jesus by surprise. He expected his gospel ministry to conform to the rhythm of raising grain crops. One group of workers sows seed, then four months later another group of farmers harvests the fields (Jn 4:35). But when Jesus farmed the gospel in Samaria, the results defied conventional wisdom. One minute he sowed the gospel into the heart of one Samaritan. The next minute the Samaritan fields were ready to be harvested. Due to the eschatological time warp, this time the planters and the reapers ended up celebrating the *same* day (Jn 4:36). Nevertheless, the old adage still holds true: one sows, another reaps

(Jn 4:37). Even though the Twelve didn't sow the gospel seed in Sychar like Jesus expected, they would still reap the benefits of his gospel ministry because of her (Jn 4:38). She did what the Twelve were sent to do even though Jesus *never sent her* to evangelize the people—a detail that is easily overlooked. Jesus didn't send the Samaritan woman to the village to tell others about the Messiah. She did that on her own. I think that took Jesus by surprise too. The one who wasn't sent did what God sent Jesus to do and what Jesus sent his disciples to do: gather fruit for eternal life. That means, of course, that the Samaritan woman ended up acting more like a disciple than the Twelve because she did the right thing without being told, revealing that she abided in his word. And what was the word of Jesus that bore fruit in her? Essentially, Jesus said, "If you knew who I was, then you would ask me for the water that will quench your thirst forever, and then you would become a well of living water" (my paraphrase of Jn 4:10, 13-14).

Some question whether Jesus' word came true in the Samaritan woman. First, one wonders whether she ever recognized the true identity of Jesus. She thought he was a prophet (Jn 4:19, 29). But she questioned whether Jesus could be the Messiah for Samaritans too (Jn 4:25, 29). Furthermore, some commentators point out that she never confessed faith in him; she only made suggestions. Second, even though she asked for the water Jesus offered, some dismiss her request as disingenuous. The woman comes off a little snarky when she adds, "so that I don't have to come all this way to draw water" (Jn 4:15), revealing that she's still thinking on an earthly level.[2] Third, did she become a well of living water? Some might say, "Yes. Look at all the Samaritans who came to Jesus because of her witness. Even the narrator points out that 'many Samaritans from that city believed in him because of her testimony' (Jn 4:39)." Yet, when it comes to the actual *conversion* of the Samaritans, the narrator seems to sublimate her witness to the authority of Jesus' word. The villagers tell her plainly: "We no longer believe because of your word. We believe because of his word" (my paraphrase of Jn 4:41-42).

[2]So also Jerome H. Neyrey, *The Gospel of John*, New Cambridge Bible Commentary (Cambridge: Cambridge University Press, 2006), 113.

Once again, we've come across an ambiguous character in John's
Gospel, one who invites speculation because she doesn't check all the
boxes of what discipleship is supposed to look like according to John's
stated purpose (Jn 20:30-31). Since she never confessed faith in Jesus as
"the Christ, the Son of God," how do we know if she ever *believed* in him?
Is confession an absolute requirement of faith according to John? If not,
how do we know whether she received eternal life? Despite these ambi-
guities, the reader is left with the impression that this woman is the kind
of disciple Jesus is looking for—and not just because she outdoes the
Twelve. It's because of the way John has set up the story of Jesus' encounter
with the Samaritan, having presented Jesus more recently as a bridegroom
prepared for his bride (Jn 3:29), but also as the temple of God looking for
true worshipers (Jn 2:13-22). As part of the background of both kinds of
stories—betrothals in the Hebrew Scriptures and Jewish traditions about
the temple as the center of the earth—a well of water plays an important
role. The well is the place where Abraham's servant finds a wife for Isaac
(Gen 24:1-67), where Jacob meets Rachel (Gen 29:1-20). According to
Jewish legend, the temple was built on top of a well, capping the pri-
mordial source of the flood.[3] When Jesus meets the Samaritan woman at
Jacob's well, all kinds of stories are splashing around in this episode, encouraging readers to connect the dots.[4] All of this has been artfully set up
by John, helping us to see this chance meeting between a "single" Jewish
man and an "unmarried" Samaritan woman as that which has been divinely arranged by Jesus' Father: "It was necessary for him to go through
Samaria" (Jn 4:4). Indeed, it was necessary because Jesus finds *in her* what
he's looking for—the reason he was sent by his Father—even though she's
a Samaritan with a checkered past, hardly the marrying type.

Abraham's servant was sent on an important mission, so important
that Abraham makes his servant swear an oath to God: go back to his

---

[3]See Margaret Barker, *The Gate of Heaven: The History and Symbolism of the Temple in Jerusalem*
(Sheffield: Sheffield Phoenix, 2008), 18-20.
[4]See Mary L. Coloe, "The Woman of Samaria: Her Characterization, Narrative, and Theological
Significance," in *Characters and Characterizations in the Gospel of John*, ed. Christopher W. Skinner (London: Bloomsbury, 2013), 186-96.

homeland and find a wife for Isaac among family (Gen 24:1-9). But where does one go to find single, marriageable women in Mesopotamia? At the well. Customarily, women would come to the well every evening to draw water for the next day (Gen 24:11). And so, once the servant finds the well at Nahor (Abraham's hometown), he prays to God to give him a sign as to which young woman should be the one. Even though the sign comes true—Rebekah offers to water his camels after he asks her for a drink from her jar, just like he expects (Gen 24:13-20)—the servant still wonders "whether the LORD had made his journey successful or not" (Gen 24:21 NASB). Once he finds out Rebekah is family (and offers her jewelry—what's an engagement without a ring?), he thanks the Lord, who "'guided me in the way to the house of my master's brothers.' Then the young woman ran and told her mother's household about these things" (Gen 24:27-28 NASB).

Some of the same features show up in other betrothal stories as well. For example, Jacob meets Rachel at a well, water is supplied to him because of her, Jacob's intentions are declared, and the young woman runs home to tell her people about him (Gen 29:1-20). During a long journey through a strange land, Moses sits down by a well and meets his future wife, and a marriage is arranged because of their "chance" meeting (Ex 2:15-22). Betrothal stories seem to follow a particular script: chance meeting of a young woman and man at a well, water offered, virgin runs home to tell her people about the man, marriage is arranged.[5] Accordingly, some scholars think John is following the same script, intentionally setting up the meeting between Jesus and the Samaritan woman as a betrothal story with a twist: she's not a virgin and Jesus isn't looking for the typical bride.

Even though the episode begins and ends like a betrothal story, it's the middle part that has led some scholars to consider another echo. In the midst of their brief repartee, where one minute the woman is asking about the living water and the next minute Jesus seems to inquire about

---

[5]See Ben Witherington III, *John's Wisdom: A Commentary on the Fourth Gospel* (Louisville, KY: Westminster John Knox, 1995) 118.

her marital history, the woman introduces another topic: Where is the true temple of God (Jn 4:20)? Even though the question was a contentious issue between Jews and Samaritans, some readers see the ploy as a diversionary tactic. Embarrassed by her personal history, the Samaritan woman was trying to distract Jesus by throwing up a theological smoke screen.[6] But such an interpretation assumes the woman should have been ashamed of herself, as if she were to blame for having been married to five men (Jn 4:18). But since divorce was only initiated by men, this poor woman was either a victim of husbands who "found some indecency in her" (Deut 24:1) or she was widowed by the premature death of her husband(s) and married five times according to the custom of levirate marriage (Deut 25:5-10). And what of her current situation? Jesus says (and the woman does not dispute), "The man you have now is not your husband" (Jn 4:18). Doesn't that mean the woman was living in sin? Not necessarily, according to Marianne Meye Thompson:

> That she is currently living with a man outside a legally contracted marriage indicates to some commentators her immorality, but to others her desperation. She needs the protection and support of a husband, but has settled for what she can get. Jesus calls attention to her problematic situation, but does not condemn her. Subsequently, commentators and preachers have hastened to fill the void![7]

Indeed, we are being presumptuous to suggest that the Samaritan woman was living immorally. In fact, if we were to give her the benefit of the doubt, perhaps the man she's living with was her brother (like Mary, Martha, and Lazarus).[8] We just don't know. Regardless of the circumstances we assign to her (whether immoral or not), her unmarried status

---

[6]Paul Louis Metzger, *The Gospel of John: When Love Comes to Town* (Downers Grove, IL: InterVarsity Press, 2010), 75-76; Andreas J. Köstenberger, *John*, Baker Exegetical Commentary on the New Testament (Grand Rapids, MI: Baker Academic, 2004), 153. See the response by Craig S. Keener, *The Gospel of John: A Commentary* (Grand Rapids, MI: Baker Academic, 2010), 1:610; Rudolf Schnackenburg, *The Gospel According to St. John*, trans. David Smith and G. A. Kon (New York: Crossroad, 1990), 1:434.

[7]Marianne Meye Thompson, *John: A Commentary*, New Testament Library (Louisville, KY: Westminster John Knox, 2015), 103.

[8]Then again, would John have used the same verb, *have*, for both situations—previous husbands and her current roommate?

still would have been a source of shame in her world—no other man would have her. But Jesus didn't shun her as a shameful, immoral woman, dismissing her "silly question." Rather, he engaged the woman as if she were a worthy dialogue partner.[9]

But there's another reason why the Samaritan woman's question seems ridiculous to us: because John has already portrayed Jesus as the new temple. Therefore, as we eavesdrop on Jesus' conversation with the woman, we can't help but think: "Poor girl. She doesn't know to whom she's talking. She's asking about the 'true temple of God,' and he's staring her in the face." Her question appears to us as rather quaint. Where does one go to worship God? On "our" mountain (where the Samaritan temple used to stand) or "your" mountain (where Herod's temple stands)? Such a turf battle makes the God of Israel look like a tribal god. According to John's Gospel, God had much bigger, more cosmic designs: "for God so loved the *world*." Sacred space is no longer about this mountain or that mountain. God is out to reclaim the *whole* world, every inch of it. So the temple question was moot—not only for us, but especially for John's first readers, who lived twenty to thirty years after the destruction of the Jewish temple. "Where?" doesn't matter anymore. Both the Samaritan temple (destroyed by John Hyrcanus in 129 BC) and Herod's temple (destroyed by Titus in AD 70) were no longer standing. Neither Jew nor Samaritan had a sacred place to "go" to worship God in his glory. Consequently, the reader easily tracks with Jesus when he says, "It really doesn't matter *where* you go to worship God" (Jn 4:21). What was once a scandalous notion (how can anyone worship God without a temple?) is now a given, not only because both temples were gone but especially because Jesus has been presented by John as the true, portable temple of God—a throwback to the tabernacle of God's glory (Jn 1:14). Like the old days, before Solomon anchored God to the ground with a stone temple, the tent of the Lord's glory was on the move again in Jesus— *another* temple that would be destroyed and yet raised up (Jn 2:19).

---

[9]Instead of playing a bridal role, "Drink, sir," the Samaritan woman "spars with Jesus." See J. Ramsey Michaels, *The Gospel of John*, New International Commentary on the New Testament (Grand Rapids, MI: Eerdmans, 2010), 239.

By his response, Jesus changes the question from "Where do *we go* to worship God?" to "Where does *God go* to find a true worshiper?" He gives two reasons why his question is more relevant (Jn 4:21-24): (1) God is Spirit, and (2) it's time. When it comes to worship, the time has come for God to be the seeker. In the eschatological age of the Spirit, "Who?" matters more than "Where?" Since God is Spirit—"the wind blows wherever it wants to go" (Jn 3:8)—only those who worship God spiritually are true worshipers, regardless of where they go. Therefore, even though Samaritans worship God on the wrong mountain, a woman like the Samaritan in this story can still be a true worshiper because "salvation is from the Jews" (Jn 4:22).

It may sound like Jesus was simply bolstering his argument, claiming Jewish privilege over Samaritan ignorance. But, since their conversation was probably in Aramaic, Jesus was claiming something more. The attentive reader hears a clever pun: Jesus was referring to *himself* when he said, "*salvation [yeshuah]* is from the Jews." While it's true that the Samaritans were looking for a Samaritan Messiah, God had a larger tent: since Yeshuah was from the Jews, then Samaritans could become true worshipers *now* because the true temple of God had come to their mountain *for a while*. God was seeking them! If they received him, then they would know that God sent Yeshuah to be "the Savior of the *world*" (Jn 4:42)—not just Jews. Indeed, since Jesus was from the Jews, he saved the whole world.

Like a well of water, Jesus is the one to whom thirsty people come to drink.[10] Once they drink of him, they carry the water to others. That's what the Samaritan woman did. She drank from the well of living water and became a well of water for her people. She did more than carry water to them; she brought them to the well, inviting them with the same words Jesus used when he met his first disciples, "Come and see" (Jn 1:39; 4:29). They came. Why? She reported that Jesus had told her "all that she had

---

[10]James Resseguie, *The Strange Gospel: Narrative Design and Point of View in John* (Leiden: Brill, 2001), 75.

done" (Jn 4:29). That's why the Samaritans believed in Jesus (Jn 4:39). It was *her testimony* that convinced the first group of Samaritans to come to the well and drink. Then, after they invited Jesus to "abide with them"—the key phrase of discipleship in John's Gospel—these same Samaritans became a well of living water themselves, leading other Samaritans to drink from the same well: "Many others believed because of his word" (Jn 4:41).[11]

That's the sequence John wanted to make plain: disciples may carry the living water to others, but everyone must drink from the well themselves: "Then they were saying to the woman, 'It's no longer just because of your word that we believe. For we have heard for ourselves and know that this man is truly the Savior of the world'" (Jn 4:42). Yet, it all started with her—a woman who met a stranger at a well and found the man she had been looking for: "I know that the Messiah is coming. . . . And when he comes, he will tell us *everything*" (Jn 4:25). Indeed he did—not only what she had done but also who he was: "I am he" (Jn 4:26). It's no wonder she left her jar at the well (Jn 4:28). Who needs a clay vessel for Jacob's well when you've become a spring of living water that lasts forever (Jn 4:14)?[12] John Chrysostom writes that the first disciples of Jesus, "when they were called, left their nets; she of *her own accord* leaves her water pot, and winged by joy performs the office of the Evangelists. And she calls not one or two, as did Andrew and Philip, but having aroused a whole city and people, so brought them to Him."[13] That's what evangelists do: they can't help but talk about Jesus and invite thirsty travelers to drink from the well of eternal life.

THE PROPHETESS

Having put a bounty on Jesus' head, the leaders of Jerusalem wondered whether Jesus would shy away from coming to the holy city for Passover,

---

[11]According to Schnackenburg, the Samaritans are "exemplary models of faith," since they didn't need signs to believe, only words (*John*, 1:456). Peter Phillips writes, "Just as the woman has begun to speak in Johannine terms, so the Samaritans begin to act in Johannine ways." See Phillips, "The Samaritans of Sychar: A Responsive Chorus," in Skinner, *Characters and Characterizations*, 298.

[12]"'Living water' cannot be contained in an ordinary vessel such as her water jar, but requires a new vessel: herself" (Resseguie, *Strange Gospel*, 80).

[13]John Chrysostom, *Homilies on St. John* 34.1, trans. Charles Marriott, emphasis added.

especially since they had "given orders that if anyone knew where he was, he should report it, that they might seize him" (Jn 11:55-57). But that didn't stop Jesus from coming to Jerusalem to observe Passover, and no one squealed on him when he showed up in Bethany only a few miles away. Instead of turning him in, his friends decided to throw a party for him when he came to town (Jn 12:1-2)—a rather in-your-face move of contempt against the religious leadership.[14] Once word reached the masses in Jerusalem that Jesus was in Bethany, the crowds flocked to see him and the man whom he raised from the dead (Jn 12:9). You would think that should have provoked the chief priests to send a posse to Bethany to take Jesus into custody. But that didn't happen. Instead, they simply added Lazarus's name to the bounty since "because of him, many were leaving Judea and believing in Jesus" (Jn 12:11).

In the public-relations contest between Jesus and the religious leaders in Jerusalem, the man who raised the dead was winning over the people despite the fact that their rulers wanted him dead. Furthermore, a banquet and a large crowd from Jerusalem gathering around Jesus would have given the impression that the people dismissed the chief priests' "idle" threats—especially when the multitude helped orchestrate the reception of Jesus into Jerusalem as the king of Israel (Jn 12:12-18).[15] After such a public spectacle, who would have believed that the chief priests could pull it off, killing the man who had power over death? Not the Pharisees: "Look! You're not doing any good. The whole world has gone after him!" (Jn 12:19).

When Mary anointed Jesus' feet with burial spices, she seemed to have ruined a good party. First of all, the narrator quickly points out the fragrance "filled the room" (Jn 12:3). Since pungent odors foul good food, one wonders whether anyone wanted to eat anymore. Second, her gesture looked like a foolish waste of money. The dead, not the living, need burial

---

[14]Reclining at table was customary during banquets: "The meal setting is probably a banquet celebrating Lazarus's resuscitation" (Keener, *Gospel of John*, 2:862).

[15]According to Michaels, the crowd's orchestrating the messianic parade was their response to the seventh sign (*Gospel of John*, 680).

spices. Finally, just when it seemed that Judas had made a good point—who could argue against using wealth to help the poor? (Jn 12:5)—Jesus latched on to the morbid implication of Mary's deed. Some could have attributed the ritual to the common act of hospitality, cleansing feet and anointing heads. Others might have interpreted it as a strange way to christen Jesus as the Messiah. But in both cases, Mary's gesture didn't add up. Heads (not feet) were anointed with oil (not spices) in both rituals.[16] Besides, Mary used way too much nard, worth about a year's wages. So why did she do it? According to Jesus, Mary was preparing his body for burial (Jn 12:7). To her Jesus was a dead man. That's why her hair was unbound; she was already grieving his death.[17] Like a prophet, Mary seemed to be the only one at the party who could see that "the poor you will always have among you but you will not always have me" (Jn 12:8). She knew that Jesus would be like no other king of Israel, so she performed "a prophetic action ahead of time to demonstrate her faith in him as the suffering Messiah," as Craig Keener puts it.[18]

Because an excessive amount of spices was customarily used to inter royalty, it smelled like a king was buried in Bethany that day.[19] Since Jesus was the anointed one—he certainly cast the odor of one who had been anointed—the crowd decided to orchestrate his arrival into Jerusalem with all the necessary messianic pomp and circumstance (Jn 12:12-13). They gathered palm branches, reminiscent of the success of the Maccabean revolt that led to the rededication of the temple (2 Maccabees 10:1-8). The multitude offered messianic praise, quoting the hallel Psalms that were sung during Passover (Ps 113–18). Joining the efforts of this staged event, Jesus himself found a young donkey and mounted it in order to punctuate the messianic imagery: "Don't be afraid, daughter of Zion. Look! Your King comes sitting on a donkey's colt" (Jn 12:15; Zech 9:9).

---

[16]Thompson, *John*, 259-60.

[17]Susan Miller, "Mary (of Bethany): The Anointer of the Suffering Messiah," in *Character Studies in the Fourth Gospel: Narrative Approaches to Seventy Figures in John*, ed. Steven A. Hunt, D. Francois Tomie, and Ruben Zimmermann (Tübingen: Mohr Siebeck, 2013), 481.

[18]Miller, "Mary (of Bethany)," 482.

[19]Keener, *Gospel of John*, 865.

What is interesting to me is how all of this was lost on the twelve disciples (Jn 12:16). Mary got it. The crowd followed her lead. But the disciples didn't understand what was going on until after the resurrection—which was par for the course according to John's Gospel (Jn 2:22; 14:26). This has happened before. A Samaritan woman understood what Jesus wanted without being told ("Make disciples!"). But the Twelve couldn't see what Jesus saw: the villagers from Sychar were a field ready for harvest *because of her*. The Samaritans declared, "This one is indeed *the Savior of the world*" (Jn 4:42). Similarly, even though he didn't ask for it, Mary did the right thing by preparing Jesus for a king's burial. Judas objected to the wasteful gesture, and the rest of the disciples couldn't smell what was going on. But the multitude understood, welcoming Jesus into Jerusalem as the anointed one *because of her*. The Judeans declared, "Blessed is he who comes in the name of the Lord, even *the King of Israel*" (Jn 12:13). The Samaritans found a Savior; the Judeans welcomed their King—all because two women did what was right without being told. Indeed, this is what it looks like when disciples abide in Jesus and his words. Because they see, others come to the Word.

THE AUTHOR

Jesus never tells his disciples to write down the gospel. Furthermore, in John's Gospel Jesus never instructs the Twelve to preach the gospel (the verb *kēryssō* never appears in the Fourth Gospel). Where Matthew ends his Gospel with the Great Commission to "make disciples" and Luke tells the story of how the first disciples made disciples by preaching the gospel, the only thing Jesus commissions the disciples to do in John's Gospel is to forgive or retain sins (Jn 20:23). In other words, it could be said that there is no worldwide gospel mission in John's Gospel—at least not one that Jesus gave to his disciples. Yet, the author of John's Gospel *expects* Jesus will make converts beyond the Twelve—not because his disciples preached the gospel to all nations or launched a missionary effort to take the gospel to the ends of the earth. Rather, Jesus will make disciples when people have eyes to *read* the Gospel according to John: "these things have been written in order that you all might believe that Jesus is the Christ, the Son of God, and in order that, believing, you may have life in his name" (Jn 20:31). The Word may have become flesh and dwelt among us, but in the end it is the Word written on paper that makes disciples. First incarnation, then excarnation. Word embodied in human flesh, words scribbled on human paper. The Gospel had to be written for people to believe the gospel.

That's why the last chapter of John's Gospel comes as a bit of a surprise. What better way to end the Gospel than with the author's stated purpose: I've written these things so that you will believe? Indeed, John 21 looks like an afterthought. Why add another story? Perhaps (1) to record a Galilean appearance of the resurrected Jesus (not just in Jerusalem), or (2) to show the rehabilitation of Simon (Peter shows no regret or remorse in John's Gospel), or (3) to give a Johannine version of the Great Commission (take care of the sheep), or (4) to offer another proof of the physical, resurrected body of Jesus (he eats with the seven disciples), or (5) to correct the legend surrounding the beloved disciple (Jesus didn't say he wouldn't die). To be sure, there's a lot going on in this story. But it's the postscript at the end (Jn 21:24-25) that seems to indicate the primary purpose of this add-on episode: to explain what Jesus meant when he said that the beloved one would abide until Jesus returns (Jn 21:23). That's why the postscript comes with a surprising revelation: the words we have been reading were written by a character in the story—the beloved disciple.[20] Since he is "the disciple who bears witness to these things *and wrote these words*" (Jn 21:24), we see what Jesus meant, how the beloved one abides until the coming of Christ. Because we have eyes to read his words, the beloved one abides with us. We hear his voice; we see what he sees. This is how he remains with us until Jesus comes. This is what Jesus meant by his prophecy (Jn 21:22), the significance of which is not only explained by the postscript but is also embedded in this strange addendum to John's Gospel.

---

[20]Resseguie, *Strange Gospel*, 85.

Throughout John's Gospel, characters typically misunderstand Jesus' words. He always seems to be talking on a different level. They hear one thing, but Jesus means something else. Even the Twelve don't get what Jesus was saying most of the time. The same thing happens in this story, but it's difficult to see because our translations obscure the double meaning of Jesus' words when he asks the seven disciples, "Children! You don't have any *prosphagion*, do you?" (Jn 21:5). In light of the story (where Peter decides to go fishing for the night and the other six tag along), we might have expected Jesus to ask, "You don't have any *fish* [*ichthyn*], do you?" or perhaps, "You didn't catch [*elabete*] anything, did you?" (see Lk 5:5).

But that's not what he asks. Instead, the author uses a word that usually referred to food that went with bread.[21] Since bread was the staple for Galileans, then *prosphagion* was anything that supplemented the meal— what we would call sides. Of course, we tend to think of bread as *prosphagion*—that which supplements our meal. But in that day, anything that went with bread (their staple diet) was *prosphagion*; and around the sea, it would have been fish. That's why translations typically render *prosphagion* as "fish," for example, "Children, you do not have any fish to eat, do you?" (NASB). Yet, Jesus didn't need any fish for breakfast. He already had some cooking on the fire—the *prosphagion* to go with the bread he already had (Jn 21:9). Why did he ask the seven, "You don't have anything to go with bread, do you?" Was he simply goading them for their unproductive night?

Many commentators think Jesus was trying to teach his disciples one last lesson, the reason John added this chapter: (1) he will always provide for them (Thompson), (2) disciples must always obey Jesus (Keener), (3) they needed to be reminded of their change in vocation (from fishing for fish to fishing for people; Michaels), or (4) in light of the peculiar

---

[21]See James Hope Moulton and George Milligan, eds., *The Vocabulary of the Greek Testament: Illustrated from the Papyri and Other Non-literary Sources* (Grand Rapids, MI: Eerdmans, 1930), 551-52; Frederick W. Danker, Walter Bauer, William F. Arndt, and F. Wilbur Gingrich, *A Greek-English Lexicon of the New Testament and Other Early Christian Literature*, 3rd ed. (Chicago: University of Chicago Press, 2000), 886. Of course, since Jesus spoke in his native tongue (either Aramaic or Hebrew), we should attribute the word choice to the Gospel writer.

reference to the number of fish caught (Jerome claimed there were 153 species of fish), Jesus was trying to teach them about the "breadth or even the universality of the Christian mission" (Brown).[22] Like many other stories in John's Gospel, this episode invites all kinds of interpretations because it provokes so many questions. Readers want to know what is going on here, wondering why the narrator mentions the number of fish caught, or why this is the only fishing story in John's Gospel (if all we had were the Fourth Gospel, we would never know that Jesus' first disciples were fishermen), or why Peter stripped to swim to Jesus, or why Jesus served them bread and fish (eucharistic overtones?), or why the disciples were confused about his identity, or why the narrator points out that this was the "third time" the resurrected Jesus appeared to them.[23] Typical of John's Gospel, there are many lessons to learn.

Yet, since the postscript is the final word of John's Gospel, perhaps these two verses indicate the prevailing point of the story: what Peter lacked, the beloved one provided. Jesus was looking for something to go with bread. Peter dragged up a netful of fish (Jn 21:11). The beloved one wrote the Gospel (Jn 21:24). Three times, Jesus had to tell Peter, "Feed my sheep" (Jn 21:15). Without being told, the beloved one would feed the sheep with his words. Peter still had lessons to learn about what it meant to follow Jesus (Jn 21:15-20). The beloved one, who already followed Jesus to the cross, would abide until Jesus comes (Jn 21:22-23). Peter's legacy would be confirmed by his death (Jn 21:18-20). The beloved one's legacy would be affirmed by a living community: "We know that his witness is true" (Jn 21:24). In other words, the beloved disciple was the only one who understood what Jesus meant when he said, "What if I want him to abide until I come?" (Jn 21:22). That's why he wrote the Gospel—the *prosphagion* that goes with the bread of life. Through his words about the Word, the beloved one abides until the end.

---

[22]Thompson, *John*, 434; Keener, *Gospel of John*, 2:1228; Michaels, *Gospel of John*, 1028; Brown, *John*, 2:1075.
[23]For the many, varied interpretations of the number of fish caught, see George R. Beasley-Murray, *John*, Word Biblical Commentary (Waco, TX: Word Books, 1987), 401-4.

John has done this before, contrasting Peter and the beloved disciple. In fact, every time the beloved disciple appears, Peter is there, functioning like a photographic negative of "the one whom Jesus loves." The difference is often startling. Peter talks a good game, promising what he can't deliver (Jn 13:37-38). The beloved one speaks only twice, offering nearly symmetrical sayings: "Lord, who is it?" and "It is the Lord!" (Jn 13:25; 21:7). Peter doesn't understand (Jn 13:6-10). The beloved one knows (Jn 13:24-26). Peter denies that he is Jesus' disciple (Jn 18:17, 25-27). The beloved one is affirmed as Jesus' brother (Jn 19:26-27). Peter sees the grave clothes of Jesus. The beloved one sees the resurrection of the Lord. Peter doesn't recognize the stranger on the shore (Jn 21:7, 12). The beloved one says, "It is the Lord!" (Jn 21:7). Peter claims he loves Jesus (Jn 21:15-17). The other disciple is the "one whom Jesus loves" (Jn 21:7, 20). The contrast couldn't be more obvious, a significant difference between the disciple who was *supposed* to be the rock and the disciple who *will* abide until Jesus comes: because the beloved one sees, others come to Jesus—the last two verses of the Gospel according to John prove it.

I read, therefore I believe.

THE EDITOR

Jesus counted on the Holy Spirit to guide his disciples after he left them: to comfort them during his absence, to help them remember what he said, to inspire them to tell the truth about him (Jn 14:16-17, 26; 15:26-27; 16:7-16). The Gospel of John testifies to the work of the Spirit; its very existence reveals that Jesus knew what he was talking about. Because the beloved one remembered what Jesus said, we have his words to comfort us in his absence. Because the beloved one "wrote these things," we are inspired to tell the truth about Jesus: he is the Christ, the Son of God. Indeed, since we have eyes to read the Gospel according to John—because we see, we come to Jesus—we heartily join the testimony of the first readers: "We know that his witness is true" (Jn 21:24). In fact, we even resonate with the claim of the first editor, the one who wrote: "There are also many other things Jesus did, which, if every single one of them were written down, I'm pretty sure no library in the world could hold all the books" (Jn 21:25).[24] Even he knew there was more to be written about Jesus. There could never be enough words to explain the eternal Word of God. Indeed, shelves in my office are filled with books about Jesus, and I can never get enough. The more I read about him, the more I want to know about him. That's why no library will ever contain all the books. No one will have the last word on Jesus. Consequently, many keep writing and we keep reading—something publishers know too well.

We had gathered for our annual meeting in Boston, a confab of biblical scholars who travel from all over the world to share research, renew friendships, meet with publishers, and buy books. As it was their custom during the conference, Zondervan (a Christian publisher) hosted a luncheon for their authors to show appreciation for our work, to give updates on the publishing industry, and to leave us with a parting gift (usually nice pens, free copies of their latest release, and other items). This time, however, they added one more gift: a coffee mug with a verse of Scripture either from the Old Testament (written in Hebrew) or the New Testament (written in Greek). It was our choice. The publisher said with a wry grin, "If you can read it, you can take it." Old Testament scholars collected their mugs with Hebrew writing, and we, New Testament writers, grabbed the ones with a Greek verse printed on the side. I expected 2 Corinthians 1:13, or 1 John 1:4, or perhaps even Revelation 1:11. When I saw John 21:25 printed on the side of the mug—a cup I would use nearly every day at work—I thought, *How clever! Every time I take sip of coffee, the words of an editor will be staring me in the face.*

I wonder about the editor of John's Gospel: Who was he?[25] What part did he play in publishing the Gospel? Why did he feel the need to add the postscript? Of course, the identity of the beloved disciple garners more attention, inviting all kinds of speculation: Who was the one whom Jesus

---

[24]R. Alan Culpepper, *John: The Son of Zebedee, The Life of a Legend* (Minneapolis: Fortress, 2000), 71-72. C. K. Barrett writes, "This gospel was in some sense a joint project." See Barrett, *The Gospel According to St. John*, 2nd ed. (Philadelphia: Westminster, 1978), 588.
[25]Probably a man, since scribal literacy was almost exclusively a masculine skill.

loved?[26] Why is he never named? If the beloved disciple were John, would he have referred to himself as "the one who Jesus loved"? Or did the author intend for us to look for someone else, teasing his readers with clues embedded in the Gospel about the "real" identity of the beloved disciple? If that is the case, could Lazarus be the beloved disciple? Three times Lazarus is identified as the one whom Jesus loves (Jn 11:3, 5, 36). Or could it have been Thomas, "the twin" who needed to see the wound in Jesus' side before he believed (Jn 20:25)—a unique detail in John's account of the crucifixion that only an eyewitness would know about (Jn 19:34-35)?[27]

Whoever he was, the editor added the postscript so that readers would know two things: (1) the beloved one is a reliable witness (Jn 21:24), and (2) much more could have been *written* about Jesus—a *unique* ability that only a few people in the first-century world would have possessed. That's because scribal literacy was rare at the time; it is estimated that only 10 percent of the population was even semiliterate (having a functional ability to read and write—some more legibly than others).[28] Given the high level of literacy in our world, when the editor claims that "much more could have been written," we wonder: "What's stopping you? Go ahead and write it down. No big deal." But due to the scarcity of writing materials and the rarity of uniquely skilled scribes, writing would have been a big deal in the first-century Mediterranean world. That makes me wonder even more about the editor: Who was he? Where did he come from? Was he a longtime friend of the beloved disciple or simply a hired hand?[29] Like a secretary, did he help the beloved one "write these things" down?[30] Having heard many, many, many stories about Jesus, did the

---

[26]Culpepper, *John*, 72-85.

[27]See James H. Charlesworth, *The Beloved Disciple: Whose Witness Validates the Gospel of John?* (Valley Forge, PA: Trinity Press International, 1995), 228-29.

[28]William V. Harris, *Ancient Literacy* (Cambridge, MA: Harvard University Press, 1991), 22.

[29]From the Codex Vaticanus Alexandrinus 14 (ninth century): "The Gospel of John was made known and given to the churches by John while he was still in the flesh, as a man of Hierapolis by the name of Papias, a beloved disciple of John. . . . Indeed, he wrote down the Gospel correctly as John dictated." See Fragments of Papias 19, in *The Apostolic Fathers*, 3rd ed., ed. and trans. Michael W. Holmes (Grand Rapids, MI: Baker Academic, 2007).

[30]Therefore, when the editor claims that the beloved one "wrote these things," he means "caused to write," similar to what Pilate said, "what I have written I have written" (Jn 19:22)—even though

editor help pare down the material? ("No. Let's add this story here; omit that story. There's so much to write, so little room!"[31]) Was the editor the beloved one's creative partner, one of those rare persons with scribal skill who knew how to write well? Are his fingerprints all over the Gospel of John? We'll never know. But like Paul's secretary Tertius, who pokes his head into the apostle's letter to the Romans just to say, "Hi, everyone!" (Rom 16:22), we see the editor of John's Gospel reminding his readers that words don't magically appear on paper. Books require authors and editors.

Since we believe the Gospel of John is the inspired word of God, then the Holy Spirit must have played a role in bringing these two together: the author and the editor. I wonder whether they ever marveled over their divine collaboration—especially if they came from different parts of the world—celebrating the lengths to which God would go to bring two people together. "A Jew from Galilee and a scribe from Ephesus! Who would have thought?" It would help, of course, if we knew the identity of both. Did author and editor come from two different worlds? Maybe so, maybe not. But it wouldn't surprise us if they did, since John's Gospel features unlikely pairings (Jesus and the Samaritan woman) and God continues to bring people together from all over the world—especially authors and editors who write books. So, when I first met Katya Covrett, I should have known the answer to the question, "How does a Russian woman become the executive academic editor for a major American Christian publisher dominated by male authors?" Some call it the providence of God. Others speak of the work of the Holy Spirit. Using John's terms, I would say she abides in Christ—doing the right thing without being told. But she spoke of her unlikely position in matter-of-fact terms, surprised that I would find her story surprising.

It could be said that Katya grew up in the typical Russian home, with parents who were atheists and a future as challenging as a Russian winter. Gifted in languages, Katya pursued studies in English at the local university,

---

Pilate didn't actually "write" what was written on the placard (see Culpepper, *John*, 71).
[31]Our Gospels are the maximum length of a papyrus roll. See Bruce M. Metzger, *Manuscripts of the Greek Bible* (Oxford: Oxford University Press, 1981), 16-17.

hoping her skills in reading and writing would lead to a good job. That, of course, eventually happened. But not in ways that anyone could have imagined. "I was a bit of a rebel," she said, "looking for opportunities beyond what was expected." She enjoyed a good party, like the rest of her friends. But she also knew that life in Khabarovsk wouldn't be enough for her—learning English was her way out. To hone her language skills, she offered her services as a translator for summer missionaries from the States. At first, she didn't think much of their gospel message. But then, after some time, as she began to reflect on her life—the sin, the emptiness, the loneliness, the yearning for something more—she wondered whether what the missionaries were saying through her might become reality in her. So, in the middle of winter, long after the missionaries had returned to their home, alone in her room, this twenty-year-old Russian woman prayed to God and was converted to Christ. No one to celebrate with—the missionaries were gone, her friends disinterested—she wondered what would become of her newfound faith. "It was so lonely," she said. "I knew little of the Christian life and really did not know where to go. I was just getting by with my little Gideon NT and the little I knew from having done translation work. I had no idea what it really meant to follow Christ."

I asked, "So, what did you do? Did you ever find Christian fellowship?" At that moment, tears welled up in her eyes as she grabbed her phone, showed me a picture, and said simply, "Yes, I did." It was a picture of more than a dozen Russian teenagers and twenty-somethings, soaking-wet hair, arm in arm, huge grins on their faces, having just been baptized. "That looks like joy," I said, to which she replied, "You want to see joy?" showing more pictures of the same group, the beginnings of a new church that met in the Khabarovsk Christian Student Center.

"How did that happen?" In the spring after her conversion, Southern Baptist missionaries were offering computer classes in a facility near the university. A friend of Katya's told her about the classes, and they both decided to go. "But the Monday night computer class he was looking for turned out to be a Wednesday night *Bible study*. My friend was immediately bored and disappointed, but I recognized the message that had changed me." That night, during the Bible study, Katya told her story, how she prayed to Christ a few months before. "That must have piqued the interest of the missionaries," I said. "Yes. It didn't take long for us to become more involved in their group. And, after several months, with more and more young people coming to the Bible study, more were converted to Christ. Not feeling like we fit well into the traditional congregation, we asked to start a new church. We were all baptized that October. Then one thing led to another. Four years later I decided to come to the States to study theology. Then, after finishing a master's degree and looking for a job, I was hired as an editorial assistant at Zondervan in 2002. Within three years, I was acquiring books. And I've been Zondervan Academic's main acquiring editor since 2005, becoming an executive editor in 2014."

I asked her, "Do you ever sit back and wonder, 'How did all of this happen? How did I get here?'" After a brief moment, in her usual matter-of-fact voice, she replied, "Sometimes, but I don't dwell on it. I'm grateful to God for the opportunity—to meet so many well-known theologians, to work with authors who publish such important works. There's a great amount of satisfaction that comes with working behind the scenes as an editor. When an author's work is widely read, when he or she receives favorable reviews, I find great joy in that. Knowing many of these books find readers all around the world . . ." her voice trailing off, I interjected, "That's the work of God." To which she quietly replied, "Yes, but I can only see it in retrospect."

As I walked away from our conversation, I kept turning Katya's story over and over in my mind. *It's a miracle—especially at a time like this, when accusations of Russian meddling in our US elections are hanging over our collective heads and women are challenging the prejudices of a male-dominant world. Who would have thought that a girl from Russia would become an editor and help lead one of the largest Christian publishers in America?* Then, lifting the coffee mug with John 21:25 printed on the side, I heard another editor say, "I would," along with a hearty "Amen" from an evangelist, a prophetess, and the disciple whom Jesus loved. It's as old as the Gospel according to John. Because they see, others come to Jesus. That's why we will abide *together* until he comes.

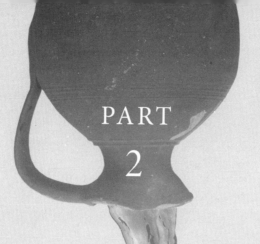

PART

2

JOHN'S LETTERS

Communing with the Word Together

JOHN KNEW WE COULDN'T BE DISCIPLES by ourselves. Even though his Gospel tells the story of how individual disciples follow Jesus, John's letters instruct the church on how to remain in Christ together—to abide by what we have in common: the Word of God. For John's community, the only way they could abide in the Word of God was to hear John's Gospel, learning how to "walk as that man walked" (1 Jn 2:6). But some members couldn't abide by John's words, no longer gathering with the community to hear the Gospel. They left the church, acting like they could abide in the Word *without* the Gospel. That left them relying on their own words, saying things such as, "Jesus Christ comes not in the flesh" and "I know Jesus." But John claimed you don't know Jesus if you deny his humanity and don't keep his commandment "love one another." How could anyone love a church they left? To abide in Christ is to remain in the church, learning how to live out the truth of John's Gospel. Indeed, true disciples of Christ abide in the Word by remaining in the community of faith. What does it take to remain in the church? To hear, confess, incarnate, and abide in the Word *together*.

5

CONFESS SIN

Hearing the Word

I MARVEL OVER OUR ABILITY to justify ourselves. No matter what we've done, if given enough time we can find a way, a reason, a circumstance that turns our bad behavior into "that's not so bad." I've seen that several times as pastor of two large congregations. Members would come to me in private, looking for absolution for their sin. But the means of their absolution didn't square with what was required by the New Testament. I thought they had come to confess their sin or to seek advice on how to deal with the lingering guilt of their sin. (And sometimes that happened.) But many times—it really did surprise me how often—what began as a "confession" would end up sounding more like self-justification. Knowing it wasn't time for a sermon when the "penitent" started justifying their sin (most often pertaining to sex or money), I would usually interject with, "But how does that square with what Jesus said or with what Paul wrote?" After referencing the text, I expected either contrition ("Yes, you're right") or a debate over the meaning of Scripture ("But I don't read it that way")—either would have been a welcome turn in the conversation. But they usually ignored the Scripture and continued with their lengthy defense. Yet, here's the real shocker: the more egregious the sin, the shorter the defense. Their open posture would quickly give way to a defiant look—a stone-cold countenance punctuating the sharp tone of their abrupt words. Even though I tried to continue the conversation, it would become apparent to both of us that our talk was over. Bringing up the Scriptures during defensive acts of self-justification rarely seemed to help, other than bringing a quick end to our conversation.

After several of these kinds of conversations, I began to realize that my expectations were not the same as theirs. For a while, I had the mistaken impression that church members were coming to me as an "expert," wanting to know what the Scriptures had to say about a certain issue. But most of the time that's not why they came. Rather, what they were *really* looking for was someone to agree with them, to rule in their favor, to support them in their cause, to vindicate them. That's why turning to the Scriptures only made things worse. For I had made the assumption that, however we interpret them, the Scriptures should always challenge our justification—as long as they are read. Indeed, I have a hard time justifying my sin while reading what Jesus said (try justifying sexual immorality while reading Matthew 5:27-30, or an indulgent lifestyle in light of the parable of the rich man and Lazarus in Luke 16:19-31). On the other hand, when the Scriptures are *not* read, self-justification is easy. Biblical illiteracy fosters sin.

Imagine, therefore, how easy it would have been to justify sin when the average Christian in John's day did not have access to the Scriptures, neither the "Old" nor the "New." Of course, the New didn't exist at the time, and the Old was only available to those who could read. Since most Christians were illiterate, the only way they would know the Scriptures was to attend a meeting (either Jewish synagogue or Christian assembly) where they could hear sacred texts read to them.[1] In other words—and this is a crucial point we tend to overlook as moderns who prize individualism—the first Christians knew they needed each other to be Christian. If a believer wanted to know, "What did Jesus say about that?" they had to find someone who either (1) heard what Jesus said (oral tradition) or (2) could read the "new" work that had recently been written—

---

[1]See the superb study by Brian J. Wright, *Communal Reading in the Time of Jesus: A Window into Early Christian Reading Practices* (Minneapolis: Fortress, 2017), 117-206.

in this case, the Gospel according to John.[2] Indeed, the only way the first Christians would know the truth was to rely on each other for the truth.

Jesus predicted the same thing—that none of us would be able to follow him by ourselves. Even though he called disciples individually, Jesus said his disciples would not live like "orphans" (Jn 14:18). He would have no lone-ranger disciples trying to go at it alone. Rather, Jesus said that, after he was gone, every disciple would need two things to follow him: other Christians ("love one another") and the Holy Spirit ("the Helper"). Even though Jesus spoke of the Spirit welling up in the individual believer, he said that wouldn't happen until *after* the resurrection (Jn 7:37-39). Indeed, throughout his Farewell Discourse, Jesus didn' talk about the future of his disciples without mentioning the work of the Spirit and their need of each other. The Spirit would teach them, help them remember what Jesus said, "guide them in all truth" (Jn 14:26; 16:13). In order to endure the hatred of the world, the disciples would eventually learn to abide in Christ's love by loving each other (Jn 15:9-12). But that wouldn't happen until later, after they "scattered, each one going to his own home, leaving Christ alone" (Jn 16:32). Then, after Jesus returned to them, their joy would return, the Spirit would come, and they would bear fruit because they would abide in him (Jn 15:5, 16; 16:19-22)—prophecies that only *partially* come true in John's Gospel. To be sure, Jesus returned (Jn 20:19-21); ten disciples received the Holy Spirit (Jn 20:22-23). But the rest of what Jesus predicted—being hated by the world, abiding in his word, loving each other, bearing fruit—didn't happen in John's Gospel.

This is where the letters of John come into play. What Jesus predicts in John's Gospel doesn't come true until we read John's letters.[3] In other words, it seems like Jesus' instruction for the Twelve about what will happen to them after he returns to the Father is more apropos for the

---

[2]So also Wright, *Communal Reading*, 191-92.

[3]Raymond E. Brown makes the same point but is pessimistic: "The body of the GJohn ended on a more positive note. Although GJohn described the rejection of God's emissary by 'his own' (John 1:11), the ultimate goal of that work was optimistic: ' . . . that you may believe that Jesus is the Christ, the Son of God, and that believing you may possess life in his name' (20:31). But a decade has passed and the Johannine Community that received the gospel has not lived up to the evangelist's hope." See Brown, *The Epistles of John*, Anchor Bible (New York: Doubleday, 1982), 602.

church than for the Twelve. John's letters reveal the rest of the story: how Jesus' disciples endured the hatred of the world, how they learned to abide in his word by keeping his commandments, why they needed to love one another, why they had to rely on the Spirit to guide them in all truth. John's letters instruct the church on how to follow Jesus *together*, a fellowship of purpose that can only be revealed corporately. As far as John is concerned, one can only abide in Christ by remaining in the church.

IN THE BEGINNING WAS THE WORD THAT WAS HEARD

What is it that holds the church together? Why are we compelled to gather together? Compared to other weekly activities, it is a rather odd thing to do. I can't think of another occasion when I join other people in a room at a certain time, sing songs together, listen to someone speak, and then part company to go our separate ways. Of course, like many others, I've been doing this thing we call church for so long it doesn't seem odd to me at all. Yet, compared to the ways of the world, it is a peculiar habit. Why do we do it? Why do Christians persist in getting together once a week, regardless of language, culture, or disposition?

We can think of several good reasons: to worship the Lord, to encourage one another, to be inspired to live for Christ, to be renewed in our commitment, to fellowship. That word, *fellowship* (from the Greek *koinōnia*), leads me to ask the question another way: What do we have in *common*? The Greek word *koinē* means "common"; therefore koinonia has to do with what we have in common, what we share together, what holds us together. For John, the reason for our koinonia, why we gather together, what holds the church together is *what we've heard and seen together*:

> What was from the beginning, what we have heard, what we have seen with our eyes, what we beheld and what our hands have handled concerning the word of life—and the life was revealed, and we have seen and bear witness and announce to you the eternal life that is with the Father and was revealed to us—what we have seen and heard, we announce also to you in order that you might have koinonia with us. And our koinonia is also with the Father and with his Son Jesus Christ. (1 Jn 1:1-3)

Scholars are divided over "what" (the pronoun is neuter) it was that existed "from the beginning," what was heard and seen, what "our hands *handled*" (1 Jn 1:1). Some hear an echo of John's prologue, where he claims the preexistent Logos became flesh and "tabernacled among us, and we beheld [*etheasametha*, the same word as 1 Jn 1:1] his glory" (Jn 1:14). So John is claiming authority as an eyewitness of the incarnation, not only a disciple who heard and saw Jesus, "the word of life," but also "handled" him. Others think John is referring to the resurrected Christ, echoing the story of Thomas when he was invited to handle the body of Christ (Jn 20:27).[4]

But, why did John use a neuter pronoun to refer to the Logos? If John were referring to Jesus, he should have written, "*He* who existed from the beginning, whom we heard, whom our eyes saw. . . ." Besides, if John were referring to the incarnation in 1 John 1:1, why would he repeat the same claim in 1 John 1:2? Some scholars, therefore, think John was referring to the gospel message that was preached—that which "we announce to you" (1 Jn 1:2-3). John is claiming that the gospel he preached to them is the same message that was heard from the beginning. That explains why John used a neuter pronoun ("that") rather than the masculine ("who"). But, if John were referring to the gospel message, how do we make sense of his claim that he not only heard the message but also saw it and handled it with his hands?

I think John was referring to the gospel *excarnated*, words written on paper, that "our hands handled about the word of life" (1 Jn 1:1). First, the Word was incarnated ("and the life was revealed," 1 Jn 1:2). Then came the excarnation—words written on paper—so that the Word of life would be once again incarnated in the community. Incarnation, excarnation, reincarnation.[5] That's why, for John, hearing the Gospel was critical to

[4]Matthew D. Jensen, *Affirming the Resurrection of the Incarnate Christ: A Reading of 1 John*, Society of New Testament Studies Monograph Series 153 (Cambridge: Cambridge University Press, 2012), 60-67.

[5]A similar correlation is made in the Epistle of Barnabas 12.9-10: "Moses said to 'Jesus' the son of Nun, when he gave him this name as he sent him to spy out the land, 'Take a book in your hands and write what the Lord says, that in the last days the Son of God will cut off by its roots all the house of Amalek.' Observe again that it is Jesus, not a son of man but the Son of God, and

their koinonia (1 Jn 1:3). The only way members of the Johannine community would be able to hear the Gospel was to listen to a literate person
read the Gospel—a rare ability at this time. John was reminding his community of his authority as a text broker, someone who not only "writes
these things" (1 Jn 1:4) but is also able to announce the gospel message to
those who have ears to hear the Gospel according to John (1 Jn 1:3)—a
message that was first heard, witnessed to, and announced by those who
saw Christ (1 Jn 1:2).[6] That would mean, of course, that those who didn't
hear the Gospel according to John wouldn't know the truth, thereby
putting their koinonia in jeopardy—with God, with Christ, and with the
community (1 Jn 1:3). If the illiterate didn't gather to listen to the Gospel
of John, then they wouldn't know "the message" John heard from Jesus
and delivered to them via his Gospel (1 Jn 1:5). They wouldn't be able to
see Jesus in the light of the Gospel.[7] Consequently, they would walk
around in darkness, unable to "do the truth" (1 Jn 1:6), because "his word
is not in" them (1 Jn 1:10)—reincarnation. Only those who remained in
community, who listened to the truth of the Gospel, could say they had
fellowship with Christ (1 Jn 1:7). How else could anyone "walk in the light"
unless they heard the Gospel of John being read to them?

The reincarnation of the excarnated word was what they had in
common, the reason they gathered together. John's Gospel was a cen-
tripetal force of their koinonia. But there were some members who had
recently left the community, convinced that they could still walk in the
truth *without hearing the Gospel*. According to John, they "went out from

---

revealed in the flesh by a symbol [*typo*]." Michael W. Holmes, trans., *The Apostolic Fathers*, 3rd
ed. (Grand Rapids, MI: Baker Academic, 2007).

[6]Jensen, *Affirming the Resurrection*, 66. Here, Jensen is arguing for a reference to the resurrection
(not the incarnation) of Jesus Christ. I think the proximal event is the reading of John's Gospel.
2 Clement 19.1 reads, "Therefore, brothers and sisters, following the God of truth I am reading
you an exhortation to pay attention to what is written, in order that you may save both yourselves
and your reader" (Holmes, *Apostolic Fathers*).

[7]Kasper Bro Larsen writes, "[The Gospel] not only claims that Jesus represents God in the story-
world, but also asserts that *the text itself*, as a testimony, represents Jesus in the reader-world. The
Gospel constitutes a second sign that points toward Jesus and compensates the reader for being
in a situation where the divine Jesus-sign is not directly accessible." See Larsen, *Recognizing the
Stranger: Recognition Scenes in the Gospel of John* (Leiden: Brill, 2008), 5-6, emphasis added.

us because they were not a part of us, for if they were a part of us, they would have remained [abide!]—but they left to reveal they were never truly a part of us" (1 Jn 2:19). That's why John wrote his Gospel (1 Jn 2:21), so that his community would know the truth and be able to recognize liars—those who "deny that Jesus is the Christ" (1 Jn 2:22). By their words, liars reveal they oppose Christ ("antichrist"), denying the unique relationship that exists between the Father and the Son (1 Jn 2:22-23). That's not the message they heard "from the beginning," the word that was heard by those who remained in the community when the Gospel was read (1 Jn 2:24).[8] If there's anything the Gospel of John makes clear it is this: Jesus is the Christ, the Son of God, and those who believe in him receive eternal life (Jn 20:30-31). "This is the promise that he promised us, eternal life" (1 Jn 2:25). It's no wonder, then, that these "liars" left the community. They couldn't stand to listen to the Gospel of John anymore, in defiance of the text broker—something Ignatius encountered as well: "For I heard some people say, 'If I do not find it in the archives, I do not believe it in the gospel.' And when I said to them, 'It is written,' they answered me, 'That is precisely the question.' But for me, the 'archives' are Jesus Christ."[9]

Ironically, the excarnation of the gospel—what was supposed to help John's community—ended up creating problems for them. It's even possible that they didn't know they had a problem until John's Gospel was read to them. According to Raymond Brown, the secessionists didn't leave the community due to "pagan" influences.[10] Their faulty theology didn't derive from a mixture of Jewish gospel and Greek philosophy. Rather, once the Gospel of John was read, the secessionists began to reveal their heretical Christology when they interpreted what they heard. In

---

[8]Since "Christian communities were often defined through and in communal reading events," Wright maintains the auditors "helped control a particular tradition, interpretation, or both" (*Communal Reading*, 203).

[9]Ignatius, *To the Philadelphians* 8.2 (Holmes, Apostolic Fathers).

[10]Brown, *Epistles*, 69-86, 92-100; see also Gary M. Burge, "Spirit-Inspired Theology and Ecclesial Correction: Charting One Shift in the Development of Johannine Ecclesiology and Pneumatology," in *Communities in Dispute: Current Scholarship on the Johannine Epistles*, ed. R. Alan Culpepper and Paul N. Anderson (Atlanta: SBL Press, 2014), 179-85.

other words, those who "went out from us because they were not a part of us" interpreted John's Gospel differently from the rest of the community—a difference that led to their departure. They weren't kicked out by John or those loyal to him. Rather, the secessionists left on their own accord—something that not only brought distress to the church (what happened to our koinonia?) but also compelled John to write 1 John.

Commentators wonder why John took such an indirect approach to dealing with heresy, first writing a Gospel to be read to the people, then sending a follow-up letter. Why not identify the culprits by name and order them out of the church? There are several reasons why—something we will sort out in the next chapter.[11] But what I find compelling is this: John presumed the reading and hearing of his Gospel would work much like the presence of Jesus (Jn 3:19-21). Those who were repelled by the Light would go out into darkness, and those who were drawn to the Light would abide (1 Jn 1:5-10). The reason? It has to do with their deeds. Those who perform evil deeds don't want their sin exposed by the Light. That's why they hide in the darkness, where the light of the Gospel is never read. But those who are drawn to the Light confess their sin—something they have in common with everyone who seeks cleansing through the blood of Jesus Christ (1 Jn 1:7). It's the hearing of Scripture (walking in the light) that brings about confession of sin and obedience. Those who don't hear the Scriptures remain in darkness, not confessing their sins because they can't see what only the Light exposes (1 Jn 1:8, 10). In the dark, it's easy to say, "I have no sin." Who can tell? Biblical illiteracy fosters self-delusion.

It's one of the great ironies of our time. Even though the Scriptures are more accessible today in our world than ever before—nearly everyone can read, and free copies of the Bible are everywhere (hard copy and electronic)—biblical illiteracy seems to have *increased*.[12] Such a

---

[11]See Burge, who maintains that John couldn't leverage pastoral authority like Paul did due to his pneumatologically informed ecclesiology: "Ecclesial correction in a spirit-filled setting requires different strategies; just ask anyone at the Society of Pentecostal Studies" ("Spirit-Inspired Theology," 182).

[12]Barna Group, "The Bible in America: Six-Year Trends," Barna, June 15, 2016, www.barna.com /research/the-bible-in-america-6-year-trends/.

phenomenon would have been inconceivable to first-century Christians. Imagine going back in time and reporting our modern convenience to the large numbers of illiterate members of the early church, some having traveled a great distance to hear a gifted person read the one copy they had of the Gospel of John. To hear the Gospel would feel to them like a tall drink of water in the desert called the world. But we have water all around us, fountains that deliver a cool sip of water whenever we want. No big deal. Yet, even though the Scriptures are so accessible today to an overwhelmingly literate population, people don't read.

I've noticed this as a college professor over the past thirty years. In light of the fact that most of our students come from evangelical churches, the steady decline of their biblical literacy is staggering. For example, since Paul quotes the Hebrew Scriptures quite often, when we're reading his letters for a college course, I have to spend quite a bit of time rehearsing Israel's story so that my students can make sense of the apostle's argument. I used to be able to say, "You know the story of Abraham. So, let's explore the significance of Paul's argument in Romans 4. For Paul, was Abraham the model sinner who realized the inadequacy of works righteousness? Or did Paul use Abraham's story to prove that the God of Israel intended to save Gentiles from the beginning?" These days, however, I have to spend quite a bit of time rehearsing Abraham's story before delving into the nuances of Paul's argument. Our students don't know the Scriptures. One day I was commiserating with faculty who had noticed the same thing when one of our colleagues said, "Our students love the Bible. They just don't care what's in it."

Ever since we placed the burden of Bible reading on the *individual* Christian—"It's your responsibility to read the Scriptures"—biblical illiteracy has increased. We have tried Scripture memorization programs for children. We have promoted Bible study fellowship for adults. But evangelical churches are producing more biblically illiterate Christians every year. In the first century, illiterate Christians gathered to hear the Scriptures read to them, instilling a sense of reverential awe for those who could read God's Word. These days, however, the thrill is gone.

Despite all of our attempts to make the Bible more readable by publishing *dozens* of translations, Christians have lost interest. We don't read. For a religion that depends on a book, that doesn't bode well for the church.

THE KOINONIA OF CONFESSED SIN

Given that he knew there were "liars" who denied that Jesus was the Christ (1 Jn 2:22), it's surprising that the first issue John confronts in his letter concerns those who refused to confess their sin (1 Jn 1:5–2:2). Having just established the verity of his Gospel (1 Jn 1:1-4)—John's word about the Word of life is the only word worth hearing—we might have expected him to blast the "liars" and the "antichrists" for their false Christology. After all, that was a *serious* problem, perhaps the main reason why he wrote this letter—a follow-up to his Gospel. But rather than deal with their false Christology, John immediately takes up the problem of their pseudospirituality. Evidently, there were false confessors among them who claimed, "We have no sin" and "We have not sinned" (1 Jn 1:8, 10). But why would anyone say that? Who could deny the obvious—that we all make mistakes, that we live in a fallen world, that we all sin? Furthermore, who in John's community would dare to say, "We have no sin," especially when they all heard Jesus say in John's Gospel that those who say they "have no sin" are *blind* (Jn 9:41)? Indeed, according to John, only those who recognize their sin truly see because the only way to see is to walk in the light. Those who live in darkness can't see a thing, blinded by the night.

Now we are beginning to see why confessing sin is the first problem John brings up in his letter. Only those who gather to hear the Gospel are able to see what is clearly revealed by the light. Those who don't hear the Gospel because they don't join the community—the only place to hear gospel truth—well, those people walk in darkness. As everyone knows, no one sees clearly in the dark. That's why those who say they see while walking in the darkness are liars (1 Jn 1:6). They're so blinded by the darkness that can't see what is true. Therefore, those who say "we see" in the dark are doubly deceived: they lie about themselves ("we have no sin," 1 Jn 1:8, 10) and about others ("we have Christ in common," 1 Jn 1:6). If they truly shared in the fellowship of Christ (1 Jn 1:7)—what the Johannine community held in common—they would (1) walk in the light (hear the Gospel), (2) confess their sins, (3) and find cleansing in the blood of Christ (1 Jn 1:7, 9). As far as John is concerned, when we confess Christ, we are also confessing our need of him. Who he is defines who we are. He is the faithful forgiver; we need forgiveness (1 Jn 1:9). He is the comforting helper; we need help (1 Jn 2:1). Indeed, when we truly see him, we truly see ourselves, because our sin is revealed in the presence of Christ. The same thing happened to Isaiah (Is 6:1-5). As soon as he saw the Lord, he confessed his sin (and the sin of everyone else!). Therefore, according to J. Ramsey Michaels, "Sin is identified as sin not in relation to the law of Moses, but only in relation to Jesus. . . . In this sense the 'coming' of Jesus creates not only 'friends,' but 'sinners' as well."[13]

The word John uses, *confess*, reveals that we have something else in common—not only who Jesus is and who we are, but what we've done. *Homologeō* means "to say the same thing." According to John, when we confess our sins, we're saying the same thing about our sin. Of course, John doesn't encourage his readers to name their sins *specifically*. Rather, he simply affirms what they should already know: since sinners sin, then when sinners come together in the light of Jesus' presence, we'll all say the same thing about sin. When we confess, we agree that what we all have in common is sin. Consequently, the koinonia of our fellowship will be evident when we confess our sins *together*. In fact, it could be said that when a bunch of Christians start confessing sins, it's a sign that Christ is present. Just like Isaiah, we can't help but confess *our* sins. Notice how often John uses plural pronouns throughout his letter—especially here when he's writing about confessing sin. "If *we* confess *our* sins" (1 Jn 1:9). Confession isn't a private matter, just between God and the penitent. Rather, John assumes a corporate context for confession, built on the conviction that public confession of sin will

---

[13]J. Ramsey Michaels, *The Gospel of John*, New International Commentary on the New Testament (Grand Rapids, MI: Eerdmans, 2010), 822.

happen when gathered Christians hear the truth about Jesus in John's Gospel.[14] Once we hear the truth about Jesus—the "faithful and righteous" one (1 Jn 1:9; 2:1)—we confess to each other our unfaithfulness and unrighteousness (1 Jn 1:9).

But our common confession doesn't end there. When we are gathered for worship, the goal isn't to get sinners to wallow in our sins. "Let's all say it together: 'We're all a bunch of lousy sinners.'" No. The reason John wants us to hear the gospel as good news is this: because of who Jesus is ("faithful and righteous/just"), we know who we are ("forgiven and cleansed") *in his presence*. You would think it should be the opposite: because Jesus is faithful, he would condemn us for betraying him. Since Jesus is just, he should make us pay for our crimes. Right? Isn't that what justice requires, especially since our sins—greed, jealousy, hatred—not only alienate us from God but also cause harm to each other? Since Jesus is just, shouldn't we all get what we deserve?

This is why John knows confession must happen during worship. When we confess our sins, we're confessing that we've hurt each other. That's what we're agreeing about—not only that we have sinned against God but also against each other. That's why we need to hear ourselves confess our sins in public worship. We're acknowledging not only our common need of forgiveness from God but also from each other. This is what we have in common. We all sin. We all need God's forgiveness. We all need to be cleansed by the blood of Christ. We can't save ourselves. We can't wash ourselves. We can't fix ourselves. It's because none of us are just. None of us are faithful. The only one who can wash us clean is the one who *is just* because he *is faithful*. "He is the atoning sacrifice for our sins—not only for our sins but for the sins of the whole world" (1 Jn 2:2). Your sin. My sin. The sins of all people. Jesus' sacrifice covers a multitude of sin. It's what we have in common. Only those who walk in the light of the Gospel of John can see that.

---

[14]So also Brown, *Epistles*, 208; Stephen S. Smalley, *1, 2, 3 John*, Word Biblical Commentary (Waco, TX: Word Books, 1984), 31; Constantine Campbell, *1, 2 & 3 John*, Story of God Bible Commentary (Grand Rapids, MI: Zondervan, 2017), 43-44.

This is liberatingly good news. But many of us miss it because we've privatized sin—a matter only between me and God. That's the way many of us would like to keep it. "I'll confess *my* sin in prayer. You confess your sin. Why should we have to confess *our* sins, out loud, together?" But keeping sin private, quarantined from corporate worship, does two things at the same time. First, privatized sin alienates us from each other, leaving me to believe that I'm the only one who deals with this particular sin. Sin has a powerfully isolating effect. *I messed up again. I'm so weak. It's all my fault. I have no one to blame but myself. I'm such a failure. Why can't I stop? I'm sick and tired of this. I don't want to do this anymore. Thank God nobody knows. No one would understand.* That's a very lonely place. When we refuse to confess our sin, it breaks our fellowship—our common confession that we all struggle, we all fail, we all need forgiveness.

Second, by keeping sin a private matter, we refuse to admit that our sin affects other people. When we say, "My sin is my sin, your sin is your sin," we act like sin can be contained, managed, controlled. Nothing could be further from the truth. Sin damages all of us because it is bigger than any one of us. Sin is a corporate reality. It's really foolish to think my sin doesn't hurt anyone else. Really? What about adultery? Theft? Deceit? Jealousy? Envy? Greed? Lust? I can't think of a sin that doesn't have a social effect. That's because sin is a contagion: it infects one, it infects us all. Your sin is my sin. My sin is your sin.[15] That's why we all need to confess our sins *together*. I can't deal with sin on my own. Of course, I still need to confess my sins in prayer to God. But John would have us confess our sins *together in the presence of Christ* because it's what we have in common—our need of the cleansing power of Christ's forgiveness (1 Jn 1:9).

"WHAT'S THAT SUPPOSED TO LOOK LIKE TODAY?"

I was teaching on John's spirituality a few years ago, talking about the importance of the confession of sin during worship, when one of the ministers of the church asked with an incredulous tone, "What's that

---

[15]"You mourned for the transgressions of your neighbors: you considered their shortcomings to be your own" (1 Clement 2.6, in Holmes, *Apostolic Fathers*).

supposed to look like today?" The reason John's advice seemed so far-fetched to him (and many others) is that, like most evangelical churches, our worship services never include confession of sin (Isaiah would find that preposterous). Oh, we'll sing about how our sin nailed Jesus to the cross. But to follow John's advice and take time during the worship hour to confess our sins? That just doesn't happen.[16]

I can't help but wonder, Why? Is it because our egos are too fragile to handle the truth? Have we given in to the idea that the "worship experience" is only supposed to make us feel good? Or, are we more concerned about our image—that a group of Christians confessing our sins might give the wrong impression, a bad witness for Christ, that we're more worldly than we're supposed to be? Besides, who would do it? Who wants to admit to a group of people, "I have sinned"? It's difficult enough to admit we've made mistakes when we're confronted by our accusers. But to voluntarily confess sin in public? Who would have the confidence to do that? Most of us would rather confess our strengths, like famous Irish author Oscar Wilde, who, upon his arrival to New York, was asked by the customs officer, "Do you have anything to declare?" and supposedly replied, "Nothing but my genius."[17]

Now we see another possibility as to why some in John's churches were saying, "I have no sin." Some scholars think their refusal to confess sin derived from their Gnostic tendencies (spiritual union trumps the material world) or perfectionistic claims (perhaps due to John's teaching, "Everyone who abides in him does not sin," 1 Jn 3:6).[18] Others think they were denying that they were liable for the *guilt* of sin because Christ had forgiven them.[19] I wonder whether some were reticent to confess their sin because it would damage their reputation—the worldly concern that John calls "the boastful pride of life" (1 Jn 2:16).[20] If they were confessing

---

[16]Of course, there are some Christian traditions that include a time of public confession during their worship services—something we experienced when we lived in England several years ago.
[17]Arthur Ransome, *Oscar Wilde: A Critical Study*, 3rd ed. (New York: Haskell House, 1971), 67.
[18]See Smalley, *1, 2, 3, John*, 28-29.
[19]Brown, *Epistles*, 206; Colin G. Kruse, *The Letters of John*, Pillar New Testament Commentary (Grand Rapids, MI: Eerdmans, 2000), 66.
[20]Taking the phrase *hē alazoneia tou biou* as an objective genitive, "boasting about one's life." For

their sins out loud, it would undermine the honor game, where public contests for social worth were crucial to self-image. Boasting in one's accomplishments was key to maintaining one's honorable reputation in public. Admitting sin publicly, however, would have been counterproductive to the pursuit of honor. So perhaps some members of John's community refused to join the group, saying, "I have no sin to confess." It's one thing to pray privately for the forgiveness of sin. It's quite something else to join in the confession of our sins together, in the presence of others, where a carefully crafted public image is crucial to social approval.[21] This may be another reason the false confessors "went out from us because they were not of us" (1 Jn 2:19). They didn't want to hear the truth about Jesus or themselves anymore.

Given our current tendencies to display our strengths and hide our weaknesses (social media make this so much easier), I wonder what would happen if Christians of my tribe began to include public confession of sin during worship services. Following John's lead, this wouldn't involve a public airing of our dirty laundry, members recounting all the sordid details of our sins. John didn't expect that, nor did he prescribe exactly how his churches would confess their sins. He simply assumes they would know what to confess. Given the content of his letter, we have a good idea of the sins they needed to confess. It had to do with what they were saying in light of what they were doing. Indeed, like the letter of James, John writes a lot about what people were saying. Notice how often he brings it up:

- 1 John 1:6: "If we say, 'we have fellowship with him,' and walk in darkness . . ."

- 1 John 1:8: "If we say, 'we have no sin' . . ."

- 1 John 1:10: "If we say, 'we have not sinned' . . ."

---

further discussion, see Brown, who opts for a subjective genitive, "overconfidence stemming from the security of one's life" (*Epistles*, 312).

[21]Judith M. Lieu writes that it's "not simply the theoretical denial of sin that the author challenges but the refusal to share in the act of confession." See Lieu, *I, II, & III John: A Commentary* (Louisville, KY: Westminster John Knox, 2008), 57.

- 1 John 2:4: "The one who says, 'I have known him' and does not keep his commands . . ."

- 1 John 2:9: "The one who says, 'I am in the light' and hates his brother . . ."

- 1 John 2:22: "Who is the liar other than the one who says, 'Jesus is not the Christ' . . ."

- 1 John 2:23: "Whoever denies the Son does not have the Father, . . ."

- 1 John 4:20: "If someone says, 'I love God' and hates his brother . . ."

Mostly, they talked about themselves: "We have fellowship with him," "we have no sin," "we have not sinned," "I have known him," "I am in the light," "I love God." A couple of times they made false statements about Jesus, denying that he was the Christ and the Son of the Father. Most of the time, what they said didn't line up with what they did. That meant their words were obviously false: for example, you can't claim to love "the Father" and hate "your brother." Beloved members of God's family love one another because God is love (1 Jn 4:7-11). At other times, what they said explained what they did: for example, since they wouldn't confess their sins or the truth about Jesus, they left the church. Liars can't stand to hear the truth (1 Jn 1:6). John presumed believers would confess their sins *together* because it's what they had in *common*: pride, lying, hatred, disobedience, selfishness, false witness. Then they would be forgiven and cleansed by the blood of Jesus Christ (1 Jn 1:9). Those who refused to confess their sins had deceived themselves (1 Jn 1:8), revealing that the Word was not in them (1 Jn 1:10)—the Word they heard from the beginning, the Gospel according to John.

Self-deception is a dangerous condition, especially for those of us who rely on our own words for the truth. Given any situation, often what we tell ourselves is what we think is automatically true. In fact, some of us presume that simply because we've said it, that's what makes it true. "I'm a good guy." "I didn't mean anything by it." "You're taking this the wrong way." "I'm not a racist." "He's being difficult." "She's clearly in the wrong." "I know I'm right." It's as if we believe our words have magical powers, casting a spell on reality. Once we say it, the truth is out there and no one can deny it. Of course, we tend to ignore the role that confirmation bias, prejudice, ignorance, and self-aggrandizement play in our pursuit of truth. We can see it in others, how their eschewed view of reality is clouding their vision. But what about me? What if I'm wrong? What happens when I've convinced myself I'm right but, in reality, I'm wrong? If I've deceived myself—a man who relies on his words for the truth— will I ever know what is true? You may tell me the truth, that I'm wrong. But I won't believe it because I've convinced myself I'm right. So, how does a man like me, who's deceived himself into thinking he's right, ever find the truth?

According to John, truth is a person. The only way we'll know the truth is if we know Jesus Christ. If we know the truth about him, we'll know the truth about ourselves. Who he is defines who we are. According to John, the only way you can know anything about Jesus is to listen to the Gospel of John. When you have ears to hear the Gospel read to you, then you have eyes to see the truth: about him and about you. Then you'll say the right things about him, "He's faithful and just," and the right things about yourself (and everyone else who says the *same* thing): "We have sinned. We are washed clean by the blood of Christ. We are walking in the light of God. We have these things in common. This is our koinonia."

Biblical literacy fosters communion.

6

DENY WORLDLINESS

Confessing the Word

IT'S TWO MINUTES TO MIDNIGHT. According to the Doomsday Clock, we've been here before. Back in 1953, the year after the United States and the USSR successfully tested thermonuclear devices, nuclear scientists moved the clock to warn us how close we were to destroying the world. Since then, time has changed—backward and forward. After the United States and the USSR signed the Partial Test Ban Treaty in 1963, the clock was moved back to twelve minutes to midnight. Then the threat of total annihilation edged the clock closer to midnight due to several wars and the development of nuclear weapons by other countries (India, Pakistan, North Korea). Test treaties and world events (such as the end of the Soviet Union and the fall of the Berlin Wall) pushed the clock back again. Then, in 2007, scientists added the threat of climate change to the equation, making our situation even more perilous—once again moving the hands of the Doomsday Clock closer to midnight, total blackout. It's a sobering thought: for the first time in human history, we have the power to completely destroy ourselves and everything with us. Modern-day prophets try to warn us about the signs of the times, two heavenly omens of the apocalypse: mushroom clouds and a hole in the ozone layer. Indeed, ever since 1947, when the *Bulletin of Atomic Scientists* invented the clock, we've lived with the stark reality that the end of the world is near. All you have to do is see what time it is.

"Children, it is the last hour" (1 Jn 2:18). When John wrote his letter, he was convinced that the end of the world was near. Even though the seer describes heavenly signs in the Apocalypse that may look to us like nuclear war (Rev 6:12-14) and a hole in the ozone (Rev 4:1), that's not what convinced John that he and "his children" were witnessing "the last hour." Instead, according to John, there was only *one* sign that the end was near: the appearance of "many antichrists" (1 Jn 2:18). What makes this eschatological sign even more surprising is that these antichrists were not external threats to John's churches—heretical strangers outside the fellowship attacking them. Rather, these antichrists used to be members of the church: "They left us but they were not of us" (1 Jn 2:19).

That's not the apocalyptic scenario we're used to. Christian films based on pop eschatology feature *one* antichrist, a man who rises to world domination, creating a one-world alliance in order to marshal forces against all Christians. The apocalyptic threat comes from without. But that's not the way John sees it. These antichrists have come from the church. They were once "of Christ" but now they're "anti-christ" because they have denied that Jesus is the Christ (1 Jn 2:22). That's what *antichrist* means to John—a term that only shows up in this letter and 2 John (but not in the Apocalypse!). To say that Jesus is not Christ is, quite literally, to be "anti-christ." So, anyone could be an antichrist. All they have to do is say, "Jesus is not the Christ." But why would anyone say that— especially someone who used to belong to the church?

Saying the Right Words About Jesus

This is the most difficult question pertaining to 1 John that scholars try to answer, why former church members would say, "Jesus is not the Christ." Who were these people? Why would any "*Christ*ian" deny that Jesus is the Christ? Well, John gives us a little more information elsewhere about these antichrists that may reveal the reason: (1) they refused to confess that Jesus is from God (1 Jn 4:3), and (2) they denied that Jesus Christ came in the flesh (2 Jn 7). It's that last clue that has led some scholars to infer that these antichrists possessed a docetic Christology.

Due to their worldview, wherein everything physical is evil and everything spiritual is good, these proto-Gnostics claimed salvation in Christ
but denied that he came "in the flesh." To them, a spiritual salvation (in
heaven) required only a spiritual Savior (from heaven). Eventually, this
heretical Christology took root and grew in the second century, when
several Gnostic teachers promoted the idea that Christ "appeared" (the
meaning of the Greek word *dokeō*, from which we get the word *docetic*)
as a man but was really a heavenly messenger—much like the angels of
the Old Testament (Gen 32:22-32).[1] Perhaps that's why John's opponents
wanted to distinguish between Jesus and Christ, saying "Jesus is not from
God," while still affirming faith in Christ. Other heretical teachers, such
as Cerinthus, who lived in Ephesus, taught that the Christ (Spirit) came
into Jesus (flesh) at his baptism (adoptionist Christology), empowering
him to perform miracles and teach the salvation of God (escape from the
world). Then, the Christ-Spirit left Jesus at Gethsemane, leaving the
Jewish man to die—thus the cross has no salvific effect. The way to
heaven is to believe everything the Christ-Spirit taught through the
human Jew Jesus. Whether they subscribed to adoptionism or docetism,
Gnostics believed knowledge was salvation—a knowledge that only
came by the Spirit (something that John emphasizes in his Gospel as well;
Jn 14:16-17; 16:13-14).[2]

If these antichrists subscribed to a docetic Christology, it would also
explain why John emphasizes later that Jesus Christ "came through water
and blood—not by water only but by water and blood, and the Spirit
bears witness to this because the Spirit is true" (1 Jn 5:6). Even though
the expression "water and blood" can mean many things, at the very least

---

[1] For a brief description of second-century Gnosticism and a survey of some Gnostic writings, see
David B. Capes, Rodney Reeves, and E. Randolph Richards, "The Gnostic Jesus," in *Rediscover-
ing Jesus: An Introduction to Biblical, Religious and Cultural Perspectives on Christ* (Downers
Grove, IL: IVP Academic, 2015), 159-75.

[2] See the discussion in Raymond E. Brown, *The Epistles of John*, Anchor Bible (New York: Doubleday, 1982), 103-6. Smalley believes John was fighting a war on two fronts: docetics, who denied
the humanity of Christ but fully embraced his deity, and Ebionites, who denied the deity of Christ
but embraced his humanity. See Stephen S. Smalley, *1, 2, 3 John*, Word Biblical Commentary
(Waco, TX: Word Books, 1984), xxiii-xxv.

it refers to the physicality of the incarnation—especially the death of Jesus, when John makes a big deal about blood and water flowing from the pierced body of Jesus (Jn 19:34-35). But if John's Gospel was read to church members on a regular basis, how could anyone claim that Jesus Christ didn't come in the flesh? From start to finish, John emphasizes the "enfleshment" of the Christ: "And the Word became flesh and tabernacled among us" (Jn 1:14); "Put your fingers here and see my hands; take your hand and put it in my side. Don't be unbelieving but believing" (Jn 20:27). Since Jesus said the Spirit would help his disciples remember what he said (Jn 14:26)—and John wrote it down—then John's Gospel would not only be Spirit inspired but also Spirit confirmed, bearing witness to Jesus Christ "coming in the flesh" (Jn 15:26). All anyone needed to believe the truth about Jesus Christ was to hear the Gospel according to John: "We are from God; the one who knows God listens to us" (1 Jn 4:6).[3]

But then again, Jesus said he didn't tell his disciples *everything* because they couldn't handle it at the time (Jn 16:12). Consequently, they would need to learn how to rely on the "Spirit of truth" to "guide them in all truth," teaching them what Jesus couldn't tell them when he was with them "in the flesh." According to his own words (written in John's Gospel!), Jesus said that his words (written in John's Gospel!) wouldn't be enough to lead the church in "all truth." Therefore, what John's Gospel lacked the Spirit would supply, teaching disciples "what is to come" (Jn 16:13). Whatever the Spirit heard—whatever he took from Jesus—he would teach the disciples (Jn 16:13-14). In other words, according to Jesus' words, it was up to the Spirit to take the truth about Jesus in John's Gospel and guide the disciples in truth.[4] What the Spirit heard in Jesus' words was what his disciples would need to learn in order to know the truth about Jesus. All they needed to do was hear what the Spirit was saying to the church *through* John's Gospel.

---

[3] J. Ramsey Michaels writes, "'All the truth' is Jesus' truth, or the truth about Jesus—the only truth that matters in the Gospel of John." See Michaels, *The Gospel of John*, New International Commentary on the New Testament (Grand Rapids, MI: Eerdmans, 2010), 837-38.

[4] Also Craig S. Keener, *The Gospel of John: A Commentary* (Grand Rapids, MI: Baker Academic, 2010), 2:1041.

Therefore, like Raymond Brown, I'm convinced that these antichrists didn't operate with a docetic Christology that led them to reject the humanity of Jesus Christ. Instead, as Brown puts it, they "refused to acknowledge that his being in the flesh was essential to the picture of Jesus *as the Christ*, the Son of God."[5] In other words, John's emphasis on Christ as the preincarnate Word of God led these antichrists to believe that the enfleshment of Christ was little more than a confirmation of the eternal gospel—a spiritual reality. According to them, the "Word became flesh" wasn't code for the miraculous birth of Jesus; John doesn't tell that story. Rather, the Word was revealed incarnate at Jesus' baptism (water and Spirit). Therefore, long after the Son returned to the Father, the Word would continue to be revealed incarnate in the church through baptism: by water and by the Spirit. These antichrists claimed that they didn't need the written Word: it was the *spirit* of Christ's words that mattered. "For it is the Spirit that gives life; the flesh profits nothing." Which is why Jesus also said, "The words that I have spoken to you are spirit and life" (Jn 6:63). Since words are spiritual things, these antichrists would have believed that reincarnation (the abiding word) should not be restrained by excarnation (the written Word).[6] They wouldn't need John's Gospel to know Christ— something we see even today. Recently, I noticed that a believer reported on social media, "I had a wonderful time with Christ this morning," which led me to wonder, "Which Gospel was she reading at the time: Matthew, Mark, Luke, or John?" Of course, I'm being a little snarky to suggest that's not what she was talking about. To her, a meaningful spiritual experience

---

[5]Brown, *Epistles*, 76, emphasis original.

[6]Or, as Gary M. Burge puts it, "The followers of John are formed by the theology of the Gospel and possess a heightened awareness of the indwelling Spirit. And while this contributes to a community of vibrancy and immediacy (John 3:3; 4:23-24), it spins off prophet-teachers who use this same inspiration to justify their novel teachings. Because they can claim that the indwelling Spirit of Jesus was with them, they can reveal to the church things about a docetic Christ no one had considered before. These controversial teachings are among the things Jesus could not say earlier but is now ready to reveal (John 16:12-13)." See Burge, "Spirit-Inspired Theology and Ecclesial Correction: Charting One Shift in the Development of Johannine Ecclesiology and Pneumatology," in *Communities in Dispute: Current Scholarship on the Johannine Epistles*, ed. R. Alan Culpepper and Paul N. Anderson (Atlanta: SBL Press, 2014), 181-82. I would say that they could "reveal to the church things about an *agraphon* Christ no one had considered before."

with Jesus may have had little to do with reading the Gospels—something John's opponents would have appreciated.

I wonder how these antichrists would have heard the part of the story when Jesus said, "But there are some among you who do not believe" (Jn 6:64). It was Jesus' offensive words that convinced some disciples to quit following him. Jesus kept trying to get them to see the spiritual: "I am the manna of life" (Jn 6:48)—to go beyond his words to hear the Spirit of truth. But they were stuck in the physical: "How is this man able to give his *flesh* to eat?" (Jn 6:52). Accordingly, Jesus knew that some of his disciples would no longer believe in him (Jn 6:64). It's only by the Spirit one is able to hear the words of Christ (Jn 6:63). But what if you don't listen to the Spirit and are constrained by the words themselves? "Because of this, many of his disciples left them and were no longer following him" (Jn 6:66). Therefore, I think these antichrists would have seen themselves in the faces of the faithful disciples of Jesus who followed him by the Spirit—just as Jesus predicted.

What about those of John's community who were stuck in the flesh, hemmed in by the written words of Christ in John's Gospel, unable to see their spiritual meaning according to these antichrists? They were the ones who "withdrew" from Christ, held back by their refusal to follow the Spirit into the world without John's Gospel. Indeed, since it was the last hour, these antichrists would have claimed that it was the rest of John's community who were left behind. How do we know that? The attempt by the antichrists to return to John's community in order to bring their unrestrained-by-John's-Gospel teaching back into the group may reveal their claim to "spiritual" perspicuity (2 Jn 7-11).

But the Elder wouldn't have it. As far as he was concerned, this wasn't just a matter of letting former members back in. These antichrists were false professors from the beginning ("they went out from us because they were never really a part of us," 1 Jn 2:19). Besides, their leaving had as much to do with what they were *going to* as what they *left behind*—something John emphasizes as well. To leave the community was the same as going into the world: "For many deceivers have gone into the world" (2 Jn 7).

What's in the world? "All that is in the world—the lust of the flesh, the lust of the eyes, and the boastful pride of life—is not from the Father but is from the world" (1 Jn 2:16). Ironically, then, it was the antichrists' love of the world—where their lustful, fleshly pride would be affirmed ("we don't need John's Gospel")—that compelled them to leave the community of faith that confesses "Jesus Christ comes in the flesh" (2 Jn 7). In fact, as far as John was concerned, the Spirit inspired *only* that confession about Christ (1 Jn 4:2). (One wonders whether these antichrists offered another confession as their counterclaim for an "unwritten" Christ: "Jesus Christ comes in the Spirit.") Like the Elder said: "Anyone who goes too far and doesn't abide in this teaching about Christ is not from God" (2 Jn 9).

These antichrists may have claimed the Spirit as their guide (1 Jn 4:2-3). But that they had gone into the world revealed that they were false prophets (1 Jn 4:1)—not inspired by the Spirit of Christ—having returned to the place where they belonged: "They are from the world; that's why they talk like the world and the world listens to them" (1 Jn 4:5). That's why the Elder wouldn't welcome these antichrists back into the fold: they were worldly people who wouldn't say the right words about Jesus Christ (2 Jn 10-11). These "deceivers" did not "abide" in the word that Jesus "taught them" when they heard the Gospel that John had written to them (1 Jn 2:24-27).[7] Only those who listened to John would know the truth about Jesus Christ: "The one who knows God listens to us; whoever refuses to listen to us isn't from God. This is how we know the difference between the Spirit of truth and the spirit of deceit" (1 Jn 4:6). John's Jesus was the gospel truth.

"WHO DO YOU SAY THAT I AM?"

Two thousand years later, I wonder what John would make of all the claims that have been made about Jesus Christ. Gnostics claimed he wasn't human. Muslims claim he never died on the cross. Mormons claim he appeared to indigenous Americans. Jehovah's Witnesses deny

---

[7]"No doubt John has in mind the Fourth Gospel." See Gary M. Burge, *The Letters of John*, NIV Application Commentary (Grand Rapids, MI: Zondervan, 1996), 131.

his physical resurrection from the dead. Some scholars deny he performed miracles. Others deny he existed at all.[8] To shore up their claims about Jesus Christ, many published their own "Gospels" to rival the Christian Scriptures. The Gnostics produced several, including the Gospel of Thomas, the Gospel of Philip, and the Gospel of Truth. Muslims revere the Qur'an. Latter-day Saints promote the Book of Mormon as "Another Testament of Jesus Christ." Some scholars produced a color-coded version of the Gospels, claiming to separate fact from fiction.[9] Not to mention the innumerable books written about Jesus by Christians and non-Christians, historians and heretics. So many voices, so many claims.

Over the years, there have been a lot of people who believe they have something to say about Jesus. In our age of tolerance, where every opinion is supposed to matter, no one can believe it all. Different versions of Christ are often mutually exclusive. You can't believe the Muslim Christ and the Mormon Christ. You can't believe the Mormon Christ and the apostolic Christ. Choices must be made. Who's right? Who's wrong? How do we know? Many of us inherit the Christ of our parents. Some of us might be drawn to the Christ of our preferences. Most of us, however, want to be more discerning. But with so many voices clamoring for our attention, the cacophony can be overwhelming, making it difficult to hear the true voice of Christ.

What would John say to us today? What advice would he give to help us cut through the noise and hear the truth about Christ?

John would put the onus on us, just as he did in his first letter to his community. Since his Gospel wasn't enough to "guide them in all truth," they also needed a letter from him, telling them what to do. Yet, we might have expected him to be a little more direct, wielding apostolic authority by naming names and directing his converts to kick out the heretics—just like Paul does (1 Tim 1:18-20; 2 Tim 2:16-18; 1 Cor 5:1-5, 12-13). But

---

[8]See Capes, Reeves, and Richards, *Rediscovering Jesus*, 159-221.
[9]Robert W. Funk, ed., *The Five Gospels: What Did Jesus Really Say? The Search for the Authentic Words of Jesus* (New York: HarperOne, 1996); Funk, ed., *The Acts of Jesus: What Did He Really Do?* (Salem, OR: Polebridge, 1998).

that isn't John's approach.[10] Instead, he counts on the church's ability not to "believe every spirit but test the spirits to determine whether they are from God" (1 Jn 4:1)—similar to what the resurrected Christ repeatedly says to the seven churches: "The one who has an ear, let him hear what the Spirit is saying to the churches" (Rev 2:7, 11, 17, 29; 3:6, 13, 22). In other words, rather than give specific directives, John trusted the work of the Spirit in the church—not only to help believers discern the truth but also to recognize when false prophets leave the church (1 Jn 4:1).[11] John presumes that false prophets will not find a hearing in his community because believers hold to the true confession about Jesus: "This is how you know the Spirit of God: every spirit who confesses Jesus Christ has come in the flesh is from God" (1 Jn 4:2). That's also why these antichrists eventually found a hearing in the world (1 Jn 4:3). It's the very reason they left the church. The truth drives them away, and the world listens to their lies (1 Jn 4:5).

To John, then, false Christology is worldly.

GREATER IS HE WHO IS IN US

The eschatological battle for the truth during the last hour results in a war of words.[12] False prophets utter lies about Jesus, and the world listens to them because they are antichrists who left the church (1 Jn 4:1, 3, 5). True confessors repeat what they heard from the beginning and overcome these worldly antichrists because they are children of God who listen to John (1 Jn 4:2, 4, 6). Who wins in the end? And how will they know when the war is over? Battles fought with conventional weapons of warfare usually result in signs of clear victory won by a superior fighting force: a defeated enemy, land protected, a nation preserved. How does one win a war of words? Shout louder? Talk longer? How will the combatants

---

[10]See Burge, "Spirit-Inspired Theology," 182-83.
[11]Notice that John didn't encourage his readers to test the spirits because false prophets were still in the church. Rather, it was because "many false prophets have gone out into the world" (1 Jn 4:1).
[12]Craig R. Koester, "The Antichrist Theme in the Johannine Epistles and Its Role in Christian Tradition," in *Communities in Dispute: Current Scholarship on the Johannine Epistles*, ed. R. Alan Culpepper and Paul N. Anderson (Atlanta: SBL Press, 2014), 192.

know the war is over? Will the antichrists give up? Will true believers have the last word?

According to John, the war will be over when Christ returns (1 Jn 2:28), and the way his community will win the war of words about Christ is by abiding in Christ until he appears (1 Jn 2:21, 24, 27). The only way to abide in Christ is to remain in the church to hear the words of Christ. That's why John is confident his community will win the war of words, because (1) they have the anointing from "the Holy One" (1 Jn 2:20, 27), (2) they have fixed their hope on Christ (1 Jn 3:2-3), and (3) they know that "greater is he who is in you all than he that is in the world" (1 Jn 4:4).

John uses a pun to assure his readers that they already knew the truth about Christ (*christos*, "anointed one") because they had the "anointing" (*chrisma*): "You all have an anointing from the holy one, and that's why you all know [the truth]" (1 Jn 2:20). But what is this anointing? Since Jesus was anointed by the Spirit, many take John's unusual term as shorthand for the Holy Spirit—Christ's gift to the church: the one who anointed the Christ is the same anointing that leads Christ believers in truth.[13] Robert Yarbrough writes, "The climactic coming of the 'Anointed One' (Greek, *christos*, from which derives the title 'Christ') results in a whole community that revels in a derivative anointing."[14] Others think *chrisma* refers to the words of Jesus, particularly John's Gospel— especially since John seems to equate *chrisma* with the teaching of Christ: "but as his anointing teaches you about everything, and it is true and is not a lie, and so, just as he taught you, abide in it [or him]" (1 Jn 2:27).[15] Here John claims that the *chrisma* continues to teach them *just as Christ taught them*. In other words, as John's community listened to his Gospel read to them, it was one and the same as Christ teaching them.[16]

---

[13]Brown, *Epistles*, 346. *Chrisma* appears only here and in 1 Jn 2:27.

[14]Robert W. Yarbrough, *1–3 John*, Baker Exegetical Commentary on the New Testament (Grand Rapids, MI: Baker Academic, 2008), 150.

[15]C. H. Dodd, *The Johannine Epistles* (London: Hodder & Stoughton, 1946), 63.

[16]Others think the anointing refers to both the word of God and the Spirit's illumination. See Karen H. Jobes, *1, 2, & 3 John*, Zondervan Exegetical Commentary on the New Testament (Grand Rapids, MI: Zondervan, 2014), 127-28.

Once again, I hear a verbal echo of the story of John 6. After the scandalized disciples leave Jesus because they are unable to hear his "spiritual" words, Jesus asks the Twelve: "You don't want to leave too, do you?" To which Simon Peter replies: "Lord, where would we go? You have the *words* of eternal life, for we have believed and have known that you are *the Holy One* of God" (Jn 6:67-69). Not only does Peter equate the words of Christ with eternal life, but he also confesses that Jesus is the *Holy One*—a phrase that appears in the Johannine literature *only* here and in 1 John 2:20. John's community should have recognized themselves in the same story: John is asking, "You don't want to leave too, do you?" And just like Peter they should have confessed, "Where would we go? You alone have the words of eternal life." Indeed, since they have the *chrisma* of the Gospel, John claims, "you have no need for anyone to teach you [about Christ]" (1 Jn 2:27). All they needed to do was abide in the words of Christ by remaining in the church until Christ came back (1 Jn 2:27-28).

John knew the war of words wouldn't go on indefinitely. His community would continue to listen to his Gospel and say the right words about Jesus Christ. These antichrists would continue to refuse to listen to John's Gospel and deny Jesus Christ (1 Jn 4:6). This is how John's community would discern the difference between "the spirit of truth and the spirit of deceit" (1 Jn 4:6): whom you hear reveals whose you are. Children of God listen to the Gospel; it's how they abide in Christ—not only by hearing the words of Christ but also by living the words of Christ: "If you know that he is right, then you also know that everyone who does what is right has been born of him" (1 Jn 2:29). By embodying the words of Christ—"walking as he walked" (1 Jn 2:6)—John's community would be the living reincarnation of the excarnation of the incarnated Word of God.

For John, then, this is what it means to abide in Christ: to hear the words of Christ and obey the words of Christ (something we'll talk about in the next chapter). Listening to the Gospel is good. But the whole point of hearing the Word is obeying the Word. The whole point of abiding in his Word is to live in the fullness, the shelter, the salvation, the hope, the beauty of his Word. That's why John believed his community would remain confident until the last day, "not shrinking away from him at his return" (1 Jn 2:28). As believers, we don't rely simply on what we say about Christ. Rather, because we live what we believe, we know that believers will make it to the end, ready to welcome Christ back to the world he died to save. Words spoken echo for a moment. The Word incarnated lasts forever. According to John, the war of words will be won by the Word of God when the first Word will have the last word. Then we'll all know—the truth tellers and the liars—that what was true "in the beginning" will be true till the end, because the words of Christ are eternal.

Until then, the war of words rages on. The battle for the truth about Jesus Christ is dualistic—set in binary terms. The way John sees it, there are no casual observers.[17] You're either for Christ or against him. It's a matter of life and death, the spirit of truth versus the spirit of deception. Right versus wrong. Obedience versus sin. Love versus hate. The children of God versus the children of the devil. The church versus the world. Some might want to chalk up all this talk to little more than a verbal disagreement. One group says this; another group says that. But, according to John, this is a cosmic battle for truth and the world. It's the reason Jesus came to earth as God's Son: to "destroy the works of the devil" (1 Jn 3:8). From the beginning, John's community heard the truth about Jesus Christ. Also from the beginning, the devil—the father of lies—has sinned. Just as God has birthed children through Jesus Christ, the devil has planted his seed in the world to birth his offspring through liars who never stop sinning (1 Jn 3:9-10). They lie about Jesus ("Jesus is not the Christ"), and they lie about themselves ("we have never sinned"). Even though their message is more popular with the world—giving the impression that true believers are losing the war of words—John is convinced his people are winning the war *now* because "greater is he that is in you all than he that is in the world" (1 Jn 4:4).

---

[17]"For the writer of 1 John, the cosmic battle between Christ and antichrist is being fought and won in the present. The author does not treat the readers as spectators but casts them in the role of participants, who are called to resist the incursions of falsehood and to overcome them with the truth that fosters faith" (Koester, "Antichrist Theme," 193).

It's one of the first songs our children learned to sing in church. "Greater is he that is in me, greater is he that is in me, greater is he that is in me, than he that is in the world." But that's not what John wrote. The second person pronoun is plural (thus the translation "you all"). Therefore, to sing the little ditty more accurately, we should say, "Greater is he that is in *us*, greater is he that is in *us*, greater is he that is in *us*, than he that is in the world." John knew we couldn't fight this battle as individuals. Instead, it's only by the power of God *in all of us* that we are able to overcome the world. I can't rise to the challenge by myself, even though a greater power lives in me. It takes every single one of us, every believer, every child of God, every truth teller about Christ to defeat our enemy, the devil. In Christ, together we overcome the world. That's why we must be vigilant without and within, to outsiders and insiders. We must always tell the truth to *others* and to *ourselves*. The Gospel is for believers as well as nonbelievers. We must gather to hear it, to live it, and to tell it. If we don't, according to John, we become susceptible to the lies: about Christ and about ourselves.[18] That's when the works of the devil (lies and sin) creep into the church—another reason why John had to remind them: "Children, let no one deceive you. He who does what is right is right just as Christ is right. He who sins is from the devil because the devil has sinned from the beginning" (1 Jn 3:7-8). It takes a church to beat the devil.

But who makes up the church? What about those who start another "church"? What if they claim the Spirit of Christ directed them to leave due to a new revelation about Christ? Can't they help defeat the devil too? Well, according to John, only those who abide in the Word overcome the enemy, and there can't be any reincarnation of the Word without the excarnated word. John heard what Jesus said and wrote it down. The Spirit confirms what Jesus said in John's Gospel, evidenced by those who abide in it. So the only way you can know what the Spirit is teaching is to hear John's Gospel. Those who refuse to gather with the church to listen to

---

[18]So also Koester, "Antichrist Theme," 194-95.

John's Gospel—having left the church—reveal that they never belonged. Only those who remain truly abide in the Word. Therefore, anyone who claims Jesus but doesn't rely on John's Gospel can't "abide" in the Word. The way John would see it, Muslims do not abide in the Word—they rely on their own Scripture. Mormons do not abide in the Word—they rely on "Another Testament of Jesus Christ." Even Jehovah's Witnesses do not abide in the Word—they deny what John affirms: the physical resurrection of Christ. "They went out from us but they were not of us, for if they were of us, they would have remained with us—but they left in order that they would be revealed that they all are not of us" (1 Jn 2:19). I realize these are harsh words and that some might say, "How dare you? What gives you the right to say who are true believers?" But, then again, that's probably what those whom John called antichrists would have said too.

This is a serious matter. John has no qualms about calling people who left the church antichrists. (One wonders what these "antichrists" called John and his community?) The Elder found them so dangerous to the cause of Christ he refused to let them back in (2 Jn 10). Neither John nor the Elder subscribed to the nicety "Let's just agree to disagree." For John, there is no agreement with antichrists. Besides, he saw our confession of Christ as a matter of life and death. Everyone who believes in Christ—saying the right words ("bearing witness") about him—has eternal life, Jesus Christ (1 Jn 5:10-12). Those who depart and do not "abide in the teaching of Christ" do not have God (2 Jn 9). Since abiding in Christ is life and departing into the world is death—"the world is passing away with all of its lusts," 1 Jn 2:17)—then these antichrists committed "the sin unto death" (1 Jn 5:16-17) when they left the faith.[19]

Of course, they wouldn't have seen it that way ("we have not sinned," 1 Jn 1:10). Perhaps, neither did some members of John's community, who evidently wanted to pray for these ex-members (1 Jn 5:16). But John wouldn't allow it. They should only pray for "brothers" committing sin,

---

[19]Also T. Griffth, *Keep Yourselves from Idols: A New Look at 1 John,* Journal for the Study of the New Testament Supplement Series 233 (London: Sheffield Academic, 2002), 144-45.

knowing that, since "brothers" remained in the community by abiding in the Word, they would receive life from God—Jesus Christ (1 Jn 5:13-16).[20] What about those who have gone into the world, having left behind true faith in Christ? They are not "brothers"; they have committed the sin of unbelief, which results in death. They can't find life in Christ since they don't abide in the Word. Therefore, there is no reason to pray for them. As Brown points out,

> While in their own self-estimation the secessionists may be Christians, in the author's estimation they do not have life (3:12-17); for they have abandoned the *koinonia* with the Father and the Son, which preserves eternal life (1:2-3). Here the author is close to Dead Sea Scroll mentality, attested by the Qumran psalmist: "I shall have no pity on those who depart from the Way" (1QS 10:20-21). Secessionists belong to the realm of darkness, the Lie, the Evil One, and death. It makes perfect sense, then, that the author discourages (and implicitly forbids) prayer for them. Jesus refused to pray for the world (John 17:9), and they belong to the world (1 John 4:5).[21]

Leaving the church because you deny Christ is a death sentence. According to John, you don't have a prayer.

HOW TO FIGHT LIKE A CHRISTIAN

Since this is a matter of life and death, and the last hour requires a war of words, how are we to battle for the truth? Should we label those who have left the church "antichrists"? Should we launch a campaign to root out the nonbelievers hiding among us? Not necessarily. Remember, John didn't advise it. He was convinced that if his readers remained true to Christ—abiding in the Word—then the false prophets would leave on their own. The truth of John's Gospel would drive them away. That's why antichrists would be easy to spot: they're the ones who have left the church because they denied what John emphasized in his Gospel, that Jesus Christ came in the flesh.

---

[20]"Sins committed by believers *as* believers are atoned for" (Griffith, *Keep Yourselves from Idols*, 145, emphasis original).
[21]Brown, *Epistles*, 618.

To be sure, there are people today who say the same thing, denying that John's Gospel is true (as well as the rest of the New Testament), claiming that Jesus Christ is a myth—that he never came in the flesh as a historical person.[22] These people are more than nonbelievers: they are antichrist. If they should ever seek a hearing in the church, hoping to spread their antigospel, we should follow the Elder's advice and stop them at the door—just like the church did to Gnostics who eventually wrote their own gospels. The same is true for Muslims, Mormons, and Jehovah's Witnesses: they have their "Gospels"; we have ours. That's why they keep trying to convert us and we keep trying to convert them. *All* of us believe—Muslims, Mormons, Jehovah's Witnesses, and Christians— that this is a matter of life and death. So the question remains. Who will save us: the Mormon Christ, the Muslim Prophet, or the Spiritual Savior? Or another way of asking the same question, Who gets Jesus *and God* right? We believe John does. That's why the war of words will continue until Jesus Christ returns and settles it—once and for all.

In the meantime, how we fight the battle of this war of words requires much wisdom, especially in a time like ours, when social media might tempt some of us to go nuclear. (One wonders, if the same weapons for verbal ammunition had existed in John's day, would he have tweeted attacks against these antichrists?) It can turn quickly into an ugly scene when Christians mount a campaign for the truth on social media. How do we win the war of words? Scream louder? Talk longer? Raise the flag of righteous indignation? Crowd-pound the truth into heretics?

Actually, the war many of us are fighting on social media has little to do with the gospel of Jesus Christ. We fight for our latest cause, our most recent outrage, our current political or social agenda. We aren't defending the gospel. In fact, the gospel rarely comes up, and when it does, it seems completely out of place in the heat of the battle. For example, several years ago, I made the mistake of trying to enter the fray and argue briefly for the verity of the gospel on Facebook. At the time, a well-known

---

[22]See Bart D. Ehrman, *Did Jesus Exist? The Historical Argument for Jesus of Nazareth* (New York: HarperCollins, 2012), 11-34.

Mormon radio/TV host was attacking the current administration for its immoral agenda, hosting a big rally in our nation's capital. I noticed that one of the posters—a Christian—claimed this celebrity was "fighting for the truth of the gospel." When I asked, "How can a Mormon fight for the truth of the Christian gospel?" the woman lashed out at me with: "Who do you think you are, judging him? He's a good man. He believes the gospel." I wrote, "He may very well be a good man, but how do you know he believes the gospel?" To which she replied, "Because he stands up for the truth!" At that point, I wanted to quote the well-known question, "And what is truth?" But I thought better of it: I didn't want to sound like Pontius Pilate. Besides, verbal wars on Facebook never end well.

Why is that so? There are several reasons—one in particular seems quite apparent: it's easier to write inflammatory words on social media than to say the same thing to someone's face. Or, to put it in theological terms, we know that incarnation tempers reckless words. Jesus didn't go around shooting off his mouth to win an argument. He was far more circumspect about what he said, speaking only the words of God (Jn 12:49-50). Why was that? It was not only due to his desire to obey his heavenly Father but also because he knew he would live what he said (Jn 13:12-17). Words matter. Embodied words matter even more: "The Word became flesh and tabernacled among us" (Jn 1:14). According to John, the same should be true for us. We should not only say the right words about Jesus—what has been true from the beginning (the Word of God!)—but we must embody the words of Jesus Christ: "Whoever keeps his word, truly the love of God has been perfected in him; this is how we know we are in him. The one who says he abides in him ought to walk just as [Jesus] walked" (1 Jn 2:5-6). That's ultimately how we fight the war of words: we live what we say is true. For just as Jesus embodied what he said, "I am the way, the truth, and the life, no one comes to the Father except through me" (Jn 14:6), so should we who claim him with words.

What time is it? According to John, we've been living the last hour for two thousand years, and we've seen many antichrists over the years to prove it. According to the Doomsday Clock, it's two minutes till the end of the world, and the reckless words of the leaders of nuclear powers could be interpreted as a sign of the times. But whether it is the last hour or the last minute, Christ believers know it's always time to live what we say we believe. The incarnation demands it.

7

KEEP COMMANDMENTS

Incarnating the Word

I usually don't pay attention to bumper stickers, but this one got to me. It only had four words: *PRO* on the left, and three smaller-font words stacked on top of each other to the right (*God, Life, Guns*). It was stuck on the bumper of a large pickup truck in front of me as we were waiting for the left turn signal, and I kept staring at this "gospel" message, wondering, "What does God think about that? How does someone move so quickly from *God* to *guns*—with *life* stuck in the middle?" I must say that when I think of God, the third word that comes to my mind isn't *guns*. Maybe *mercy* or *grace* or perhaps even *resurrection*—that sounds biblical to me: God first, through life, then at last resurrection. But the sequence "God—life—guns" made no sense to me. That's when I begin to wonder about the driver, a middle-aged man waiting for the turn signal. "What kind of Christian is he? Probably a churchgoing, right-leaning, family man," I thought to myself. Then I imagined having a conversation with him, where I tried to get him to explain his "gospel" message: "Where do you find that in the teachings of Jesus?"

Then again, I know how that would go. I've talked to several men like him who are quick to point out that we wouldn't have the freedoms guaranteed by the First Amendment (to religion, speech, press) without the freedom assured by the Second Amendment (to bear arms). "Jesus saves my soul," they say; "but the Second Amendment protects my family. God and guns."

In my mind, however, God and guns don't go together. Even though Jesus did instruct his disciples *one time* to "sell his coat and buy a sword" (Lk 22:36), it wasn't a major teaching of our Lord. He didn't go around constantly encouraging his followers to buy weapons, making sure they always had a sword on hand. Can you imagine? "Blessed are the sword-makers, for theirs is the kingdom on earth." Ask anyone to list the major teachings of Christ and "the right to bear arms" wouldn't make the top ten—probably not even the top one hundred. But that doesn't matter to many Christians. For we all have the ability to keep what we believe about Christ separate from the daily realities of life, even though much of Jesus' teaching had to do with *how* we should live every day. In my little evangelical world, what Jesus did for us (he saved us from sin by dying on the cross) takes precedent over what he taught us (deny yourself, pick up your cross, and follow me)—the contemporary songs we sing during worship services reveal our bias. We'd rather sing about his cross but not about ours. We have *many* songs about the ugly sin of our lives but very few about his beautiful life before he died. We emphasize having a personal relationship with the Christ who reigns in heaven without regard for the Jesus who lived on earth. In other words (to put it in scholarly terms), we have separated the Christ of faith from the Jesus of history.

I have wondered, therefore, whether evangelical Christians should admit that we don't need the Gospels. As long as we have Paul to explain how the death of Jesus atones for our sin and why the resurrection of Christ matters, what difference does it make whether we read the Gospel according to John? Since Jesus lived the perfect life as the "one-of-a-kind Son of God" (probably the intended meaning of "only begotten")—a nonrepeatable event—then some might say, "Should we really be expected to follow Jesus Christ, the Son of God?[1] Who could live a perfect life? Not me and certainly not you. Isn't that the point of John's Gospel, to show us that Jesus did for us what we couldn't do for ourselves? 'For

---

[1]On "only begotten," see Marianne Meye Thompson, *John: A Commentary*, New Testament Library (Louisville, KY: Westminster John Knox, 2015), 33-34.

God so loved the world. . . . ' Isn't that the gist of John's stated purpose? 'These things have been written so that you would believe that Jesus is the Christ, the Son of God (Jn 20:31).' That's why John wrote his Gospel. The words and works of Jesus were supposed to lead *nonbelievers* to faith in Jesus Christ. What about those of us who already believe? Do *we* still need John's Gospel?"

The people who left John's community didn't think so. Evidently, these secessionists, whom John called antichrists, believed the Spirit would be enough to lead them in truth without the Gospel of John. But John contended that, since Jesus Christ "came in the flesh," the only way to know the truth would be to hear his Gospel—to learn what Jesus Christ said and did "in the flesh." But why would that matter? If the secessionists already believed in Christ, why would they need to sit and hear the same story over and over again? This is why most scholars argue that John's purpose was more than evangelistic. He wrote his Gospel in order to correct the heretical Christology of the secessionists, perhaps targeting proto-Gnostics, who denied the humanity of Christ; Ebionites, who denied the deity of Christ; or even apostate Jews who no longer believed that Jesus was the Messiah.[2] But if that were the case, would John's Gospel help? It wasn't the heretics who stuck around to hear it. Indeed, since they had already left the community, John was essentially preaching to the choir when he sent his Gospel. So perhaps John's purpose was also pastoral, to encourage his faithful community to *continue* to believe the right things about Jesus and not follow the secessionists. If that were the case, then John's Gospel was not only written for nonbelievers (evangelistic) and against heretics (theological) but also for believers (pastoral). Yet, John seems to give *another* reason *in his letter* as to why he wrote his Gospel: so that his people would know how to "walk just as that man walked" (1 Jn 2:6). In other words, John's Gospel was supposed to serve an ethical purpose too.

---

[2]T. Griffith, *Keep Yourselves from Idols: A New Look at 1 John*, Journal for the Study of the New Testament Supplement Series 233 (London: Sheffield Academic, 2002), 173-79.

THE JESUS WAY

According to John, those who truly believe in Christ will "keep his commandments" (1 Jn 2:4). Saying the right words about Jesus matters. But ultimately words are not enough. True believers must do the right thing too: "Little Children, let us love not only in word or tongue, but also in deed and in truth" (1 Jn 3:18). That's how the faithful recognize false professors. They may claim with their words, "I have known him." But if they don't "keep *his* word," they reveal to everyone that they are "liars" (1 Jn 2:4-5). For no one can claim to know Jesus unless they (1) know what he said and did, and then (2) *do* what he said and did. Of course, John presumes his readers will know the words and works of Jesus as long as they abide in the community. The only way to abide in Christ is to abide in his words. And the only way to abide in his words is to abide in the church where John's Gospel is read (1 Jn 3:24). This is why John claims he isn't writing anything new in his letter: "Beloved, I am not writing a new commandment to you but an old commandment that you had from the beginning—the old commandment is the word that you heard" (1 Jn 2:7).

Perhaps "old commandment" is John's way of referring to the "new commandment" Jesus gave to the Twelve: "I am giving you a new commandment, that you love each other just as I loved you in order that you love each other" (Jn 13:34). Since this is the only "commandment" Jesus gives to his disciples in John's Gospel, then that's the old commandment that John referred to as both old and new (1 Jn 2:7-8). The old commandment in John's Gospel, then, was reinscribed as new in John's letter.

But John also refers to keeping "his commandments" (1 Jn 2:3-4; 3:22), indicating more than one.[3] So, if Jesus gave only one commandment in John's Gospel, what are the other commandments of Jesus? There are several possibilities (the laws of the Old Testament embedded in Jesus' teaching, the imperative verbs in John's Gospel, taking the wisdom of

---

[3]Raymond E. Brown finds no significance between the singular and plural. See Brown, *The Epistles of John*, Anchor Bible (New York: Doubleday, 1982), 250-51.

Jesus as commandments).[4] But I wonder whether John was referring to his entire Gospel—especially when he seemed to correlate keeping "his commandments" and "his word" with "walking as that man walked" (1 Jn 2:3-6). For, as far as John was concerned, hearing his Gospel was the same as hearing what Christ commanded—not only through his words but also by his deeds. *Everything* Jesus said and did—the Jesus way—is the revelation of the Word of God in human flesh. When the Gospel of John was read, those who were present would hear the Word of God speak to them through John's words. As a result, John's Gospel would function as the commandments of Christ, summed up in John's *letter* as a twofold commandment: "This is his commandment: that we might believe in the name of his son, Jesus Christ, and love each other—just as he gave the commandment to us" (1 Jn 3:23).

But there's a problem. Even if John was making an oblique reference to his Gospel, Jesus "offers virtually no specific moral instruction either by word or deed," as Brown says.[5] There's not much ethical instruction in the Fourth Gospel. (Imagine how different John's Gospel would sound if he had included something like the Sermon on the Mount.) Most of what Jesus teaches has to do with *who* he is and not *what* is required of his disciples. In fact, as we've already noticed, the only thing Jesus requires of the Twelve is exactly the same commandment John repeats in his letter: believe in Jesus and love one another. That's it. Compared to the Synoptic Gospels, it doesn't take much to follow Jesus according to John. There's no talk of "taking up your cross" or "denying yourself" or "losing your life to find it." One doesn't get the impression when reading John's Gospel that disciples are supposed to "follow Jesus." In fact, only once in John's Gospel does Jesus tell his disciples to follow his example (Jn 13:12-17).

Beyond that, even if listeners were to try to imitate the Jesus of John's Gospel, Brown claims it wouldn't result in a circumspect moral life.[6]

---

[4]See Robert W. Yarbrough, *1–3 John*, Baker Exegetical Commentary on the New Testament (Grand Rapids, MI: Baker Academic, 2008), 82-83.
[5]Brown, *Epistles*, 286.
[6]Brown, *Epistles*, 286.

There are no stories of Jesus dining with tax collectors or welcoming children—living parables with a moral to the story. Most of the deeds of Jesus in the Fourth Gospel are miraculous signs performed in order to reveal his true identity. Furthermore, Jesus never sends the Twelve out to perform miracles and cast out demons—as if it were a part of their training—even though he predicts the disciples "will do even greater works" than he does (Jn 14:12). So, when John encourages his readers to "walk as that man walked" (1 Jn 2:6), what does he expect them to do? Perform signs? Give long soliloquies about Jesus as the way, the truth, and the life? What would it mean to "keep his word" (1 Jn 2:5), when the only word they needed to hear was the Gospel according to John? Is that the reason they didn't need anyone to teach them (1 Jn 2:27)?

According to Cornelis Bennema, John thought that his Gospel would inspire "virtuous thinking" among his listeners, trusting it would lead to virtuous behavior. "Perhaps this explains why neither John nor Jesus spells out the particulars of virtuous behavior."[7] Having heard about how Jesus faced certain situations in the Gospel, John's community would be inspired to translate lessons learned for their context. For example, hearing about the time when certain disciples left the group due to Jesus' teaching, those listening to John's Gospel would be affirmed as faithful followers because they continued to abide by the words of Christ. Or, taking to heart how Jesus refused to condemn the adulterous woman, John's community might be encouraged to confess their sins. In other words, John was counting on the power of the Gospel *story* to direct the lives of his people—not only inspired by Jesus but also by those who followed him. Indeed, we've already seen how characters in John's Gospel can function as virtuous examples of what it means to abide in the Word of God.[8] In the same way, then, John's episodic narrative "commands" his listeners to obey Jesus by living the *same* story. That would mean, of

---

[7]Cornelis Bennema, "Virtue Ethics and the Johannine Writings," in *Johannine Ethics: The Moral World of the Gospel and Letters of John*, ed. Christopher W. Skinner and Sherri Brown (Minneapolis: Fortress, 2017), 275.
[8]See above, chapter 4. So also Bennema, "Virtue Ethics," 275-78.

course, that John's auditors would have not only asked themselves, "What *did* Jesus do?" but also "What did the Samaritan woman do?" and "What did the man born blind do?"—connecting the dots of their experience with the one and only true story of their lives.

We underestimate the power of visualizing the gospel story when John's community gathered to hear his Gospel. Think about how differently they would have heard the Gospel compared to us. First of all, we hear the Gospel story in our heads because most of the time we read it to ourselves silently. That means, of course, the voice of the narrator, some of the characters, perhaps even the voice of Jesus sounds like the voice in our heads—our voice. In their day, the voice of narrator, the characters, even Jesus would have *always* sounded like the literate man who could read the Gospel. The literate *always* read texts out loud (whether intended for an audience or not), having to vocalize the words in order to understand what they were reading (Acts 8:30). No one read silently to themselves.[9]

Second, consider how our visual library works when we read the Gospel. What did Jesus look like? Probably the actor from our favorite Jesus film or the portrait that hung in the children's building of our hometown church. And what of Peter or Nicodemus or the Samaritan woman? Again, our visual library is informed by fictional characters culled from films and paintings. But when John's community gathered to hear stories about Christ, their imagination would have been fueled by people they knew—Jews, Samaritans, Greeks, and Romans. Fleshing out the characters of John's Gospel with real people would have brought an incarnational dynamic to the power of the narrative. In other words, unlike us, they would be able to see themselves in the story of John's Gospel because they had met people like the characters of John's narrative world. When we visualize ourselves in the Gospel story, I think we unconsciously cast ourselves in a film—something imagined because we've seen it *visually* on television or at the movies. But when John's

---

[9]H. Gregory Snyder, *Teachers and Texts in the Ancient World: Philosophers, Jews and Christians* (London: Routledge, 2000), 30-31.

hearers heard the Gospel, they would be able to visualize the real, flesh-and-blood story of their lives—something *incarnated* because they could imagine it on the streets of their city.

So, if John's community "walked just as that man walked" (1 Jn 2:6), which meant keeping the "old commandment" that they heard from the beginning (1 Jn 2:7), then they would see the "true light" that shines in the darkness—both in him and in them (1 Jn 2:8). That's the same progression regarding the light that we've seen before (1 Jn 1): from Jesus, through the Word, in them. Incarnation ("in him"), excarnation ("I'm writing again the new commandment"), reincarnation ("in you"): "The darkness is passing away and the true light shines already, which is true in him and in you" (1 Jn 2:8). Notice, once again, that the second-person pronoun is plural. John claims that the true light shines in *all* of them—not only because they gather to hear the word they heard from the beginning but also because the true word shines *in them*. Indeed, due to the reincarnation of the word, they become the word of God for each other. According to Sherri Brown,

> The Christian community continues to receive Christ, the Word of God, through each other, activating their ongoing believing by cultivating their love for one another and responding both to each other's needs and each other's teaching. The Fourth Evangelist teaches that in the ongoing lives of the community, believing is practiced by receiving the Word of God, *by receiving one another.*[10]

Bennema adds, "The presence of Jesus in the community of faith provides believers with continued access to his example. For as believers imitate Jesus, they also mediate him. To perform an authentic act of love that imitates Jesus *mediates* the experience of Jesus and his love to the beneficiary."[11]

The light of Christ is the light of the church. In the world, he shines nowhere else.

---

[10]Sherri Brown, "Believing in the Gospel of John: The Ethical Imperative to Becoming Children of God," in Skinner and Brown, *Johannine Ethics*, 23, emphasis original.

[11]Bennema, "Virtue Ethics," 278-79, emphasis original.

Proof that the true light not only shines among them but in them and through them is evident when "the darkness goes away" (1 Jn 2:8). Of course, the absence of light creates darkness. Unlike light, which derives from a source, darkness has no originating power. There is no planetary source for darkness. We don't look up into the night sky and say, "It sure is dark tonight. Where is the black hole this evening?" Rather, we know it gets dark when the sun goes down. Applying the same imagery to the world, John would have us recognize that the only reason the world is dark is the absence of light. When the light shines, darkness "goes away"—or in the words of John's Gospel, "the light shines in the dark and darkness did not overpower it" (Jn 1:5). In the eternal battle of light versus dark, darkness can only win when light is no longer present. Darkness cannot invade light. But light *always* invades darkness. Indeed, when light appears, darkness loses—more than that, it ceases to exist, it "passes away." Since light and dark are mutually exclusive, darkness *always* dies in the presence of the light—a light that shines en masse.

That's why *individuals* who claim to walk in the light while living in darkness are "liars who do not practice the truth" (1 Jn 1:6). The only way to "walk in the light" is to abide where the light of Christ is, that is in the church—what John called koinonia (1 Jn 2:7), where brothers and sisters love each other (1 Jn 2:10). You can't have koinonia by yourself. You can't walk in the light by yourself. That's why those who walk away from the church, no longer remaining "in the light"/walking in darkness, no longer love brothers and sisters. As far as John was concerned, only those who remain in the church—abiding in the Word, walking in the light— can love one another. More than that, those who walk in the dark reveal that they actually hate their brothers and sisters (1 Jn 2:9, 11). The love of Christ *only* happens in community. Love is a "one-another" commandment exemplified by Christ and in Christ—the old commandment that is made new every time we gather together to hear the Word that we've heard from the beginning (1 Jn 2:7).

No one can find the light of love in the dark.

THE WAYS OF THE WORLD

John worked with the presumption that the world does not know what love is because true love can *only* be found in the church, where the love of Christ abides. That's where love is perfected, where the one-another love of Christ abides (1 Jn 4:16-17). All that is in the world, on the other hand, is lust—the insatiable desire for self-gratification (1 Jn 2:16). The world and its lusts are fleeting, passing away, elusive, never fulfilled (1 Jn 2:17). That's why the world is filled with violence. Without the love of Christ, hatred incites brother to kill brother (1 Jn 3:12). Without the light of Christ, haters stumble around in the dark, not knowing where they come from or where they are going (1 Jn 2:11). Without the truth of Christ, the lost can't see they live with liars who deny who they truly are because they can't see who Christ truly is (1 Jn 1:10; 2:22). Without the church, the self-deceived persist in sin (1 Jn 3:6-7). Without God, sinners prove they are children of the devil (1 Jn 3:8). In fact, that's the way John sees it: we're in the midst of a conflict between God and the devil, between children of God and children of the devil, between Christ and the world, between truth and error, between love and hatred. Even though John doesn't use the language of warfare, he believed that the children of light must fight for true love.

Of course, the *way* we fight for love is not like the world. The world kills for what it wants, just like Cain, who "slaughtered" his brother (1 Jn 3:12). A world of evil deeds seeks to destroy what is good (1 Jn 3:12). A world of hatred tries to turn brothers into enemies (1 Jn 3:13). A world of death claims love doesn't change a thing (1 Jn 3:14). But the world doesn't know true love. The world knows erotic love. The world knows self-love. The world knows romantic love. The world even knows family love. But the world doesn't know brotherly love *in Christ*.

Even though John never contrasts these other worldly loves with the love of Christ, we see why he was convinced that "the one who loves his brother abides in the light, and there is no offense [*skandalon*] in him" (1 Jn 2:10). It's because all of us, at one time or another, have been scandalized by the love of the world. For example, even though the world tries to prop up romantic love as eternal, we know better. Attempts made by married couples to keep the romance alive prove that kind of love always fades. Yet, jilted lovers are always offended by cheaters, knowing their love didn't last. Loveless marriages usually end in divorce. What surprises me is how many people blame *God* for failed marriages. I've seen it too many times. A young man discovers his wife has broken their vows. Heartbroken, he tries to reclaim his wife's affection, but to no avail. Friends take sides in the war that leads to divorce. In the aftermath, the man gets mad at God, leaving the faith and drowning his sorrows in alcohol. Sadly, the scenario I just described sounds cliché because it's so common. Yet, both in song and in film the world still dangles the elusive carrot of romantic love in front of our faces, and we keep beating a dead horse hoping to win the prize. We are desperate for love even though we are constantly offended by it.

But John thinks there are several reasons why no one should ever be offended by love in Christ (1 Jn 2:10). First, "love one another" is nothing new; it's the same message that was heard from the beginning (1 Jn 3:11). Second, brotherly love is life giving, which proves it's from God (1 Jn 3:14). Hatred, on the other hand, is life taking and belongs to the world of death. Obviously, killers don't have Jesus Christ—eternal life—living in them (1 Jn 3:15). Third, we fight for true love the same way Christ did: by sacrificing ourselves for each other (1 Jn 3:16). Worldly people may boast in their worldly goods (1 Jn 2:16), but brothers in Christ give their worldly goods to help brothers in need. The hardhearted are selfish, proving that the love of God doesn't abide in them (1 Jn 3:17). But true love always does what is right, which is why words alone are never enough (1 Jn 3:18). Love *must* be incarnate. Stephen Smalley writes, "God's life does not dwell in a murderer (v 15); but neither does God's love dwell in a miser (v 17)."[12] This is how we can be confident that God is at work among us, knowing that we are true: if we love one another as Christ loved us (1 Jn 3:19-24).

---

[12]Stephen S. Smalley, *1, 2, 3 John*, Word Biblical Commentary (Waco, TX: Word Books, 1984), 197.

Trying to convince his community not to be like Cain, John *didn't* write, "Be like Abel"—even though he reminds his converts that they shouldn't be surprised when a violent world hates them (1 Jn 3:13). Instead, John holds up Jesus as the antithesis of Cain, knowing his community has already heard from his Gospel that Jesus' "brothers" didn't take his life. He laid it down (Jn 10:17-18). We must be very careful, therefore, not to confuse the difference between the two. Abel was a righteous man (1 Jn 3:12), the victim of an injustice that should never be repeated. Jesus is the righteous Christ, the obedient Son of God who suffered injustice, a willing sacrifice that should be imitated (1 Jn 3:16). Remembering what Christ has done for us—God's love for us—is the only motivation we need to open our hearts and sacrifice our life's possessions to help our needy brother (1 Jn 3:17). In John's world of subsistence, where most people needed to pray for daily bread, giving away what is necessary for life would be the same as giving away your life—something lost on us because we live in a land of plenty.[13] John knew that the only way his community would make it was to rely on each other for everything. The love of God abiding in everyone—loving one another in word and deed just like Christ—would ensure that no one suffered like Abel (1 Jn 3:17-18).

But there have been many Abels in our churches, victims of such egregious offenses that it makes one wonder whether the love of God abides in us at all. Who could say that true love can only be found in the church when another scandal comes to light? Recently, over three hundred priests in Pennsylvania were accused of sex crimes against children and adults. Stories of sexual abuse committed by a well-known pastor of a megachurch in Chicago have surfaced. The president of the United States—backed by evangelicals—has needed a slush fund to pay off porn stars and abused women. In *every* situation, so-called Christian leaders tried to cover up sin. Therefore, it should come as no surprise that the #MeToo movement quickly found support in #ChurchToo.

---

[13]Revealed by the fact that most commentators claim that John certainly wasn't encouraging them to die for one another. But I think that's exactly what John was saying.

With all the abuse, all the offense, all of the scandal, all of the *sin*, it would be easy to forgive outsiders for claiming there is no difference between us and the world. We who are supposed to be the people imitating Christ—sacrificing ourselves for one another—have so many Abels abused by "brothers" that it's enough to tempt me to join the skeptics who say, "What difference does faith in Christ make? None at all." Even nonbelievers know the people who claim to follow Christ are not supposed to act like the world. The ways of Christ and the ways of the world are supposed to be mutually exclusive. In fact, that's exactly what John claims, when he asks, "How can the love of God abide in him?" (1 Jn 3:17), the one who hardens his heart just like the hardhearted world. Our hearts are not supposed to condemn us because we're living the truth (1 Jn 3:19). Even when our hearts condemn us, God is greater than our hearts because *he knows everything* (1 Jn 3:20). My heart can hardly take the news when such horrendous abuse is uncovered in the church. Imagine the heart of God—what it must feel like to know *everything*, all the sin, all the abuse, every offense, every heart.

In light of these latest scandals, I kept turning the question over and over in my head, "Why didn't the Scriptures make a difference?" How can a priest who spends so much time reading the Bible sexually abuse little boys? How can a preacher who delivers so many sermons that teach the ways of Christ also sexually abuse women in his own congregation? You would think spending that much time in the Gospels would be enough to convince the pervert that those who abuse children are going straight to hell—Jesus says so (Mt 18:6). You would think preaching from the Gospels would be enough to convince the adulterer who abused women to pluck out his eyes and cut off his hands lest he wind up in hell (Mt 5:27-30).

Then it dawned on me that even John knew his Gospel wouldn't be enough to convince his community not to treat one another like Cain. Hearing stories about how Jesus Christ laid down his life for his friends wouldn't be enough to inspire them to lay down their lives for each other. It would take more than a preacher, more than a written Gospel. The reincarnation of the Word requires the Holy Spirit, the gift of God that empowers us to abide in the Word we hear, keeping his commandments (1 Jn 3:24). Without the Spirit, we would be trying to keep the commandments in our own strength. Without the Spirit, we would be simply gathering to hear the words. Without the Spirit, we would be nothing more than a book club.

For all John's talk about the importance of abiding by his written words, he knew we would need the Word abiding in us to make a difference (1 Jn 3:24). You can read the words; you can hear the words. But unless you have the Word in you—reincarnation—you're not living the words. It's the Spirit *in us* that makes that happen. To be sure, Christ abides in the individual person who keeps his commandments (1 Jn 3:24). But the only way we know Christ abides in all of us is when we love one other *by the Spirit* (1 Jn 3:23-24). This is the reason we can be confident that God is at work among us: we love each other. Self-confidence is never enough—satisfied with myself that I obey Christ. The only way I can find confidence in my relationship with God is when Christ abides *in all of us*, when *we* all do the things that please him: believe in Christ and love one another (1 Jn 3:22-23). I can't believe in Christ by myself (no man is an island). I can't experience the love of Christ by myself (his love is our communion). That's why John believed our confidence in faith is only found *together*. By the Spirit *in all of us*, we overcome the world together: "Greater is he that is *in us* than he that is in the world" (1 Jn 4:4). We overcome the world when we love one another.

WHAT ABOUT THE STRANGER?

The scenario John used to convince his community to give their worldly goods to the needy depended on one brother recognizing another as his brother. The reason he doesn't harden his heart against the destitute is that he sees him—his brother—in need (1 Jn 3:17). John assumes he will give his life like Christ because they have Christ in common. In other words, in this letter, John assumes brotherly love is an intramural reality. But what happens when the needy man is outside the walls of our

gathering? Should the love of Christ be extended to people we don't
know? It's one thing to deny hospitality to an antichrist who used to
belong to our group (2 Jn 10), but what about the stranger who comes to
our door looking for help, claiming to be our brother? If brotherly love
should *only* happen between brothers, did John expect *un*familiarity to
breed contempt? Perhaps Diotrephes thought so. He was acting like the
gatekeeper of his house church, refusing to let "brothers who are strangers"
join the gathering (3 Jn 5, 10). Not only that, but if any member welcomed
one of these "strangers" into their homes, Diotrephes threw them out as
well (3 Jn 10). That made the Elder angry, which is why he dashed off a
letter to Gaius, a man who welcomed visitors sent by the Elder (3 Jn 3).

Offering acts of hospitality to honorable visitors was customary. Honorable men traveling through an unfamiliar town could always expect
locals to provide food and lodging even though they were strangers. Travelers of low social status, on the other hand, would have to seek shelter in
the public house—a seedy place that would often function as a brothel.
That's what made the practice of early Christians so unique. They were
known to offer hospitality to *all* people, regardless of the traveler's social
status (see Jas 2:2-3). Since churches met in homes, Christians hosting a
visitor was the same as welcoming a stranger to church. Of course, since
the Elder had already instructed his house churches to refuse hospitality to
former members who were antichrist (2 Jn 7-11), then it became apparent
that not everyone was welcome in church. Perhaps that's what Diotrephes
thought he was doing, serving as the door monitor for his church that met
outside Ephesus—probably a town in the surrounding region. Even though
the Elder had written "something to the church," Diotrephes appears to
have disregarded the Elder's previous letter (what the Elder writes literally
is, "but Diotrephes—the man who loves to be first—does not receive *us*,"
[3 Jn 9]). Diotrephes went too far, not only rejecting letters but also
"brothers" who were strangers to him. To the Elder, ignoring his letter was
the same as rejecting him. Furthermore, to reject a brother sent by him was
"doing what is evil" (3 Jn 11). In word and deed, Diotrephes dishonored the
Elder when he rejected brothers who were strangers to him (3 Jn 10).

Since Ephesus and the surrounding region was a place where Christianity first flourished due to Paul's ministry, one can't help but wonder whether Diotrephes belonged to one of Paul's churches in Asia Minor.[14] We know that there were several different brands of teachers in and around Ephesus at the time: Pauline, Johannine, Cerinthinian. There was even a group in Ephesus who seemed to have belonged to "the church" of John the Baptizer (Acts 19:1-4). Scholars wonder about the relationship between these different churches. To what extent did they get along? Did they know each other, visit each other, worship with one another, share John's Gospel? We know that Cerinthus was dismissed as a heretic early on.[15] But what about the relationship between Paul's churches and John's churches? Did they see each other in adversarial terms? Or did they consider themselves one church with many locations, united as the body of Christ?

It's easy for us to assume they affirmed each other, since both Paul's letters and John's writings made it into our Scripture. But, when we read in the Revelation of John that Christ was angry with churches in Pergamum and Thyatira because they ate "things sacrificed to idols" (Rev 2:14, 20), and yet Paul told the Corinthians that eating idol meat was okay under certain conditions (1 Cor 10:25-27), we can see why Paul's and John's churches may have been suspicious of each other—especially when it came to sharing the Lord's Table. There's no way to know for certain about their relationship (I agree with Paul Trebilco, who thinks they did get along).[16] But, if they were on brotherly terms, there's a real possibility that many of these house churches would have turned into a blended fellowship. John's house churches would have mingled with Paul's churches and vice versa—especially since Christians were known

---

[14]Paul Trebilco assumes a segregated church, all the way to the time of Ignatius: "Thus, even though (we have suggested) at the time Ignatius wrote, one group in Ephesus looked back to Paul (the spiritual children of the addressees of the Pastorals), and another looked back to 'John' (the spiritual children of the addressees of 1-3 John), it was Paul who was the stronger focus for unity because he established the Christian group in the city." See Trebilco, *The Early Christians in Ephesus from Paul to Ignatius* (Grand Rapids, MI: Eerdmans, 2004), 677.

[15]Trebilco, *Early Christians in Ephesus*, 290-91.

[16]See Trebilco, *Early Christians in Ephesus*, 589-627.

to expect hospitality from one another when they traveled.[17] Perhaps that was the problem between the Elder and Diotrephes. The Elder assumed that his letters would be received by all churches in Ephesus *and the surrounding region*, whether Johannine or Pauline, because they were one people in Christ ("I wrote something to the church," 3 Jn 9—he doesn't say "churches"). But, Diotrephes dismissed the Elder's presumption that he had anything to teach them (1 Jn 2:27). That doesn't surprise us. We all know churches of different denominations sometimes treat one another like strangers—acting like we have nothing to learn from one another—even though we are brothers and sisters in Christ.

When I look at my bookshelf, I see what the Elder presumed would be true. Standing side by side are Presbyterians, Methodists, Pentecostals, Baptists, Christian Church, Anglicans, Episcopalians, and Catholics—all offering their teachings. Some of them are familiar to me, friends who have written helpful books. Most are strangers. Some are still living. Most are dead. But, when I want to hear the voice of God in Scripture, I don't reach first for the living, the friendly, and the Baptist voices to see what they say before I consider the dead, the stranger, and the outsiders. Without regard for their identity, I read what they all have to say about God's Word. Of course, sometimes their Catholic or Presbyterian voice sounds peculiar to my Baptist ear. I hear the stranger knocking at the door. But, when I open the door and see "that we believe in the name of his Son, Jesus Christ and love one another—just as he gave the commandment to us" (1 Jn 3:23), then I'm ready to welcome the stranger and share the fellowship of the Word by his Spirit. Strangely enough, it wasn't my childhood church that taught me to be like Gaius and open my door to strangers. Rather, it was my *denominational* seminary that encouraged me to listen to Christians from other traditions, knowing that the truth isn't fragile. In fact, my professors would say, if your doctrine is so fragile

---

[17]"Everyone who comes in the name of the Lord is to be welcomed. But then examine him, and you will find out—for you will have insight—what is true and what is false. If the one who comes is merely passing through, assist him as much as you can. But he must not stay with you for more than two or, if necessary, three days." Didache 12.1-2 in *The Apostolic Fathers*, 3rd ed., trans. Michael W. Holmes (Grand Rapids, MI: Baker Academic, 2007).

that you won't listen to strangers, then maybe what you believe isn't true. Baptists don't have the corner on truth—and neither do Presbyterians, or Methodists, or Anglicans, or the rest. Heaven will reveal the difference because only the truth is eternal.

I grew up in church hearing a joke about heaven that made fun of the tribalism that often accompanies denominationalism. A Baptist dies, and St. Peter meets him at the pearly gates to take him on a tour of heaven. They walk by a towering cathedral, majestic choir accompanied by organ music bellowing from the building. The Baptist asks St. Peter, "What's going on in there?" St. Peter says, "The Anglicans are taking communion." A few miles down the road they come across a modest building, shouts of praise, loud applause, and a pounding piano shaking the walls. "Who's that?" St. Peter replies, "That's the Pentecostals having church." Later, the Baptist and St. Peter pass by a simple structure, where only human voices can be heard singing songs without any instruments. The Baptist shouts above the loud chorus, "Who's in there?" St. Peter says, "Shhhh! Be quiet! That's the Church of Christ, and they think they're the only ones here." Even though we Baptists loved to tell that joke, as I think about it now, the joke was really on us. Our Baptist view of heaven wasn't heavenly. We acted like we were taking the higher moral ground by affirming that Christians of other denominations would make it to heaven. But, apparently, it would only be heaven to us as long as everyone still worshiped with their own tribe. Or another way to put it, on any given Sunday we Baptists believed that we were *already* experiencing heaven on earth—a realized eschatology of segregated Christianity. I think Diotrephes would have been proud.

Since then, I've met Baptist versions of Diotrephes and Gaius, the recipient of the Elder's letter who welcomed brothers, especially when they were strangers, which earned him the reputation of loving the *whole* church (3 Jn 1-6). The Diotrepheses among us promote tribalism. The Gaiuses among us love all the brothers and sisters. The Diotrepheses among us act like the church boss, running strangers out of the church to protect their turf. The Gaiuses among us recognize those who "walk in the truth," sending "them on their way in a manner worthy of God" (3 Jn 6). The Diotrepheses among us fight like the world, attacking others with "wicked words" (3 Jn 10). The Gaiuses among us sacrifice their worldly goods to help "fellow workers of the truth" (3 Jn 8).

Simply put, Diotrephes hates his brothers and sisters; Gaius loves them. Therefore, according to the Elder, we should imitate Gaius and not Diotrephes because "the one who does good is of God; the one who does evil hasn't seen God" (3 Jn 11). Indeed, as far as John is concerned, the only way to "see God" is to recognize Christ in one another: "No one has ever seen God. If we love one another, God abides in us and his love is fully revealed" (1 Jn 4:12). Those who can't see the love of Christ in another brother or sister—especially the stranger—can't see God. Ironically, the one who can't see God is the very person who needs to come to church so he can meet him—which is why the Elder doesn't advise the church to kick out Diotrephes. For even Diotrephes needed the love of Christ that can only be found in the church.

A few years ago I was walking through the parking lot to speak to a Baptist church when I noticed several bumper stickers with similar messages: Pro-Life, Pro-Guns, Pro-Freedom. Then I remembered the man in the truck and thought to myself, "He could be in the congregation today. That guy could be a member of this church." I fantasized for a moment about the possibilities, taking a prophetic word into the pulpit in order to challenge my bumper-sticker brother's "guns and God" approach to life. But that's not what I had prepared to preach. My remarks that day were based on Matthew's Gospel, highlighting the warning Jesus gave to anyone who offends "little ones" who believe in him (Mt 18:6). Since I had been studying John's spirituality, echoes of his letters flooded my mind too—especially the passage where John says there is no offense in the man who loves his brother (1 Jn 2:10). That convergence of the Word of God, Jesus' warning and John's claim, rattled around in my head as I approached the church building, savoring the irony: *Here I am. A Baptist professor, getting ready to preach to a Baptist church, and if most of these members have the same bumper-sticker, "God and guns" sentiment*

I saw in the parking lot, I may feel more like a stranger than a brother among them.

But that didn't happen. Instead, the worship service was wonderful. Their hospitality was graceful. Diotrephes wasn't there. Rather, several Gaiuses sent me on my way with their worldly goods, having treated me like a brother. They trusted me; I trusted them—not simply because we're Baptist, but because Christ abides in us. The politics of the world may try to divide us. But the love of Christ unites us. That's how we know we're abiding in the Word.

I think the Elder would have been pleased.

8

LOVE ONE ANOTHER

Abiding in the Word

THE YOUNG GROOM WAS MAKING VOWS to his bride, repeating what the preacher told him to say, line by line, until he got to the end: " . . . [in sickness and in health] in sickness and in health, [to love and to cherish] to love and to cherish, [till death do us part] till death do us part, [in the name of the Father]," at which point the confused groom asked the preacher, "Whose father? Hers or mine?" Everyone at the wedding laughed nervously at the young man's question—even the preacher.

As the video made the rounds recently on social media, posters ridiculed the groom's ignorance of the traditional Anglican wedding ceremony. But when I saw the video, I relished the irony of his innocuous query. The groom wouldn't mindlessly repeat what the preacher told him to say. When it came to pledging love to his bride "in the name of the Father," he had to ask, "Whose father?" I think that's a very good question. Since the groom was making a vow to love his bride to the end, knowing that love didn't start with him—we love because we are loved—he needed to know the standard of love to which he would be held: the way his father loved him or the way his future father-in-law loved the daughter he was giving away that day. The way love is modeled by parents—whether good or bad—creates expectations of the way love should be.

Of course, the preacher that day was trying to get the young groom to seek a higher love. Indeed, the Anglican wedding ceremony is built on the presumption that the only way a young man can love his wife forever is by the love of God. Only God is eternal. Since God is love, then the only way mere mortals can truly love one another "till death do us part" is by the love of God. More than that, the love of God transcends death. For even if a husband loves his wife till she dies, he is free to marry another when she's gone. Death brings love to an end. But when it comes to the love of God *in Christ*, death made love eternal. Death may separate husbands and wives. But the death of Christ unites brothers and sisters forever. It's the love of the Father revealed by his Son that creates the possibility of true love for all men and women. So, when the groom asked, "Whose father? Hers or mine?" the preacher should have said, "Yes." For God is our Father, and his love lasts forever.

FEARLESS LOVE

According to John, to know true love is to know God because God is love (1 Jn 4:7). Or, to put it in negative terms, you can't know true love unless you know God. Of course, there are several ways that we know God: through creation, through Scripture, through one another. Since no one has seen God, we rely on these visible demonstrations of an invisible God to know him. When we see creation, we recognize the work of our Creator. When we listen to Scripture, we hear the Word of God. But when we love one another, we realize the *presence* of God. That's what sets the love of God apart from everything else. Creation may come from God, but God is not creation. The Scriptures may be inspired by God, but the words of God are not the Word of God. But, when it comes to love, John claims *God* is love. Love isn't something God simply gives or does. Love isn't an attribute of God, like mercy and grace.[1] According to John, God *is* love. The only way to know love is to know God. You can't have one without the other. Creation is a thing. The Bible is a thing. Love isn't a thing. Love is a person. Therefore, love is relational. That's why, when brothers and sisters love one another, John claims God abides in them (1 Jn 4:12). It's the proof that Christ believers know God, when his love is revealed in

---

[1]Constantine Campbell, *1, 2 & 3 John*, Story of God Bible Commentary (Grand Rapids, MI: Zondervan, 2017), 143.

them for one another (1 Jn 4:9). Those who don't love the church, on the other hand, don't know God (1 Jn 4:8).

Since God is love, and love is relational, then it shouldn't surprise us that God's love for us was first revealed through his only Son (1 Jn 4:9, 19). That act—God's sending his Son into the world to save us—reveals several things about God's love according to John. First, God took the initiative to love us first (1 Jn 4:10, 19). God's love wasn't given in response to our seeking a relationship with him. Rather, God made the first move, revealing his love for us through his Son—an approach that was completely backward according to first-century social standards. Typically, the lowlifes were the ones to make the first move, seeking out the higher-ups in hopes of establishing a relationship with benefits. The only way to get on the good side of the rich and powerful was to shower them with gifts. Money had to flow up before it would come back down. The poor and lowly were constantly sending gifts up the ladder in hopes that those at the top would help them one day when they really needed it. Most religions were built on the same presumption: sacrifice to the gods first, then blessings might come later. But, according to John, that's not the way our God works. He made the first move. He gave to the world. He sent his Son to save us. Because he first loved us, he expects us to return his affection by loving one another. Indeed, we know what love is and are enabled to love others because he loves us.[2]

Second, because God loved us first, it means that God established the precedent when it comes to the *way* we should love one another. The love of God isn't some abstract concept we get to define for ourselves. God has already shown us what love is through the sacrifice of his Son. God sent him into the *world* as a sacrifice for *our sin* (1 Jn 4:10). Even though the world is pictured in John's writings as a hostile place, dominated by evil powers that oppose God, "John's spirituality is 'consciously rooted in the world,'" as Stephen Smalley puts it.[3] John didn't spiritualize love—as

---

[2]Cornelis Bennema, *Mimesis in the Johannine Literature: A Study in Johannine Ethics*, Library of New Testament Studies 498 (London: Bloomsbury T&T Clark, 2017), 173-74.

[3]Stephen S. Smalley, *1, 2, 3 John*, Word Biblical Commentary (Waco, TX: Word Books, 1984), 259.

if love were just a feeling. God didn't dispose of the world, treating it like an enemy that must be destroyed. Instead, "God so loved the world that he gave his only begotten Son" (Jn 3:16). God's love is a this-worldly phenomenon. It is physical; it is incarnational. That doesn't mean that the world and God are on friendly terms. Indeed, the death of his Son reveals that the world is hostile to his purpose. But for those of us who believe in Christ, his sacrifice means the forgiveness of our sins (1 Jn 4:10). Therefore, since God loves us like this—a sacrificial love that covers a multitude of sin—we ought to love one another the same way (1 Jn 4:11). That means giving up our lives for each other in a world that is hostile to God *in order that the world might see the love of God in us* and recognize Jesus as the Savior of the world (1 Jn 4:12, 14).[4] This is how God's love is *clearly* seen—"perfected in us"—when we love one another like God loves us (1 Jn 4:12), signifying, as David Rensberger writes, "that *God's ultimate plan and desire for the world has been attained*" in us.[5] This is how we bear witness to the truth of the gospel, that God sent his Son as "Savior of the World"; it's when we love one another like Christ (1 Jn 4:14). In fact, God's love first incarnated in Christ and reincarnated in the church proves that he abides in us because the Spirit lives in us (1 Jn 4:13).

Third, the love of God in us is the *presence* of God among us for the sake of the world. The same was true of God's Son. He came into the world so that the world might know the love of God in him. Just as Christ is the incarnation of God—the very presence of God's love—so also are we who believe in Christ the embodiment of true love (1 Jn 4:16). "Just as that man is so also are we in this world" (1 Jn 4:17). When the world sees us love one another, the world sees Christ. Just as Christ is the visible presence in the world of the invisible God (Jn 14:9), so also are we who love one another.[6] Because God is in us—evident by the way we love

---

[4]So also Bennema, *Mimesis in the Johannine Literature*, 118-20.

[5]David Rensberger, "Completed Love: 1 John 4:11-18 and the Mission of the New Testament Church," *Communities in Dispute: Current Scholarship on the Johannine Epistles*, ed. R. Alan Culpepper and Paul N. Anderson (Atlanta: SBL Press, 2014), 250, emphasis original.

[6]Also Bennema: "In their mimesis of God's love, believers provide a visible, concrete expression on earth of who God is" (*Mimesis in the Johannine Literature*, 120). See also Jan G. van der Watt, "On Ethics in 1 John," in Culpepper and Anderson, *Communities in Dispute*, 209-19, where he

one another—we are the visible presence of the invisible God.[7] That's
the implication of John's argument concerning the man who claims "I
love God" but hates his brother (1 Jn 4:20). For how can a man claim to
love the invisible God (whom no one has seen) when he hates his brother
(whom everyone has seen)? Therefore, according to John, the *only* way
to love the invisible God is to love the visible brother. When the world
sees how the church loves its own, it sees the invisible God. Just like
Christ, we have been sent into the world to reveal the love of God. When
the world sees us love one another, they will see the Savior of the world
(1 Jn 4:14). According to John, then, *we* are the hope of the world in
Christ—the reincarnation of the invisible God (1 Jn 4: 15-16).

Finally, in light of this progression of divine love—from priority, by
precedence, to presence—love-one-another Christ believers should live
as if we have nothing to fear. John assumes that people are inclined to
live in fear of the judgment of God (1 Jn 4:17-18). But since we are the
very embodiment of God's love, evident by the fact that his love "has
been perfected in us," John claims that love-one-another Christ believers
should live confidently—boldly—until Judgment Day (1 Jn 4:17). In fact,
he contrasts fear and love as if they are mutually exclusive when it comes
to our relationship with God *and with one another* (1 Jn 4:16-18). You
can't claim to experience the love of God individually and corporately
while living in fear of God and each other. More than that, "perfect love
casts out fear because fear has to do with punishment" (1 Jn 4:18). That
means the love of Christ in the community should be so powerful that
fear cannot abide there. Love drives fear out the door. Therefore, the
Christian who lives in fear is not letting love do its perfect work (1 Jn
4:18). John seems to imply that those who live in fear will end up hating

---

sums up the Jesus ethic as: walk like Jesus, be righteous like Jesus, be pure as Jesus, love like Jesus,
and die like Jesus.

[7]Cornelis Bennema writes, "The presence of Jesus in the community of faith provides believers
with continued access to his example. For as believers imitate Jesus, they also mediate him. To
perform an authentic act of love that imitates Jesus *mediates* the experience of Jesus and his love
to the beneficiary." See Bennema, "Virtue Ethics and the Johannine Writings," in *Johannine Ethics:
The Moral World of the Gospel and Epistles of John*, ed. Sherri Brown and Christopher W. Skinner
(Minneapolis: Fortress, 2017), 278-79.

their brother because the love of Christ is not in them (1 Jn 4:20). Even though the love of Christ covers a multitude of sin in the community of faith, the fear of punishment will lead to hatred of one another. You may say you love your brother and sister. But, if you live in fear, you'll end up hating the very ones you're supposed to love. If you're constantly afraid of being punished by God, you won't love your brothers and sisters. Fear frustrates the love of God in the church.

TRUE LOVE

As I read Wesley Hill's *Spiritual Friendship: Finding Love in the Church as a Celibate Gay Christian*, I kept thinking to myself, *He sure has to spend a lot of time allaying the fears his readers might have about Christian friendship.* Of course, the subtitle reveals why his book might provoke fear in the hearts of his readers—not to mention that Hill contends we need to rediscover the ancient art of friendship in the church and pursue spiritually intimate relationships *outside* marriage. That produces all kinds of anxiety for an evangelical church that has sanctioned *marital* love as the only kind of intimacy that is socially acceptable within the confines of our faith. Since we want to protect the sanctity of marriage no matter what, the idea that a married man could have a spiritually intimate relationship with someone other than his wife sounds incredibly dangerous. Since our culture tends to sexualize all relationships (thanks to Freud), we are suspicious of deep friendships occurring between two people who are not married to each other. If we see friendship developing between a single man and a single woman, we think marriage is right around the corner. If a married woman is friends with another man, we wonder whether her marriage is in trouble. If two men develop a strong affection for one another, we assume they're homosexual.

Sex always enters the picture because we think sex trumps everything, even our spiritual lives. How sad is that? We're afraid the lust of the flesh is more powerful than the gift of the Spirit. Given our oversexed view of the world, would Christian men and women (married or single, opposite-sex or same-sex attracted) even dare to love one another as intimately as

Christ loves us? Or have we given up on the Spirit among us, believing that *only* married couples should share in the intimacy of Christ's love for one another? If that's the case, where does that leave single members—especially a man such as Wesley, who is attracted to other men and is committed to a celibacy because he affirms a traditional view of marriage? Can he ever know the intimacy of Christ's love with another believer? Or should he be resigned to a life of longing for something (someone?) he can never have?

Of course, married couples know their spouses don't meet all their relational needs. That's why deep and abiding friendships form outside marriage among Christ believers who are married. Those kinds of relationships seem natural to us—when couples find other couples to share life together in Christ. So, marriage affords two opportunities for intimate relationships among Christians: between spouses and between married couples. Ultimately, then, *marriage* establishes the context for meaningful relationships in the church, where individuals learn to sacrifice their wants and desires for the other—first family, then friend. More than that, marriage forges the bonds of friendship in the church.

Sadly, though, that's why those who aren't married have a harder time finding meaningful relationships among the very people who are supposed to embody the sacrificial love of Christ for one another. Wesley writes, "I talk regularly with these people: men and women who have passed the usual age for marriage and child rearing and who turn to the church, hoping to find a robust vision of committed friendship, only to encounter a looser, more casual form of social life that seems to say, *We can be friends, so long as it doesn't require too many sacrifices.*"[8] Of course, intimacy can't happen without sacrifice, which explains why there are many lonely people in our churches. We tend to sacrifice for the people who matter most to us. Since friendships are formed primarily due to marriage, it's easier to care less about those who live outside marital bonds:

---

[8]Wesley Hill, *Spiritual Friendship: Finding Love in the Church as a Celibate Gay Christian* (Grand Rapids, MI: Brazos, 2015), 14, emphasis original.

What I and others like me are yearning for isn't just a weekly night out or a circle of people with whom to go on vacation. We need something more. We need people who know what time our plane lands, who will worry about us when we don't show up at the time we said we would. We need people we can call and tell about that funny thing that happened in the hallway after class. We need the assurance that, come hell or high water, a few people will stay with us, loving us in spite of our faults and caring for us when we're down. More than that, we need people for whom *we* can care.[9]

Hill reminds us that Jesus said, "There is no greater love than this: that a man would give his life for his *friends*" (Jn 15:13). You would think, then, that a group of people who embody the love of Christ would be the best place to find that kind of friendship—no greater love than *his*, a man who was never married.

But fear bridles our love for one another. Fear of rejection. Fear of intimacy. Fear of judgment. Fear of failure. Fear of inadequacy. Fear of loneliness. It's the vulnerability required by true love that strikes the deepest fear in our hearts. (Wesley tells of how men might be afraid to embrace one another for fear that people will think they're gay.) Even though love is supposed to cover a multitude of sins, some of us are tempted to think, *I'm afraid that if Christians get to know me, they wouldn't want me in their company. I'm a far cry from what a believer is supposed to be.* Of course, the same could be said for all of us. Most of us have secret sins and past failures that, if they were made public, would damage anyone's reputation—pastors know that better than most. Several years ago, after a difficult week of dealing with all kinds of problems in the church where I was pastor (marital, financial, social, sexual, familial), I said from the pulpit one Sunday, "If you knew the people who attended this church—all of their problems—you probably wouldn't want to worship God with them." I was making a point at the time that we all do a very good job hiding from one another, projecting the "I'm okay" image that we think is required when we attend worship

---

[9]Hill, *Spiritual Friendship*, 42-43, emphasis original.

services. But who we really are is a collection of humanity who desperately needs the love of Christ. When I read a book like Wesley's, it's a stark reminder that we aren't being honest with ourselves or with one another. If we were, we wouldn't fear a celibate gay believer looking for true love—the intimate love of Christ—in church.

So what should we do? Follow the example of God's love. Don't be afraid. Take the initiative. Love your brother before he loves you. Seek out a relationship with a believer who isn't like you. Take the risk and make friends with a gay man. Help the single mom with her children. Find ways to sacrifice for someone other than your family. Don't treat people like a project. Create a safe place of trust for believers to share their struggles and then be vulnerable enough to share yours. Accept charity. Take an interest in uninteresting people. Offer common gifts of kindness to the strangers among you. Don't be afraid to love those who don't love you. Make love personal. Look into their eyes. Open your heart. See the face of Christ. Welcome them to your table.[10] Worship God together. Rely on one another for all things. Love the church more than you love yourself. Then the world will see the love of Christ *in us*. Then the world will know the presence of God *among us*. Then the world will hear the truth of the gospel *for us*. Love became a man and dwelt among us so that we could take in the glory of the only begotten, full of grace and truth, *in one another*.[11] So why should we be afraid? If God is for us, who can be against us? Since God is our Father and we are his children, it should be evident to everyone that we have been born of a *fearless* love (1 Jn 5:1-2).

If loneliness is supposed to be the casualty of divine love, why are there so many lonely people in our churches?

---

[10]Joshua W. Jipp, *Saved by Faith and Hospitality* (Grand Rapids, MI: Eerdmans, 2017), 82.
[11]Raymond E. Brown writes: "In speaking of the revelation of God's Son as an act of love, the epistolary author wants to say more than John 1:14: 'The Word became flesh and made his dwelling *among* [in] *us*.' When he says, 'God sent His Son . . . that *we may have life through him*' (4:9), he shows that part of the revelation is what happens within Christians." See Brown, *The Epistles of John*, Anchor Bible (London: Doubleday, 1982), 553, emphasis original.

THE PROBLEM WITH IDOLS

When John ends his letter with the admonition, "Little children, protect yourselves from idols" (1 Jn 5:21), it seems to come out of nowhere. Up to this point, John hasn't mentioned the threat of idolatry at all. Other enemies have been named: the devil/the evil one, the world, false prophets, antichrists, liars, and haters. But in all of John's warnings about needing to overcome their enemies, the problem of idolatry was never mentioned—until the end. Why? Was it an afterthought? "Oh, yes. One more thing. I'd better warn them about idols before I sign off. After all, that's the lesson we Jews finally learned after hundreds of years of worshiping false gods. Don't mess with idols. Idolatry only leads to immorality."[12] Yet, John doesn't warn them about the perils of idolatry (*eidōlolatreia*). It's the idol itself that poses a threat to his community.[13] So what does John mean by the term *eidōlon*?

Brown lists ten possibilities, sorting out whether John was referring literally (the image made of wood or stone) or referentially to an idol (code word for any physical object, or pagan lifestyle, or the mystery religions, or food sacrificed to idols, or the Jewish temple, or Gnostic ideology, or the secessionists, or sin, or anything that takes the place of devotion to God).[14] Yet, despite all of the possibilities—whatever John meant by the term—it makes perfect sense that he would refer to the threat of idols having just reminded his people that they know the "one true God" (1 Jn 5:20). For those who don't know the "one true God," the only alternative left to them is false gods, that is, idols.[15] Who is the "one true God" and how do we come to know him?

The answer may seem obvious. John was referring to the God of Israel, the invisible God (1 Jn 4:12, 20) who must be worshiped above all other

---

[12]A common theme in Jewish polemics against idolatry: "For the idea of making idols was the beginning of fornication, and the invention of them was the corruption of life" (Wisdom of Solomon 14:12 NRSV); see also Rom 1:21-25.

[13]Terry Griffith, *Keep Yourselves from Idols: A New Look at 1 John*, Journal for the Study of the New Testament Supplement Series 233 (Sheffield: Sheffield Academic, 2002), 57.

[14]Brown, *Epistles*, 627-29.

[15]Griffith, *Keep Yourselves from Idols*, 57.

gods and cannot be represented on earth by any visible image (Ex 20:2-6). But it's just as likely that John was referring to Jesus Christ as the "one true God" (1 Jn 5:20), especially since Jesus is not only the Son who has "given us insight that we might know the true God" but also the "one who is eternal life" (1 Jn 5:20).[16] This is something John has claimed several times before (1 Jn 1:2; 2:24; 3:24; 4:15; 5:1, 10-12): to know Christ is to know God. To be in Christ is to be in God. To have Christ is to have eternal life. John also claims the converse: to not know Christ, to not be in Christ, to not have Christ means not knowing God, not being in God, not having eternal life (1 Jn 2:23; 4:3; 5:12). Since "we know that the Son of God has come" (1 Jn 5:20), that God "sent his only begotten Son into the world" (1 Jn 4:9), whom John claims "we have seen" (1 Jn 1:2), the visible Christ is the revelation of the invisible God. Or, to use a non-Johannine term, the Son is the *icon* of the Father. Since Christ believers "are in the world just as he is" (1 Jn 4:17), that means the church is the visible revelation of the icon of the invisible God.

This may explain why John ends his letter with a warning about *eidōlon*, which derives from the root *eidō*, meaning "what is seen."[17] Since Jesus Christ is the true God—the "what-can-be-seen" of the invisible God—then all idols stand in opposition to the claims of that one-of-a-kind divine revelation. That's why John pits the icon of the invisible God against all other pretenders, *eidōla* that pose as icons of invisible deity. That would mean, of course, that those not "given the insight" (*dedōken hēmin dianoian*) that Jesus is God's Son, refusing to confess that "he is the true God and eternal life" (1 Jn 5:20), do not know "the true God" and therefore belong to a world that is filled with idols and "lies under the power of the evil one" (1 Jn 5:19). John sees things from a very Jewish perspective, a binary world of worshipers of the one true God and the idolaters. You either believe in Christ or venerate idols.[18]

---

[16]Brown, *Epistles*, 640.

[17]For an excellent survey of the meaning and background of *eidolon*, see Griffith, *Keep Yourselves from Idols*, 28-57.

[18]Griffith, *Keep Yourselves from Idols*, 204-12.

You either belong to Christ or fall under the power of the evil one. You are either in Christ or in the world. There is no middle ground with John. It's Christ versus idols, God versus the evil one, the church versus the world. That's why there are two kinds of sins: the sin that leads to death and sins that do not lead to death (1 Jn 5:16-17). Since Jews believed that idolatry led to immorality, John believed that those who refused to confess Christ were consequently consigned to a life of sin, for which there was no forgiveness because they rejected Christ—the sin unto death. Idols, then, were not only false gods designed to attract false worship. Idols pulled devotees down into the world of sin and death—co-regents of the evil one. Idols were the devil's magnet, drawing people away from the one true God. Idols populated the earth, intending to replace the icon of God. Like an army of the devil's minions, idols were taking over the world.

This is why John uses military terms to describe the Christ believers' fight against the forces of the evil one. We must *guard* (*phylaxate*) ourselves from idols—the noun (*phylax*) refers to a sentinel (1 Jn 5:21). Our faith in Christ is the *victory* (*nikē*) that conquers the world (1 Jn 5:4-5). In the midst of the battle, God's commands are not difficult to carry out (1 Jn 5:3). The devil may fill the world with idols, but our God populates the earth with his children. Since "everyone who has been born of God conquers the world" (1 Jn 5:4), we know we will overcome. Indeed, John gives several reasons why we can "have confidence" in the midst of the battle—it's based on what "we know." We know God hears us if we make requests "according to his will" (1 Jn 5:14). We know the evil one cannot touch us (1 Jn 5:18). Even though the world lies in the power of the evil one, we know that we belong to God (1 Jn 5:19). We know that God is the source of our convictions (1 Jn 5:20). Yet, despite all that we know, idols can still pose a threat to us because we are still "little children" who need to be vigilant and protect ourselves against idols (1 Jn 5:21). This is the *only* worship war that matters because *whom* we worship is a matter of life and death: "And who is the one who conquers the world if not the one who believes that Jesus is the Son of God?" (1 Jn 5:5).

Not only do believers bear witness to the one in whom we trust (the Son of God), but God has given eternal life (Jesus Christ) to us, made evident by the Spirit, who is "the witness" in us (1 Jn 5:10-11). In other words, Jesus is the gift of eternal life for those who believe, and the Spirit in us is the proof that we believe. "The one who has the Son has life and the one who doesn't have the Son of God doesn't have life" (1 Jn 5:12). Indeed, without the Son, all that nonbelievers have are dead idols.

In light of the final warning of John's letter, I wonder whether the threat of idolatry lies behind John's claim that three witnesses corroborate Jesus as God's Son: the water, the blood, and the Spirit. "This one [referring to Jesus as the Son of God; 1 Jn 5:5] is the one who came through water and blood, Jesus Christ—not by water only, but by water and blood; and the Spirit bears witness because the Spirit is truth. For the witnesses that testify are three—the Spirit and the water and the blood—and these three witnesses are in the one thing [*kai hoi treis eis to hen eisin*]" (1 Jn 5:6-8). This famous passage invites many interpretations because John's language is so vague (not to mention the notorious variant reading, known as the Johannine comma, that transformed the obscure verse into an affirmation of the doctrine of the Trinity). We have some good ideas about what he might be referring to regarding "the water and the blood," and perhaps even why he appears to emphasize the blood, but what he means by the enigmatic line "and the three are into the one thing" (a literal rendering of *kai hoi treis eis to hen eisin*) is anyone's guess.

The water and blood could refer to the ways Jesus Christ "came" as the Son of God (1 Jn 5:6): (1) through his baptism and crucifixion, (2) through his birth and death, (3) through the incarnation, or (4) through the sacraments (baptism and Communion).[19] Since John never mentions the birth of Jesus, and baptism doesn't appear as a requirement for discipleship in his Gospel, I think John is making an oblique reference either to the death of Jesus (blood and water flowing from his side) or to his

---

[19]See Brown, *Epistles*, 575-78; Campbell, *1, 2 & 3 John*, 156-58.

whole Gospel (the story of Jesus from his baptism to his death).[20] Either way, that's why John adds the Spirit as the third witness; it's the Spirit who testifies to the truth of John's Gospel (1 Jn 5:6). It's one thing to "receive the testimony of man" in a written document (1 Jn 5:9). It's quite something else to receive the "greater" testimony of God about his Son (1 Jn 5:9). As far as John was concerned, then, his Gospel wasn't just the testimony of man. His Gospel was affirmed by the Spirit as God's testimony about his Son because believers had the "witness" in them (1 Jn 5:10).[21] They heard the story in John's Gospel about how Jesus came in water and in blood. The Spirit bore witness in them to the truth of John's Gospel. Water, blood, and Spirit—they needed all three witnesses to believe the Gospel truth.

In John's Gospel we read the story of how the Word became flesh and dwelt among us, seeing with our mind's eye the visible glory of the invisible God. In John's letters we're told that if the church obeys the commandment of Christ to love one another as he has loved us, then the visible presence of the invisible God—his love—will abide among us (1 Jn 4:16).[22] That's why we don't need idols to make visible the invisible God. We have eyes to see the gospel truth incarnated in the church. But what happens when we don't love one another, when the love of Christ isn't present, when the absence of God is evident? In the vacuum of the absence of God's love, John is concerned that we will turn to idols—vacuous promises of divine presence. That's why, I think, John keeps reminding his community about the love of God, the command to love one another like Christ, the danger of claiming to love God but hating our brother, and the importance of abiding in the word they heard from John's Gospel.

---

[20]Matthew D. Jensen thinks "water and blood" refers to Jesus' resurrection since the scars of crucifixion—not only the wounds from impalement but also the spearing of Jesus' side—were offered as proof of his identity to his disciples. See Jensen, *Affirming the Resurrection of the Incarnate Christ: A Reading of 1 John*, Society of New Testament Studies Monograph Series 153 (Cambridge: Cambridge University Press, 2012), 181-83.

[21]Colin G. Kruse, *The Letters of John*, Pillar New Testament Commentary (Grand Rapids, MI: Eerdmans, 2000), 181.

[22]Much of the material in the remainder of this chapter I first shared on my blog at www.agenuine faith.blogspot.com.

Joshua Jipp writes, "This vision of place, friendship, mutuality, and service that is *embodied* in residential communities all over the world is rooted in the belief that Jesus's gift of friendship and love creates new and surprising forms of friendship between those who would otherwise be alienated from one another."[23] Indeed, if people don't find the love of Christ in the church (incarnation!), they'll look to idols—any *visible* hope of deity—that alienate them from God and from us.

If John were to write his letter to the church today, one wonders what the last line would be: "Little children, protect yourselves from _____." Since idols that were once ubiquitous in his world no longer populate our world, I wonder what John would see as the major threat to Christ believers today. Just like idols of his day, everywhere we look we would see them—a visible display of an invisible power. These "idols" would stand in opposition to our claim that Jesus is one of a kind. Christians might be susceptible to them, needing the warning to "protect yourselves." People disillusioned with the church would turn to them when they didn't see the love of Christ in us. Promoters would hold them up as paragons of divine favor. The masses would worship them. Christians would be attracted to them. The ways of the world would be empowered by them. So, what are the present-day American idols that John would be compelled to warn us about?

I think he would write, "Little children, protect yourselves from *heroes*." Our culture is obsessed with heroes: courageous men and women who risk their lives to save us from peril, mighty soldiers who protect us from hostility, brilliant geniuses who create a better world for us, and gifted artists who entertain us. We cry out for heroes. We hope for heroes. We venerate heroes. These larger-than-life superheroes are our gods. Lovers desire them. Fans adore them. Our children want to be them. Mythologies promote them—in politics, in sports, in music, and in film. The

---

[23]Jipp, *Saved by Faith and Hospitality*, 94, emphasis added. Here Jipp is referring to residential communities such as L'Arche. But I wonder whether his description of their ministry shouldn't also be the reality of the church. In other words, perhaps residential communities have something to teach us about what it means to be the embodied love of Christ.

images of our heroes are everywhere, demanding our attention. We spend a lot of time and money in our devotion to them. We build shrines to their popularity. We offer praise to their superiority. Is it any wonder, then, that hero worship is our new religion? Just listen to the masses praise them.

AMERICAN IDOL

On July 4, 2007, during our family vacation, some of us dropped into the Apple Store to check out the brand-new invention that had been released just days before: the iPhone. Dozens of people were huddled around the display table, trying to get their hands on the new device. We were waiting our turn, watching over the shoulders of customers playing with the iPhone and marveling over the miraculous (something as simple as shifting the position of the phone from vertical to horizontal to make the screen move from portrait to landscape mode was astonishing— remember?). Then, in the exuberance of collective gasps and "Oh my, look at this," a young man shouted (to no one in particular), "Steve Jobs is a god!" at which point the enthusiastic crowd offered audible affirmations of approval.

Postmortem, Steve Jobs has been enshrined as an American god— much like the caesars of old. Almost immediately after his death, as pundits recounted his accomplishments, his story began to sound more and more messianic: a fatherless boy born to a young single woman, he grew up believing he was destined to change the world. He bucked the establishment and took on the imperial domination of the computer world (and therefore, our world): Caesar IBM and its Herodian servant, Microsoft. His loyal disciples followed his every move, longing for the times he would take the stage and perform miracles (remember when he pulled the first-generation iPod Nano out of his pocket and the crowd roared with approval?). He wasn't formally educated but still spoke wisdom to this generation, challenging dogma and established religion. He garnered the devotion of the masses because he brought heaven to earth (no, he didn't heal anyone. But to the American consumer, having entertainment at your fingertips—at a reasonable cost, with very little know-how required to operate the latest, greatest device—that is heaven on earth). He even defied death. In the face of the death sentence that is pancreatic cancer, Jobs refused to fear it, modeling for everyone what it takes to live courageously to the end: listen to the inner voice (his version of the Holy Spirit?) within all of us.

Steve Jobs didn't rise from the dead. But he at least achieved immortality —if you believe what the pundits say: Jobs single-handedly changed the world (not counting all the geniuses he hired to do the work). He made our life better (without Pixar, where would the movies be today?). He will always be with us (millions carry his creation in our pockets; I'm writing this on a MacBook Pro). He has devoted followers who will carry on his work no matter what, reminding us that *at the very least* he's done something tangible, something you can hold in your hands, something you can experience with your eyes ("that's better than most messiahs," they say, "especially the Jewish one who live two thousand years ago"). The accolades will continue to ring through the halls of stardom. There's never been anyone like him. He is one of a kind. He is the perfect version of the American dream, from orphan boy to corporate wunderkind. We must worship him, for this is the kind of messiah we want, we need—one who makes our lives better and requires only a little money in return.

But John claims worship of the one true God is greater. He calls for total sacrifice, laying down our lives for one another like Christ (1 Jn 3:16). He says our devotion must amount to more than the words of our lips— that which is easily offered to heroes. Heroes soak up our adoration, but according to John we love God by loving one another in deed and truth (1 Jn 3:18). The heroes of our world fade over time; tell-all docudramas reveal that idols such as Steve Jobs were not as perfect as we made them out to be. But our God covers a multitude of our sins; the sacrifice of his Son proves it. Since he loved us like that—forgiveness!—we ought to love one another the same way (1 Jn 4:9-11).

iPhones may serve as a witness to the genius of Steve Jobs (and many of us gaze on them as if they were idols). But sooner than later, time will make them obsolete. On the other hand, there are three witnesses to the eternal work of God's Son, and their testimony will last forever because we have the gift of eternal life abiding in us (1 Jn 5:6-12). Impulsively, we may idolize the heroes of our world—whenever a celebrity is spotted, we whip out our iPhones to record their brief presence (or, even better, try to snap a selfie with the image of our god in the frame). But Christ believers worship a God whose presence cannot be captured by a camera. Idols are attractively present. Jesus Christ is illusively veiled. Heroes are easily worshiped. The Son of God compels our devoted sacrifice. We wouldn't have it any other way. This is our conviction from God (1 Jn 5:20). Put your phones down. Pick up the Word of God. For this is what we know: the one true God is our Father, Jesus Christ is his Son, and we are his children—born not by the will of man or by the will of flesh, but by his Spirit. Our love for one another proves that we have turned from idols to serve a living and true God.

There is no greater love than his. His word is our koinonia. This is how we abide *together*. Idols were not there in the beginning. The devil has been a liar from the beginning. But we know what has been true from the beginning: Jesus is the Christ, the Son of God—the Alpha and the Omega. Because we abide in his Word, the one who is eternal life abides in us.

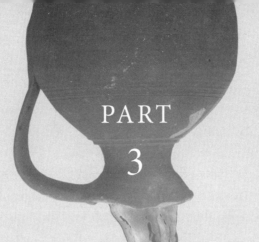

PART
3

JOHN'S REVELATION

*Remaining in the Word Until
the End of the World*

AT THE BEGINNING OF HIS FIRST LETTER, John makes the claim that his words about Jesus are foundational to the church's faith because he not only heard the Word of life but *saw* the Word *on earth*. Therefore, the only way his "children" will be able to abide in the Word of life is to abide by his words about the Word incarnate. For him, the incarnation of the Word of life was the beginning and ending (Alpha and Omega) of faith—the Word of God heard and seen, vouchsafed by John's words that become incarnated in those who abide in Gospel words.

But how do we remain in the Word when the visible world is a counterwitness to the words we inhabit? It's one thing to hear words and perhaps even obey words, but how do we go about "taking up residence" in words (Christ has overcome the world) when the world we see defies the words we hear? That's why John needed to hear the Word again, this time seeing Christ *in heaven*, coming to earth to defeat the enemies of God and conquer the world—a revelation that inspires those who have ears to hear and eyes to see the kingdom come.

According to John's Revelation, the purpose of the church is to bear witness to Christ until he comes. Only those who abide in the Word reveal the light of Christ. There is no other testimony to the truth. In fact, John's evangelistic strategy is based on the singularity of the Word incarnated in the church. The disciples' witness to Christ as the Lamb of God—a living sacrifice on earth—is embodied in the church. As a result, since we "follow the Lamb wherever he goes," giving our lives for Christ as he gave his life for us, disciples bear witness to two realities at once: the world is passing away, and we have eternal life. Therefore, we are the final revelation of the end of the world in Christ. When Christ returns and heaven invades the earth, it will be all over. Until then we hear, confess, incarnate, and abide in the Word.

9

CALL TO WORSHIP

Hearing the Word

CHILDREN ARE OFTEN ENCOURAGED to draw pictures to help them deal with death and devastation. As they lack the words to describe their emotions, crayons and paper enable little artists to say what's on their minds. Whether picturing the death of a parent, the aftermath of destructive hurricanes and tornadoes, or the painful suffering that comes with fighting a terminal illness, drawings not only give us a window into their world of how bad it hurts but also provide an outlet for expressing their unspeakable grief. Oftentimes, the pictures are hard to look at: deathly images in dark hues, scribbled lines of chaos and violence, angry faces, monstrous creatures, ominous skies, ghastly specters. The child may go about their task without any emotion, drawing their picture almost nonchalantly—without a care in the world—stubby fingers gently cradling their crayons, eyes focused briefly on their work, their angelic face showing no signs of anguish. But when they're finished, it's hard to reconcile the art and the artist. "Such a sweet little girl drew that?" Adults in the room might be tempted to gently correct the child: "Oh sweetie! Things aren't that bad, are they?" But the experts know: things may look calm on the outside, the child quickly moving on to other things, happily playing with their toys, but the picture they drew tells the true story of what is unseen. Those who have eyes to see understand: things are not as they appear. Something deeper is going on inside the visible world.

After John saw God's picture of the end of the world, I wonder
whether he thought to himself, *I had no idea it was that bad.* Or did the
ghoulish visions and night terrors confirm what he already knew to be
true? Rome's pretentious claim of ruling the world by providing peace
and safety was a lie, especially for a prisoner exiled on Patmos "because
of the word of God and the witness of Jesus" (Rev 1:9). Of course, once
John wrote everything down and sent it to the seven churches, the
question remained as to whether Christ believers would make sense of
what he saw. Were Christians so embedded in the Roman way of life
that John's visions would appear completely foreign to them—the bizarre hallucinations of a crazed prophet? Or would they receive the
Revelation in the same manner in which it was given to the seer: a word
from God about Jesus Christ, through a messenger, to the church, not
only about the end of the world but also their place in it (Rev 1:1-2)?
Would they understand the hidden message of the mysterious Apocalypse? Or would they dismiss John's story of lambs and dragons, angels
and beasts, scrolls and bowls, heaven and hell as nothing more than the
whimsical tales of fantasy? Did John see the real world as it really is,
pulling back the veil to reveal the power behind the throne—both in
heaven and on the earth—something that takes eyes of faith to see? Or
was John simply pulling the wool over our eyes, making believe that a
slaughtered lamb could defeat both Leviathan and Behemoth? Is this
happening now? Or are we peering into the future? Since the unveiling
comes to us in such veiled language, how could anyone tell the difference between prophecy and fiction? Is this the word of God or the
fantasy of a man?

According to John, the only way to see it is to hear it read to you (Rev
1:3). The time to hear it is on the Lord's Day—just like he did (Rev 1:10).
It's no coincidence that John received these visions on Sunday. For when
the church gathers to worship the enthroned Creator and the roaring
Lamb, we discover that, because we have ears to hear God's Word when
it is read to us, we can see what he's doing in *his* creation. Indeed, for John
and for us, worship changes the way we see the visible world.

"On Earth as It Is in Heaven"

The end of the world begins with a book.[1] The first beatitude promises a blessing to the lector and those who gather to hear the "words of the prophecy and keep them" (Rev 1:3). The first thing Christ says to the seer is, "Write in a book what you see and send it to the seven churches" (Rev 1:11), repeating the command after the Christophany (Rev 1:19). Christ commands John to "write" a special message to every church (Rev 2:1, 8, 12, 18; 3:1, 7, 14). Christ repeatedly warns each congregation that they had better listen to what they hear when the book is read to them (Rev 2:7, 11, 17, 29; 3:6, 13, 22). Furthermore, books play a crucial role in the unfolding drama of the Apocalypse. Christ warns the church at Sardis that those who fail to "overcome" risk having their names erased from the book of life (Rev 3:5). While sitting on his throne, God holds a book in his hand that must be unsealed before its contents can be read (Rev 5:1). The only one worthy to open the book is the Lamb (Rev 5:2-5). When the Lamb takes the book from God, it causes the heavenly host to worship God and the Lamb (Rev 5:7-14). The unsealing of the book triggers the judgment of God on earth (Rev 6:1, 3, 5, 7, 9, 12; 8:1). When a strong angel comes from heaven to stand on earth, holding an open book in its hand, the seer is told by a heavenly voice to take the book from the angel, who then feeds it to John (Rev 10:1-11). Those who worship Leviathan prove that their names were not written in the Lamb's book of life (Rev 13:8; 17:8). The dead will be judged by deeds recorded in books, and those whose names are not recorded in the book of life will be cast into the lake of fire (Rev 20:12-14). Those whose names are recorded in the Lamb's book of life enter the new Jerusalem (Rev 21:27).

Finally, the Revelation ends with a flurry of references to the importance of the book: a beatitude and angelic warning to keep the words of the book, a directive not to seal up the book, and a warning to those who hear the book read to them not to add or omit any words of the book (Rev 22:7, 9, 10, 18-19). Even when John sees heaven split apart, he com-

---

[1] Of course, the word translated "book," *biblion* (from which we get the word *Bible*), referred to a scroll in John's day.

pares it to "a book being rolled up" (Rev 6:14), something his hearers would have seen often during worship services.[2] Quite obviously, then, the Revelation of Jesus Christ to John for the churches about the end of the world depended on books written, read, heard, digested, and kept.

For a world that was predominately illiterate, having to depend on books to be faithful to God must have been incredibly intimidating. Those who couldn't read would not only need to rely on a literate member of their church to read John's Revelation to them, but they would have had to develop an auditory acuity to take in the strange world of the Apocalypse. Can you imagine hearing the Revelation of John for the first time? You're accustomed to gathering with other believers to hear Gospel stories about Jesus Christ and letters sent by John. Then there's word that another book has been written by "John," sent specifically to seven churches in Asia Minor. As the Apocalypse makes the rounds (did the Ephesians make a copy and send it on to the next congregation?), word spreads that your church is one of the named recipients. When it finally arrives, you gather expectantly on the Lord's Day to hear the new book. The reader has spent several days rehearsing, working through the manuscript to make sure he has all the line breaks memorized. (Early Greek manuscripts were written in continuous script, all capital letters, no punctuation, words crammed together without any space between them, no proper line breaks. No matter how gifted an orator, no reader would be able to pick up a manuscript cold and start reading. It would have taken a lot of time to prepare to read a lengthy work like the Apocalypse—not counting all the necessary preparation to interpret all the bizarre imagery with the right tone.)

Once the reading begins, you hear the blessing sent to you and the lector—a comforting word. But soon you are confused by what you're hearing. Even though it starts out sounding like a letter, all of the sudden the reader recounts strange visions of the seer. When the reader gets to the part where the one "like the Son of Man" addresses your congregation

---

[2]Brian J. Wright, *Communal Reading in the Time of Jesus: A Window into Early Christian Reading Practices* (Minneapolis: Fortress, 2017), 198.

directly, you try to soak up every word. The orator keeps repeating the refrain, "He who has an ear, let him hear what the Spirit is saying to the churches," and you can't tell whether it's a threat or a word of encouragement. As you puzzle over the meaning of these oracles of Christ— filled with warnings and promises of blessing—the reader doesn't give you time to think about it, moving on to even more bizarre and strange images of books and seals, horsemen and locusts, dragons and beasts, trumpets and bowls, death and destruction, judgment and reward. When it's finally over (possibly taking as long as two and a half hours to read the entire Apocalypse in one sitting), with so many thoughts swirling through your head, you walk away from the meeting wondering, "What was that? A comedy or a tragedy?"[3]

It would have taken a lot of imagination to hear the Apocalypse. Those accustomed to plain talk when receiving instruction about how to be a disciple of Jesus would have been so confused. John's strange work probably provoked much discussion, requiring more meetings to hear the Revelation again and again to sort out the meaning of the message. At first, the congregants may have focused on the first part—the Christophany and the letter to the seven churches. Having dirty laundry of other churches aired for all to see, some congregations were probably angry: "What good does it do to send one letter to all seven churches? If John wanted to send a letter to us, fine. But to send a circular letter for the whole world to see? That's not honorable." Some cities may have found solace by comparison: "Well, at least we're not as bad as Thyatira." Other believers may have despaired over the gloomy picture of the churches in their region: "I had no idea we were that bad." But the more they heard the Revelation, the more they would have made the connection: as Richard Bauckham points out, "The domestic problems within the churches in part parallel Revelation's depiction of the world

---

[3]The Greek text of the Apocalypse is around 10,250 words, reading at sixty to seventy words per minute with no breaks. James L. Resseguie thinks the Apocalypse follows a comedic plot (U-shaped), where things start out well, quickly fall apart, then recover in the end (the inverse of tragedy). See Resseguie, *The Revelation of John: A Narrative Commentary* (Grand Rapids, MI: Baker Academic, 2009), 45-47.

ruled by the devil and the beasts."[4] In other words, several churches seemed to have more in common with Babylon than the new Jerusalem. That should have been especially discouraging to the churches who knew they were supposed to be an alternate reality, a counterwitness to the way things are in the world.[5]

The problems in the churches were not new. Some of these same issues show up in the letters of Paul: false apostles, false teaching, eating meat offered to idols, immorality, persecution, Christ coming like a thief. Paul tackles all of these issues, trying to get his converts to see why they are wrong and he is right—sometimes by "the word of the Lord" (1 Thess 4:15), other times by offering advice based on his own opinion (1 Cor 7:12). But John makes it plain that he was nothing more than a secretary taking dictation: from Christ's mouth, to the seer's ears, to the page, to the eyes of the reader, to the ears of the churches. This couldn't be dismissed as one man's opinion. These were the very words of Christ written in a book and read to the seven churches.

While some of Paul's converts ridiculed the apostle's pretense of sending such "weighty" letters (2 Cor 10:10), the seven churches would have heard the authoritative voice of Christ speaking *directly* to them: "*I know* your works . . . *I know* your poverty . . . *I know* where you live" (Rev 2:2, 9, 13, 19; 3:1, 8, 15).[6] When certain rebels were called out as false teachers and false prophets, everyone heard *Christ* give them the nicknames Balaam and Jezebel (Rev 2:14, 20). One wonders if the monikers stuck. The next time a false prophet opened his mouth in Pergamum, someone from the congregation might have shouted: "Hey, Balaam. Why don't you sit down and shut up?" Indeed, Christ put the onus on members

---

[4]Richard Bauckham, *The Theology of the Book of Revelation* (Cambridge: Cambridge University Press, 1993), 123.

[5]Steven Friesen writes, "John considered the churches to be an alternate sovereignty, a polity resisting the imperialism of his time. It was not a choice between religion or politics; it was a choice between legitimate and illicit authority." See Friesen, *Imperial Cults and the Apocalypse of John: Reading Revelation in the Ruins* (Oxford: Oxford University Press, 2001), 181.

[6]David A. deSilva writes, "Christ's position in the worldview shared by John and the congregations allows him indeed to command, whereas John, even if a respected leader, could only come alongside to persuade." See deSilva, *Seeing Things John's Way: The Rhetoric of the Book of Revelation* (Louisville, KY: Westminster John Knox, 2009), 179.

to police themselves. Rather than give instructions to overseers and elders to straighten out congregational problems, the seven churches heard Christ challenge every member to "overcome" their deficiencies to receive their reward (Rev 2:7, 11, 17, 26; 3:5, 12, 21).

Even though different churches had different challenges to overcome, every member from every church was summoned to have "ears to hear what the Spirit says to [all] the churches." That's because the problems in one congregation threatened the witness of the whole church. Ephesus and Sardis were no longer doing the deeds they did at first (Rev 2:5; 3:2). Smyrna and Philadelphia faced persecution from the "synagogue of Satan" (Rev 2:9-10; 3:8-9). Pergamum and Thyatira were dealing with false teachers and false prophets (Rev 2:14-15, 20-24). Laodicea boasted in its wealth (Rev 3:17). All of these threats put the reward of every member in jeopardy. Five times Christ warns the churches to repent: of dereliction (Rev 2:5; 3:2-3), of eating idol meat and immorality (Rev 2:14, 20-21), and of opulence (Rev 3:17-19). Two times Christ encourages the churches to be faithful in the midst of persecution (Rev 2:10; 3:11). How every member responded to these challenges determined whether they would be rewarded by Christ: those who overcome dereliction will eat of the tree of life in paradise and will walk with Christ in white garments, and their names will remain in the book of life (Rev 2:7; 3:4-5); those who abstain from eating idol meat and immorality will receive hidden manna, a white stone with a new name written on it, authority to rule over the nations, and the morning star (Rev 2:17, 26-28); those who overcome tribulation will be given a crown of life, will not be hurt by the second death, and will become a pillar in God's temple that has the name of God inscribed on it (Rev 2:10; 3:11-12); and those who give up the riches of the world for the riches of Christ will sit down with Christ on his throne (Rev 3:18-21).

On the other hand, those who refuse to repent will face the judgment of Christ: he will remove their lampstand (Rev 2:5); he will make war against them with the sword of his mouth (Rev 2:16); he will persecute them and kill their children (Rev 2:22-23); he will come like a thief

(Rev 3:3); and he will spit them out of his mouth (Rev 3:16). Just as Christ warned the church in Thyatira (the faithful and the unrepentant), both rewards and punishments will be *earned:* "I will give to each one of you according to your works" (Rev 2:23). Furthermore, *Christ* will be the one to hand out rewards and inflict punishment. Indeed, for Christ the life of the church is *personal.* He is the one who must take care of the matter before it's too late. It's why he sent them a letter. Things were not the way they were supposed to be. The church on earth was not reflecting its heavenly vision.

If all we had were the first three chapters of the Apocalypse—if that's all John saw on the Lord's Day—some might give up hope that the church will ever be what we're supposed to be. Has anything changed over two thousand years? John's picture of the church back then looks a lot like the church today. We seem to suffer from the same challenges: some of us are being persecuted, martyred for faith in Christ; some of us have lost our first love, a church dead in tradition; some of us are plagued by false teaching, where idolatry has led to immorality; and those of us who live in the land of plenty, well, we live as if we don't need Christ at all. Consequently, we might be tempted to subscribe to some sort of fatalism, claiming that the apocalyptic picture of the church in John's Revelation is timeless: the church as it was, is, and ever shall be. It may seem like these problems will never go away. After two thousand years, one wonders whether we have ears to hear what the Spirit is saying to the church today. We hear what Christ said. Why don't we do what he commands? What will it take for the church to overcome the world? Will the church on earth ever live up to heaven's purpose? When will we have ears to hear?

WHEN WE HAVE EYES TO SEE

That's the significance of the order of the Christophany: in this case, vision comes before audition. The *first* thing John sees is the seven golden lampstands in heaven, and then he hears Christ say these lampstands are the seven churches. John sees Christ reigning in heaven and then hears Christ dictate the letter. This is crucial—for John and for us. The seer saw

the seven churches reign with Christ in glory, lighting up heaven. Then
John heard Christ tell them how to light up the world, reigning as priests
on earth. That's what the seven churches would have experienced as well.
Having heard the Apocalypse read to them, they would first envision
themselves reigning in heaven with Christ. Then they would hear what it
would take for them to reign on earth as a kingdom of priests—the very
thing we were made for (Rev 1:6). What was true for John and the seven
churches is still true for us today. We won't have ears to hear what the
Spirit is saying until we have eyes to see the church reigning with Christ—
on earth as it is in heaven. From the very beginning of the Apocalypse—
no matter how tattered and abused and confused we may be—we are
confronted with the vision that the church reigns with Christ in heaven.
That should be enough to encourage us to obey our King on earth, especially when we take in the startling vision of the apocalyptic Christ.

Even though the lampstands were the first thing John saw (Rev 1:12), it
was the vision of Christ that captivated him—and with good reason. This
is not the way any of us would have pictured a heavenly version of Christ.[7]
In fact, when I think about how I imagine the resurrected Christ in
heaven, the image I have in my head comes closer to the way the Gospel
writers describe Jesus' appearance during the transfiguration: a human
figure glowing with resurrection glory. Sure enough, at first the seer seems
to give a similar description: "one like a son of man, wearing a robe" and
shining brightly (Rev 1:13). But as John shifts his focus from what Christ
is wearing and begins to describe his physical features, that's when the
Christophanic revelation turns dreadful (Rev 1:14-16). Fire shooting out
of his eyes. A sword for a tongue. Thunderous voice. The power to hold
seven stars in his right hand. A face so bright you couldn't look at it
without burning your retinas. No wonder the seer fell down like a dead
man (Rev 1:17). Christ scared him to death—a far cry from the man who
appeared on the Galilean shore, made breakfast for worn-out fishermen,

---

[7]See our chapter on the apocalyptic Jesus in David B. Capes, Rodney Reeves, and E. Randolph
Richards, *Rediscovering Jesus: An Introduction to Biblical, Religious and Cultural Perspectives on
Christ* (Downers Grove, IL: IVP Academic, 2015), 139-52.

and gently scolded Simon Peter for denying him (Jn 21:1-17). Rather than
dreams of heaven, the apocalyptic Jesus would more likely show up in our
worst nightmares, even haunting us after we wake up, making us puzzle
over why Jesus would come to us like that. *He looked angry. Why did he
have to scare me like that? I thought we were on good terms.*

I wonder whether that's the impression the apocalyptic Christ would
have made on those gathered to hear John's Revelation on the Lord's Day.
This was no feel-good service. Seeing Christ like that—appearing as the
legendary Son of Man during his coronation by the Ancient of Days
(Dan 7:9-14)—must have sent shivers through the crowd as they listened
to the apocalyptic Christ's thunderous warnings. This was more than a
sermon. Christ told John to "write this down," a book they would need
to hear again and again. The more they heard the book, the more they
would have recognized that overcoming the challenges they faced was
predicated on who Christ is.[8] That is to say, the Christophany revealed
the Christ they needed to see in heaven in order to live victoriously on
earth. To the church in Ephesus, he's the one who holds seven stars in his
right hand and walks among the seven golden lampstands—powerful
and yet intimately involved in their lives (Rev 2:2). He not only knows
their deeds, but he knows matters of the heart—good reasons to repent.
To the church in Smyrna, he's the first and the last, the one who was dead
and came back to life—a comforting reality for those facing martyrdom
(Rev 2:8, 10). For the churches of Pergamum and Thyatira, where false
teachers and false prophets are finding followers, Christ has a sword for
a tongue as well as eyes and feet on fire (Rev 2:12, 18). Appearing like the
Son of Man who frightened Daniel to death (Dan 10:5-8), Christ will
defeat his enemies with his words. To the weak church in Sardis, he's the
powerful Lord who holds stars in his hand (Rev 3:1). For the church in
Philadelphia, Christ holds the key that opens the door of their faithful
witness (Rev 3:7-8). And to the church in Laodicea, Christ is the last
word ("Amen") because he is the origin of all creation (Rev 3:14)—a

---

[8]David E. Aune, *Revelation 1–5*, Word Biblical Commentary (Dallas: Word Books, 1997), 121.

sobering thought for these wealthy Christians when Christ comes like a stranger knocking at their door, looking for hospitality (Rev 3:20). Will they recognize his voice and open the door?

The message to the churches is unmistakable: to reign on earth as they do in heaven, these seven churches needed to see their weaknesses in light of Christ's strength, their war against the world as the result of Christ's victory. The only way they could see it was to gather together to worship God, having ears to hear the Revelation of John *one more time.*

WORTHY TO OPEN GOD'S BOOK

The Romans thought the royal pageantry required by Eastern kings made them look like wimps. All of the accessories kings relied on to prove that they ruled the world were contemptible to the Romans: jeweled crowns, lavish thrones, shiny robes, and sparkling jewelry. Plutarch ridiculed Mark Antony for dressing up his sons like Eastern kings in Egypt, claiming he "incurred people's hatred for the provisions he made for his children in Alexandria, which seemed to be theatrical, overdone, and anti-Roman."[9] Mark Antony not only presented them with lavish thrones, making them wear jeweled crowns and flowing robes, but proclaimed them "king of kings"—a derogatory term for Roman rulers. The glory of Roman rule was to be preserved by the Senate, not by a succession of kings of royal pedigree. Power should be claimed, not inherited. When the republic evolved into an empire and senators accused the emperor of trying to establish a monarchy, Caesar deflected their accusation by emphasizing how he refused the title *king.* To be sure, Rome allowed compliant Eastern kings who ruled as clients of the empire to keep all the trappings of royalty, sitting on their thrones with crowns on their heads. But everyone knew Rome was the power behind the throne. Even though imperial provinces at times would welcome Caesar as their king (with all the pomp and circumstance associated with royalty), emperors usually avoided appearing

---

[9]Plutarch, *Antony* 54, in *Roman Lives: A Selection of Eight Lives*, trans. R. Waterfield and P. A. Stadter (Oxford: Oxford University Press, 1999), 406.

like monarchs.[10] Imperial rulers never wore jeweled crowns. Roman gov-
ernors sat on backless chairs, not thrones (to the Romans, chairs with
curved backs were for women).[11] Indeed, by the first century, the glamour
of Eastern kings in many provinces was eventually replaced by the drab,
businesslike duties of Roman procurators (at times dressed like soldiers)
who reminded imperial subjects of the undeniable power of Roman
justice every time they rendered a verdict based on Roman law.[12]

When John was transported to heaven, he saw God sitting on a throne,
ruling all creation like one of the antiquated Eastern kings (Rev 4:1-3).
Thrones were once the quintessential symbol of power in the Mediterranean world. A king's throne was his earthly claim to a heavenly power,
a lavishly decorated version of the chairs found in the homes of the
wealthy. Nearly all chairs were made of local or imported wood. The seats,
backs, and armrests of chairs were decorated with ivory, gold, silver,
copper, or bronze inlay. The ends of the armrests were often shaped like
heads of lions and bulls, giving the appearance that the enthroned king
was stroking the heads of these great beasts as if they were his pets.
Carved into the backs of the chairs would be depictions of the royal
family or national symbols (winged griffins, lions, sphinxes, flowers, ro-
settes). High-backed chairs originated in Egypt and were often decorated
with gems, semiprecious stones, faience, and colored glass.[13] Throughout
the ancient Near East, legs of chairs were carved to look like animal legs
(bulls, lions, gazelles), sometimes made of hippopotamus ivory, accented
with gold and silver gilding.[14] The Romans, however, tended to prefer

---

[10]Plutarch rakes Mark Anthony over the coals for enjoying royal honors given to him by the
Ephesians when they welcomed him to town (*Antony* 24).

[11]Ann Killebrew, "Furniture and Furnishings: Hellenistic, Roman, and Byzantine Periods," in *The
Oxford Encyclopedia of Archaeology in the Near East*, ed. Eric M. Meyers (New York: Oxford
University Press, 1997), 2:358-59.

[12]Chester G. Starr, *Civilization and the Caesars: The Intellectual Revolution in the Roman Empire*
(New York: Norton, 1965), 58-61. Emperors preferred monuments, statues, and arches as symbols of their authority.

[13]Geoffrey Killen, "Furniture," in *The Oxford Encyclopedia of Ancient Egypt*, ed. Donald B. Redford
(Oxford: Oxford University Press, 2001), 1:583.

[14]Harold A. Liebowitz, "Furniture and Furnishings," in Meyers, *Oxford Encyclopedia of Archaeology*, 2:353.

chair legs that were either turned on a lathe or were rectangular in shape (less ostentatious?). Sometimes human figurines (royal attendants and subjected peoples) were carved into the side of the throne, placed under the armrests, or etched beneath the seat of the throne. Many kings also used footstools, designed and decorated in similar style to the throne, with miniature human figures carved into the side. The symbolism was obvious: the king rules over all subjects, creatures, and lands of his kingdom, and his enemies are his footstool.

Even though John never gives a description of the throne of God, what he saw surrounding the throne matches the distinctive features of the thrones of Eastern kings: dazzling jewels, precious stones, colored glass, bulls, lions, winged creatures, and royal attendants (Rev 4:1–5:6). To a prisoner of Rome exiled on the island of Patmos, seeing God seated on a throne like one of the great kings of old must have appeared counter-imperial. Rome may have claimed sovereign control over the world at that time, but John saw all heaven worship God as the *pantokrator*: worthy of worship because he created all things (Rev 4:11)—even the earth dominated by Roman rulers.

But such a vision presented a problem. If God ruled all creation as a great king sitting on his throne in heaven, why didn't he do something about the wicked Roman Empire on earth? Many times before, the God of Israel had been pictured as a king, ready to execute his will on earth as it is in heaven (Is 6:1-13; Ezek 1:4–3:15). In fact, that's the first image of God we see in the Scriptures. In Genesis 1, God acts like a king when he creates the world by issuing his divine decree: let there be light, and it was so. If God created all things through the power of his word, first-century hearers of John's Revelation may have wondered: Why doesn't he speak the word, bringing judgment against his enemies on earth? Is John's vision supposed to be taken as an ironic picture of God, making the Almighty appear like an ancient Eastern king who seems out of touch with the current realities of a world run by the Romans—a ruler more interested in holding onto the trappings of royalty than directly challenging Roman power (ironically, this king will subvert the empire via sacrifice)? Or is John's vision more about setting up the next scene (Rev 5:1), where God sits on his heavenly throne holding in his hand a divine decree for all the peoples of the earth, waiting for someone who is worthy to execute his will on earth as it is in heaven—the Almighty has a plan? Perhaps it's both.

When the strong angel asks, "Who is worthy to open the book?" (Rev 5:2), we might think the answer is obvious. Who is worthy? God is worthy. He's the King. He should open the book. But throne-room scenes in the Hebrew Scriptures often included the commissioning of an agent of God to carry out his will on earth. When Isaiah saw God reigning as King, he heard the Almighty ask, "Whom shall I send, and who will go for Us?" (Is 6:8). Having seen God's throne, Ezekiel fell on his face and heard God say, "Son of man, stand on your feet that I may speak with you! . . . I am sending you to the sons of Israel" (Ezek 2:1, 3). The reason has to do with the covenant God made with Adam and Eve. Made in his image, humanity was appointed by the Creator to rule the earth (Gen 1:26-28). As co-regents of God, then, humans reflect his image when we fulfill his purpose for all creation: flourishing and ruling. Kings rule the earth by divine design; they are accountable to God for their power. Therefore, it came as no surprise to John that the strong angel would have vetted any would-be agent of God with the question: "Who is worthy to open the book?" It's what God does. Come before his throne and you'll hear the commissioning question, "Who will do my will?"

The seer must have known he didn't qualify. He doesn't respond like Isaiah: "Here I am. Send me." Instead, John waits for another co-regent of God to step forward, the one prepared to do God's will on earth. Yet, this time, surprisingly, "No one was able in heaven or on the earth or under the earth to open the book and read it" (Rev 5:3). The issue was more than a question of literacy: "Who can read?" It was a question of power: "Who can break the seals?"—not to mention the fact that the worthy one had to be strong enough to take the book from God's right hand. For, when the time comes, it is significant that the King doesn't *give* the book to his co-regent; the one who is worthy has to *take* it from God (Rev 5:7).

It must have seemed like a hopeless situation: God sitting on his throne, his royal decree—God's will—in his right hand, and no one worthy to carry out his divine purpose on earth. That would mean, of course, that Rome would continue to rule the earth unchecked. Evil would persist without opposition. The righteous would have to suffer, knowing that things would never get better on earth. No help. No hope. No justice. That's why the seer wept (Rev 5:4). With no chance of good overcoming evil, what else was there to do but cry your eyes out in despair? How could the Almighty Creator, sitting up there on his throne in heaven, allow such evil and suffering on the earth of his creation? Is it enough for the Creator of all things to be worshiped only in heaven? Shouldn't he be worthy of worship on earth as well? What would it take for *that* to happen? What will God do to prove he's still worthy of worship on earth as he is in heaven? Well, according to the vision, it's not just what God will do. It's what God has already done that joins heaven and earth to worship the one who sits on the throne. There is no reason to weep because the Lion has *already overcome* the world as the slaughtered Lamb: that's why he's worthy to open the book (Rev 5:5).

Throughout the Apocalypse, hearing and seeing often don't match up.[15] Ten times, John hears one thing then sees something else. He hears a trumpet voice and turns to see seven golden lampstands (Rev 1:10, 12). He is told he will see the future but then witnesses the timeless worship of the one who sits on the throne (Rev 4:1-11). He hears the Lion of Judah is worthy to open the sealed scroll but then sees a slaughtered Lamb seize the scroll (Rev 5:5-6). John hears the census of Israel going to war—144,000 from twelve tribes—but then sees a countless multitude of martyrs from every nation worshiping God and the Lamb (Rev 7:4, 9-17). The seer hears the angel with the sixth trumpet order the release of four angels bound at the Euphrates River but then sees an army of two hundred million horsemen kill a third of humankind (Rev 9:14-19). In Revelation 14:13, he hears the beatitude, "Blessed are the dead who die in the Lord," then sees

---

[15]See Resseguie, *Revelation of John*, 52-53.

a sharp sickle harvesting grain and wine for divine judgment. In Revelation 16:15, he hears Christ's warning, "Behold, I am coming like a thief," then sees the enemies of God knowingly gather for war at Har-Magedon. John is told he will be shown a harlot who sits on many waters but then sees a queen riding on a beast into the desert (Rev 17:1-5). In Revelation 19:9, he hears the invitation, "Blessed are those who are invited to the marriage supper of the Lamb," but then sees vultures eating human flesh. Finally, John is told he will see the bride of the Lamb but then sees a jeweled city—a new Jerusalem—falling from heaven to earth (Rev 21:9-11).

Outsiders would be perplexed by these contradictions. How can a Lion be a Lamb? But, for those who have ears to hear the Revelation, the juxtaposition of audition and vision would have been both affirming and subversive. The rhetorical strategy would have been apparent: John must interpret what he hears by what he sees—a contrast built on irony.

Irony can be used as a weapon as well as a source of appeal. The rhetorical effect reveals the difference. Insiders relish ironies because they exploit the ignorance of their enemies while sharpening the focus of their group identity. In fact, the ironist depends on a common sociology of knowledge whereby stock images and local symbols are reinterpreted by the group's ideology. Revelation makes heavy use of the Hebrew Scriptures, Jewish and Roman symbols, and common mythologies, reinterpreting them in light of the vision. For example, when the seer hears the trumpet of God on the Lord's Day, shouldn't he expect to see the parousia (especially when the first vision is set up by the expanded quotation of Dan 7:13, "Behold, he is coming with the clouds, and every eye will see him, even those who pierced him," Rev 1:7)? When John hears that the Lion of Judah is worthy to open the scroll, shouldn't he expect to see the Messiah sitting at the right hand of God?

But then again, insiders know why the ironic imagery makes sense—how seven candlesticks reigning with Christ reveal the end of the world, or why a slaughtered Lamb is the Lion of Judah, the destined co-regent of God.[16]

---

[16]What Leonard L. Thompson calls "kerygmatic irony." See Thompson, *The Book of Revelation: Apocalypse and Empire* (New York: Oxford University Press, 1990), 189-91.

What we believe deconstructs the pretense of the world ("you may think it takes a Lion to destroy evil") and reveals the work of God that can only be seen with eyes of faith ("the slaughtered Lamb has overcome all enemies of God, and we shall reign with him forever"). All of this happens on the Lord's Day, when the people of God hear the word so that they can see the kingdom. Indeed, by inviting the seven churches to hear the audition in order to see the vision of God's reign—all in the context of Christian worship—the seer challenges the world as it appears with the world as it really is since God is King.[17] When we worship the one true God—"true knowledge of who God is is inseparable from worship of God," as Bauckham says—we see the truth about God, the Lamb, ourselves, and the world.[18]

After John is told to stop crying because the Lion of Judah has overcome to open the scroll (Rev 5:5), he sees appearing in the middle of the throne—perhaps like a family figure carved in the back of the chair—a Lamb standing as slain, having seven horns and seven eyes. God does not hand the scroll to the Lamb. Instead, the Lion/Lamb takes it from the right hand of God, which causes the heavenly council to fall down in abject submission, singing a new song to the slain Lamb and the one who sits on the throne. The song not only reveals why the Lamb is worthy to open the book—what he has already done ("because you were slaughtered and purchased for God with your blood from every tribe and language and people and nation," Rev 5:9)—but also what his purchased slaves are redeemed to be: "a kingdom and priesthood to our God, and they shall reign on the earth" (Rev 5:10). What the slaughtered Lamb *has done* reveals what *will be*. This is the content of our worship; this is what believers sing about. When we offer songs about Christ (who he is and what he has done), we're also singing about ourselves—what we are meant to be. His lordship reveals our discipleship. His kingdom is our

---

[17]"On earth the powers of evil challenge God's role and even masquerade as the ultimate power over all things, claiming divinity. But heaven is the sphere of ultimate reality: what is true in heaven must become true on earth" (Bauckham, *Theology of the Book*, 31).

[18]Bauckham, *Theology of the Book*, 32. Thompson writes, "True worship reveals the way things really are, and true worshippers form an egalitarian *communitas* around the center" (*Book of Revelation*, 71).

priesthood. His sacrifice is our destiny. The way he overcame the world is the way we overcome the world, redeeming all creation for heaven's purpose. That's why all creation joins in the chorus once the song is sung, once the one who sits on the throne and the Lamb are worshiped as worthy rulers (Rev 5:11-14). Indeed, it is only after the Lamb seizes the sealed scroll and "begins the work of messianic repairs to the cosmos" that worship of God is extended to all creation—in heaven, on the earth, under the earth, and on the sea (Rev 5:13).[19] This makes the sequence of the liturgy significant: after the antiphonal praise of the one who sits on the throne and the Lamb, then the Lamb opens the sealed scroll and judgment follows (Rev 6:1–8:1).

The irony is picture perfect: the Lamb has overcome his enemies even though he appeared to be overcome by them. The Lamb was slain but still stands. Only he is worthy to open the book. Only those who have ears to hear can see the vision and join in heavenly worship, envisioning the justice of God coming to earth *through them* because of him—a kingdom of priests offering sacrifice. According to Thompson, "By placing the slain Lamb in the throne scenes in different ways, heavenly worship becomes a way of expressing the irony of kingship through crucifixion."[20] What a strange way to rule the world! Christ reigns through sacrifice—his and ours.

No wonder the Apocalypse is such a strange book. Defeating the Roman Empire by becoming a victim of Roman "justice" sounds completely backward, upside down, counterintuitive, otherworldly.[21] That's why the Revelation of John is filled with such bizarre imagery and weird characters. Heaven crashing into earth cannot be revealed through ordinary measures, conforming to worldly expectations. Rather, to see a slaughtered Lamb still standing, a kingdom of priests still reigning through self-sacrifice takes quite a bit of imagination—and a new song:

---

[19]Resseguie, *Revelation of John*, 46.
[20]Thompson, *Book of Revelation*, 65.
[21]"The world below, and to a certain extent this world, is 'the reverse side' of the world above" (Resseguie, *Revelation of John*, 43).

"Worthy is the Lamb that was *slain* to receive *power*" (Rev 5:12). Power through sacrifice: Who could see *that* unless it is revealed by God? Indeed, that's why imagining the kingdom of heaven on earth happens every time we gather to worship God and sing praises to our King. That's what happened to the seer. Therefore, according to John, that's the surest way to envision the kingdom of heaven on earth: to have ears to hear what the Spirit is saying to the churches when someone reads the book of Revelation.

Because of John, all of us are seers.

10

DECLARATION OF WAR

Confessing the Word

MY BIGGEST FEAR IS SELF-DECEPTION. Given the many warnings in Scripture about the perils of self-deception, we should all be concerned about our human inclination to deceive ourselves. Since we tend to prefer the voice in our heads—how we make sense of the world, what we think about others, how we see ourselves—we're less inclined to consider outside voices that challenge our self-made perceptions. In fact, our natural reflex, our first impulse is to justify ourselves when confronted with an opposing opinion—a human weakness explored by David Foster Wallace during his now-famous 2005 commencement address to the graduates of Kenyon College:

> There are these two young fish swimming along, and they happen to meet an older fish swimming the other way, who nods at them and says, "Morning, boys, how's the water?" And the two young fish swim on for a bit, and then eventually one of them looks over at the other and goes, "What the _____ is water?"
>
> If at this moment you're worried that I plan to present myself here as the wise old fish explaining what water is to you younger fish, please don't be. I am not the wise old fish. The immediate point of the fish story is that the most obvious, ubiquitous, important realities are often the ones that are the hardest to see and talk about.[1]

---

[1]David Foster Wallace, "This Is Water," *Kenyon Alumni Magazine*, 2005, http://bulletin-archive .kenyon.edu/x4280.html.

At this point, Wallace explores the human condition in existentialist terms, how we tend to make sense of the world around us through our own sense of well-being. We can't help but see ourselves as the center of all things. We were born that way, preprogrammed to think everything revolves around us. Plus, we've been conditioned to think that way, looking on the outside world from the only vantage point that we have: our own perspective. We are self-centered people because everything that happens *around* us also happens *to* us. We are the subject of all things; each one of us gives meaning to everything. We never question our self-made reality, that our own perspective is the only way we make sense of the world. But the truth of the matter is, none of us is the center of all things. What I'm certain of in light of my experience isn't the same as what you're certain of based on your experience. So, none of us sees things as they really are, even though we go around pretending like we do. And, to make matters worse, we don't acknowledge this fatal flaw in humanity because we don't see it. It's the water we're all swimming in.

Wallace goes on to offer reasons why we should try to break out of our self-imposed self-centeredness, even suggesting that worshiping God could be effective in countering our self-delusion. Convinced that there are no atheists—we all worship something—Wallace claims that worshiping God or some higher spiritual power may be our only hope because

> pretty much anything else you worship will eat you alive. If you worship money and things—if they are where you tap real meaning in life—then you will never have enough. Never feel you have enough. It's the truth. Worship your own body and beauty and sexual allure and you will always feel ugly, and when time and age start showing, you will die a million deaths before they finally plant you. On one level, we all know this stuff already—it's been codified as myths, proverbs, clichés, bromides, epigrams, parables: the skeleton of every great story. The trick is keeping the truth up-front in daily consciousness.[2]

---

[2]Wallace, "This Is Water," emphasis original.

If "the trick is keeping the truth up-front in daily consciousness," then how will we know the truth unless there is someone outside ourselves to tell it? There may be older, wiser fish trying to get us to recognize the water we're all swimming in (and Wallace claims he's not one). But who can answer the younger, "woke" fish when they ask, "*What* in the world is water?"

John believes the only way we can know the truth about ourselves is through "the Revelation of Jesus Christ" (Rev 1:1). Indeed, the Apocalypse begins with the presumption that we need a word from outside ourselves—a word from God—to tell us the truth about ourselves (we are slaves of Christ) and about the "the things that must occur soon" in the world (the water we swim in) because "the time is near" (Rev 1:1-3). We tend to forget who we are in Christ—we are his slaves—because the world would have us believe we can be masters of our world. We are told to believe in the power of choice (Wallace believes it's our only hope). We are told we can create our own destiny (Wallace is suspicious of such a self-centered agenda). There are masters of our domain—much like the Roman Empire in John's day—who are held up as paragons of human achievement (they are the ones invited to give the commencement addresses at college graduations).

Consequently, even though we know that Christ is our master, we're tempted to give up serving him and to give in to the way of the world: to pursue our kingdom and not his, to treasure the earthly and ignore the heavenly, to idolize things rather than worship God. It's the same problem John addressed in his letter to the church: how to be *in* the world but not *of* the world (1 Jn 2:15-17). That's why the Revelation is so important—then and now. We need a vision from God to help us see the water we're all swimming in—something we can't see by ourselves. Indeed, according to an ancient Chinese proverb, "If you want to know what water is, don't ask the fish."

WORSHIP AS WARFARE

After Christ reveals the truth about the seven churches (Rev 1:9–3:22)—strengths and weaknesses, opportunities and threats—the seer's first glimpse of what's really going on in the world comes from a heavenly perspective.[3] Having been called up to witness the worship of God and his Lamb (Rev 4:1–5:14), John looks down on the world as the sealed scroll is opened, bringing about the judgment of God on earth (Rev 6:1–8:1). It's significant that John's vision of things to come happens during heavenly scenes of worship. Even though John is called up to heaven, passing through the heavenly portal that brings him into the throne room of God, even though he sees and hears different kinds of heavenly creatures offer unceasing praise and adoration, the worship of God is not shut up within the heavenlies. Devoted worship of the Pantocrator and the Lamb extends to the earth, with "every created thing which is in heaven and on the earth and under the earth and on the sea" joining in festal praise (Rev 5:13). The interplay between scenes of heavenly worship and the things "that must take place" reveals the eschatological purpose of worshiping God. According to John's vision, when we worship God we are able to see the end of the world. Not only that, but those who have ears to hear the reading of John's Revelation and join in heavenly worship end up participating in the unfolding drama of this eschatological narrative—the story of heaven invading earth.[4] In this way, then, according to Thompson, "the kingdom of God and the rule of the Messiah—future, eschatological claims—are acclaimed in heavenly liturgies as present, 'eternal' realities."[5] Every time we gather to worship God, we're declaring war on the world, like street prophets holding up signs that say, "The End Is Near."

That's why worship is an act of war in the Revelation of John.[6] Notice how all seven visions of the end of the world begin with a heavenly

---

[3]Some of the material in this chapter I first shared on my blog at http://agenuinefaith.blogspot.com.
[4]Leonard L. Thompson, *The Book of Revelation: Apocalypse and Empire* (Oxford: Oxford University Press, 1990), 66. Steven Friesen writes, "So 'worship time' is the first and most important kind of time in Revelation, unique because it spans heaven and earth." See Friesen, *Imperial Cults and the Apocalypse of John: Reading Revelation in the Ruins* (Oxford: Oxford University Press, 2001), 158.
[5]Thompson, *Book of Revelation*, 65.
[6]Richard Bauckham, *The Theology of the Book of Revelation* (Cambridge: Cambridge University Press, 1993), 67-70.

scene.[7] Sometimes John saw the heavenly temple of God (Rev 8:3-5; 11:19; 15:5-8). Other times he saw the throne of God and his heavenly council (Rev 4:1–5:14; 14:1-5; 15:1-4; 19:1-10). Whether in the temple or around the throne, each vision begins with a festal gathering of worshipers. Then God executes judgment on the earth, launching his invasion with armies of heavenly beings—from horsemen to angels—so that "the kingdom of the world has become the kingdom of our Lord, and of His Christ" (Rev 11:15). In the unfolding eschatological drama, two overlapping worlds (spatial and temporal) blend into one: heaven crashes into earth; the future is precipitated by the present. The dystopian scene is replicated over and over again. After the saints worship God and the Lamb, all hell breaks loose on earth. The way John sees it, the Apocalypse is an unveiling of—a behind-the-scenes look at—what happens when we worship God. The seer is pulling back the veil, helping us see the invisible war occurring in the visible world as the reign of God is established on earth as it is in heaven.

More than that, the seer's vision is a call to participate: when we worship God we wage war against the powers that oppose him and us. Worship, therefore, becomes a subversive act whereby we overcome the idolatrous powers and their pretentious rule. Despite the ruinous effects of evil powers trying to destroy God's creation, we are declaring in worship, "Our God reigns!" Indeed, the apocalyptic vision of a dystopian world is a Christian hope of God turning the world right side up, when earth is elevated to heaven's purpose through divine purification. Furthermore, the promise (perhaps even evidence) of a dystopian world is, therefore, the apocalyptic sign of God's reclamation of all creation. That evil is putting up a fight by trying to muck up the place is proof that God, the Lamb, and his slaves are winning the war.[8] It's just a matter of time

---

[7]I follow Charles H. Talbert's schema, "Seven Visions of the End Times," in *The Apocalypse: A Reading of the Revelation of John* (Louisville, KY: Westminster John Knox, 1994), 26.

[8]Edith M. Humphrey writes, "Paradoxically, what could be seen as an argument against the fact of God's rule is redirected as a reason for it: the earthly rampage of Satan is the demonstration of God's victory, and the fall is linked inversely with the effective blood of the Lamb and the martyrdom of the faithful. This passage of the Apocalypse argues that things are not as they seem: martyrdom and death equal victory; the very fury of Satan's earthly activity signals that God is

until everyone sees it on the last day, when heaven and earth become one. In the meantime, one must have ears to hear in order to envision the end—now and then.

War is hell on earth. That's what it looks like when the Lamb breaks the seven-sealed book and forces of destruction are unleashed on the earth. Military imagery dominates the unfolding cosmic invasion—like a scene from the Lord of the Rings trilogy: (1) horsemen conquer, wielding swords, killing, and taking "peace from the earth" (Rev 6:5); (2) the land is devastated by war, resulting in famine, pestilence, and economic ruin (Rev 6:5-8); (3) innocent casualties of war are slaughtered, their blood crying out like Abel's (Gen 4:10) as it drips off the altar of sacrifice and pools with one voice on the floor of God's heavenly temple ("How long, holy and true Lord, before you avenge our blood, judging those who live on earth?" Rev 6:10); (4) darkness blocks the sun, the earth quakes under the feet of kings and commanders doing battle, as the apocalyptic end of all things becomes apparent to everyone (Rev 6:12-17).

Then, just when it looks like it's all going to hit the apocalyptic fan once the seventh seal is opened, there is a reprieve—a break in the action. After a rapid-fire sequence of war scenes unveiled by the first six seals, a lengthy interlude appears between the sixth and seventh seals (Rev 7:1-17). In fact, if we pay careful attention to narrative time, we can't help but notice that the interlude seems to last as long as the war. Just when it looks like the earth is going to hell in a handbasket due to war—destructive powers have ruined a fourth of God's creation, injustice reigns on the earth—the seer sees divine forces marshaled for a counter-attack against the powers of darkness (Rev 7:1-8). It's as if God is finally going to step in and do something to overcome the rulers who oppose him, before the "great day" of the wrath of God and the Lamb dawns on the earth (Rev 6:16-17).

But those who have ears to hear know that's not the case. God is not aloof, looking down on earth from the comfort of heaven, intervening at

---

already the Victor." See Humphrey, *And I Turned to See the Voice: The Rhetoric of Vision in the New Testament* (Grand Rapids, MI: Baker Academic, 2007), 169.

the last minute. Indeed, this devastating war happened because the Lamb opened the sealed scroll that came from God's right hand. Therefore, it could be said that all of this happened by divine decree. This is God's will. But why? Why would God want to unleash such destructive forces on earth, waging a war that seems to do nothing but hurl humanity toward the apocalyptic end of all things?

The interlude answers the question, "Why?" as well as "How long, O Lord?" and "What happens now?" Before he answers the "Why?" question, God first answered the martyr's question, "How long?" with a promise. He will avenge their blood "in a little while," once enough martyrs have shed their blood on earth (Rev 6:11). In other words, the war will not go on forever. God is keeping count of the victims, knowing when the number of martyrs will be "complete" (Rev 6:11). That's why they are counted and sealed as God's slaves (Rev 7:3-8). For "the 144,000 are an army."[9] As Bauckham rightly notes, Israel took a census before going to war. The book of Numbers wasn't just a matter of preserving genealogies and tribal identities. God was preparing Israel for war, taking a census before taking the Promised Land by conquest (Num 1:2-3).

That God is marshaling an army of faithful witnesses to fight the war on earth reveals how the interlude answers the question "Why?" Why did God and the Lamb start this war by breaking the seals? An answer could be inferred in light of the visions that occurred before the interlude: as the Pantocrator, God can do whatever he wants with his creation. But God didn't do this alone. The Lamb—the worthy agent of God—took the book and broke the seals. The reason he was worthy to start the war was that he was "slaughtered, and [he] bought for God with his blood" a people from all over the earth (Rev 5:9). Why was he slaughtered? Brian Blount sums it up well: "This lamb is no innocent; he *earns* the slaughter that comes his way."[10] The Lamb was God's first warrior to oppose the evil powers on earth, overcoming them through his death and resurrection,

---

[9]Bauckham, *Theology of the Book*, 77.
[10]Brian K. Blount, *Can I Get a Witness?: Reading Revelation Through African American Culture* (Louisville, KY: Westminster John Knox, 2005), 83, emphasis original.

in order to establish a "kingdom of priests" who will "reign on the earth" (Rev 5:10), replacing the rulers who oppose God. In John's day, the power that slaughtered Jesus was still the ruler of the earth: Rome.

By opening the six seals, the Lamb launched an invasion against the Roman Empire, the rulers who pretentiously claimed dominion over the earth. Rome promised peace and safety for the world. The unsealed book unleashed horsemen who "took peace from the earth" (Rev 6:4). Rome promised economic prosperity. The unsealed book unleashed horsemen who wreaked havoc on commerce, driving prices for bread through the roof (Rev 6:4-6). Rome executed Christ for treason. Rome persecuted Christians for the same reason, "slain because of the word of God and their faithful witness" (Rev 6:9)—the army of God who will win the war and overcome the world just like Christ. That's what the interlude envisions: an army arrayed for battle goes to war and emerges as victorious in heaven; having "come out of the great tribulation, they have washed their robes and made them white by the blood of the lamb" (Rev 7:14). Like Christ and because of Christ, God's army wins the war through sacrifice.

Finally, the interlude answers the question, "What happens now?" With the world falling apart, unmasking the arrogance of Rome's claim, one would think Christians would be encouraged to celebrate during the desolation, able to see clearly the purpose of the messianic war. J. Nelson Kraybill writes,

> The central political reality in the author's day—the late first century—was the indomitable Roman Empire and its "divine" emperors. The pressing issue for John's readers was how Christians, who gave their highest loyalty to Jesus, should conduct themselves in a world where economic and political structures assumed that everyone would worship the emperor. While no Western nation has outright ruler worship today, we do have political, military, and economic powers to which millions give unquestioned allegiance.[11]

---

[11]J. Nelson Kraybill, *Apocalypse and Allegiance: Worship, Politics, and Devotion in the Book of Revelation* (Grand Rapids, MI: Brazos, 2010), 15.

That's the tension the Revelation creates: Whom do we trust when the world seems to be coming apart at the seams? In the days of the Roman Empire, citizens and subjects looked to the emperor for help. After all, Caesar ruled the world as a god, a divine agent of blessing. The people were more than willing to worship Caesar in order to curry imperial favor for their cities. Furthermore, Roman rulers knew that "bread and circuses" would never be enough to placate the masses.[12] That's why they promised a good life to devoted citizens and subjects.

This religious/political/economic/social quid pro quo arrangement of the first-century world was, to recall Wallace's analogy, the water all fish swam in—even Christians. Or, to use a common expression of our day, "That's just the way the world works." You have to pay to play. Get involved or get left out in the cold. Even those who refuse to play the game today—hermits, anarchists, loners, the Amish—still have to enter society now and then to make ends meet. Withdrawal isn't feasible. Like fish out of water, we all know we can't live without the world. That's why most of us, when the world begins to fall apart, can't help but worry about our futures, turning to the experts who promise to make it all better. The stock market crashes, hurricanes and tornadoes destroy homes, terrorists attack retail shoppers, war breaks out in another country, another epidemic morphs into a pandemic, an asteroid makes another flyby, cancer returns with a vengeance—all of these catastrophes strike fear in our hearts, inciting us to wonder whether the end is near. That's when the masses turn to our modern-day caesars, scientists and politicians, technocrats and visionaries, military and might, moguls and gurus to save our world. Indeed, our greatest fears reveal our ultimate dependency on the rulers who promise to protect our fragile world—even from so-called acts of God.

What happens now? Will Christians swimming in the same water join the school of fish that place their hope in the rulers of the earth, allured by their pretentious claim "to make the world a better place"? Will we

---

[12]Juvenal, *Satire* 10.81.

join the masses in venerating these gods, swearing allegiance to their ideology, their politic, their way of life, convincing ourselves that we can serve God and Mammon just like the Laodiceans? Or will we worship the one true God in defiance of the world, believing he does all things well even though the wicked enjoy prosperity and the righteous suffer unjustly? According to the interlude, we who belong to God's army should march into the war with great confidence, knowing that "as the seals are unsealed, the saints are sealed" (Rev 7:3).[13]

This doesn't mean, however, that Christian soldiers are kept from harm during the war. Even though the interlude doesn't explain how they die (or even why they die), the scene of the countless multitude "clothed in white robes" in heaven—dressed like martyrs (Rev 6:11)—implies the 144,000 gave their lives for the Lamb (see also Rev 14:1-5). Once again, the correlation of audition and vision is built on irony. John hears the census of 144,000 "from every tribe of the sons of Israel" (Rev 7:4) and sees a numberless multitude rewarded in heaven, where "God shall wipe away every tear from their eyes" (Rev 7:17). The ironic juxtaposition of audition and vision reveals why God will win the messianic war launched from heaven even though his army keeps "losing the war" (being killed) on earth: his army consists of a numberless multitude. He'll keep sending his saints into battle, and these faithful witnesses will continue to be slaughtered like the Lamb they follow knowing that, in the end, the victorious will drink from the "springs of living water" and never suffer again (Rev 7:16-17). God will win the war because he'll never run out of soldiers who follow the Lamb *faithfully*.

It is significant that these victorious soldiers come from "every nation and tribe and people and language" (Rev 7:9), indicating that Christians from all over the world will have resisted rulers who oppose God. Today, it's easier for us to see the faithfulness of those who suffer violence at the hands of oppressive governments—such as the Coptic Christians murdered by Egyptian terrorists or Christian dissidents imprisoned by the

---

[13]James L. Resseguie, *The Revelation of John: A Narrative Commentary* (Grand Rapids, MI: Baker Academic, 2009), 125.

Chinese government. Like Smyrna in John's day (Rev 2:9-10), there have always been places where Christians have been persecuted for the faith. The stark contrast between faithful confession and denying the faith is evident to everyone. We all know that when the Antipas of our time is martyred (Rev 2:13), he has kept the faith.

But what about Christians who are not persecuted for their faith, like the church in Laodicea? What does their faithful resistance to ungodly rulers look like? Since Christ considered wealth and luxury to be serious threats to our faith (Rev 3:17-18), and rulers are in power to provide and protect such an opulent lifestyle, what should faithfulness look like in places like Laodicea? How should Christ's soldiers fight against rulers who promote wealth and luxury? What does it mean to "buy from [Christ] gold refined by fire" (Rev 3:18)? Was Christ calling for his soldiers to incite persecution—essentially picking a fight with pagan rulers that may lead to martyrdom ("wear white garments")—because they were too comfortable living in the land of plenty, not realizing how "miserable and pathetic and poor and blind and naked" they really were (Rev 3:17)? According to Christ, they needed salve for their blind eyes (Rev 3:18). What was it that these rich yet poor Christians couldn't see?

BLIND IDOLATRY

American politics has a blinding effect on Christians. Donald Trump's presidency divided the church, revealing our true allegiances. Whether Democrat or Republican, Christians toeing the party line can't see how their political ideologies end up eclipsing our shared faith. Take, for example, the loyalty of Trump supporters. My wife and I have been baffled over how easily Christians who support the president set aside basic Christian beliefs. Jesus taught us to care for children because, more than anyone else, they embody the kingdom of heaven (Mt 18:1-6). Yet, when the Trump administration separated immigrant children from their parents at the southern border, Christian supporters of the president turned a blind eye to the tragedy. Jesus taught us to welcome the stranger, helping them with food and water, clothing and shelter (Mt 25:31-46).

Yet, when Trump cast aspersion on all aliens, lambasting them as rapists and lawbreakers, his Christian supporters justified the administration's decision to put the "intruders" in cages, treating them like animals. We have Christian family members who strongly support the president, and when we bring up these basic Christian convictions, they completely ignore what Jesus said, defending Trump no matter what. I'll say, "But that's not what Jesus taught," and they ignore the point. It's as if the only thing that matters is their faith in the president. Not even the teachings of Jesus can make them question their political allegiances.

The same is true for Christian Democrats. Jesus taught us to humble ourselves—even plucking out our eyes and cutting off our hands—to protect the weak and vulnerable (Mt 18:7-14). And yet, when Democrats shout down those who oppose abortion on demand, left-leaning Christians ignore the plight of the unborn child and join the chorus of hate speech directed against their brothers and sisters who dare to question a woman's right to choose. Jesus taught us that calling someone a fool makes one liable to hell (Mt 5:22). Yet, Christians who hated Trump while he was president skewered his supporters with such venomous words that it makes calling someone a fool pale in comparison. This type of thing happens all the time. Ironically, in our attempts to point out the shortcomings of others based on our religious convictions, our political preferences end up blinding us to Christ's teachings about his kingdom.

The same thing happened in John's day because people were just as invested in religion and politics as we are today. Of course, we live in a society that celebrates the separation of church and state (a very Baptist conviction!)—something first-century people would have found to be very odd.[14] Who can separate religion and politics, especially a Christian? We live for the kingdom of God, a political reality. We preach the good news of Jesus Christ, a political claim (*Christ* referred to the ideal Jewish king). For us, swearing allegiance to Christ must take precedence over

---

[14]Regarding the indivisibility of religion and politics in the first-century world, see the helpful description by Larry W. Hurtado, *Destroyer of the Gods: Early Christian Distinctiveness in the Roman World* (Waco, TX: Baylor University Press, 2016), 44-49.

everything—even country, law, and flag. For, if King Jesus is Lord of all, then any nation or government or ruler that tries to compel its citizenry to swear allegiance to them is challenging the exclusive claims of Christ. At least, that's the way early Christian Tertullian saw it. He objected to the way Roman standards (flags) were held up as unquestionable symbols of Roman sovereignty, worthy of supreme devotion (especially for Roman soldiers): "Roman religion, every bit of it a religion of the camps, venerates the standards, swears by the standards, sets the standards before all gods."[15] That's why Jews and Christians avoided military service. Even though becoming a member of the Roman army eventually afforded some opportunities for upward mobility, the blatant idolatry promoted by military officers compelled Jews and Christians to turn to the only other option to improve their livelihoods: business.[16]

Religion was deeply embedded in the politics of commerce as well. Trade guilds honored patron gods. Business owners were expected to pay respects to the ancestral gods of their financial backers. Cities promoted the worship of local deities through special festivals and games, often rewarding businesses for sponsoring certain events. The emperor promoted the economic welfare of cities that built shrines and temples for the imperial cult.[17] In other words, in the first-century Mediterranean world, business and idolatry were indivisibly linked. To engage profitably in commerce was to venerate gods.[18] Since Jews and Christians refused to worship these ubiquitous gods, they were despised as atheists, scapegoats of public wrath when the economy faltered or other disasters threatened their welfare.[19]

Wealthy Jews and Christians tried to ameliorate tensions by offering support for civic projects that were less "idolatrous," such as funding public buildings, paving streets, or underwriting the expenses of certain

---

[15]Tertullian, *Apology* 16.8, trans. T. R. Glover.
[16]J. Nelson Kraybill, *Imperial Cult and Commerce in John's Apocalypse*, Journal for the Study of the New Testament Supplement Series (Sheffield: Sheffield Academic, 1999), 90.
[17]Friesen, *Imperial Cults*, 23-131.
[18]Kraybill, *Imperial Cult and Commerce*, 102-41.
[19]John M. G. Barclay, *Jews in the Mediterranean Diaspora: From Alexander to Trajan (323 BCE–117 CE)* (Berkeley: University of California Press, 1996), 267-81.

public offices.[20] Yet, financial support of pagan cults was unavoidable in most civic and business affairs.[21] Even conscientious objectors were forced to support idolatrous liturgies—especially after the Jewish temple was destroyed, when Rome redirected the Jewish temple tax to support the construction of a temple to Jupiter in Jerusalem.[22] Furthermore, Roman coins functioned as portable idols, the image of Caesar stamped on one side with an inscription that extolled the emperor as a god.[23]

So it shouldn't come as a surprise that, in the minds of Jews and Christians, money and idolatry were two sides of the same coin. We tend to think the reason warnings appear in early Christian literature about the idolatry of money has to do with how easily believers can fall into the trap of giving their lives to the pursuit of wealth, as if money were the god of blessing. To be sure, early Christians were leery of money for that reason. But for them there was more to it than that. Since idolatry was embedded in daily commerce, in business, in government—even stamped on the Roman coins they used—early Christian Polycarp claimed that "anyone who does not avoid love of money will be polluted by idolatry."[24] Therefore, being rich in faith and rich according to the world were mutually exclusive. You cannot serve God and Mammon.

This is why the trumpet plagues were unleashed on earth: to get humanity to give up their idols. "And the rest of humanity, the ones who did not die from these plagues, refused to repent from the works of their hands, that they would no longer worship demons or idols made of gold, silver, brass, stone, or wood—images that are not able to see or hear or walk" (Rev 9:20). To us, these catastrophes appear to be little more than a more intensive version of the broken seals; this time a third of the earth is devastated (Rev 8:7-12; 9:15). But in a world where everything was animated by divine powers, the trashing of trees and grass, seas and rivers,

---

[20]See Thompson, *Book of Revelation*, 137-54.

[21]Kraybill, *Imperial Cult and Commerce*, 80-87, 90-101.

[22]Barclay, *Jews in the Mediterranean Diaspora*, 310-12.

[23]See Rodney Reeves, *Matthew*, Story of God Bible Commentary (Grand Rapids, MI: Zondervan, 2017), 437-38.

[24]Polycarp, *To the Philippians* 11.2.

moon and stars not only had a ruinous effect on daily commerce but also challenged the sovereignty of the gods. Their turf had been invaded. Promises of economic prosperity that were tied to religious devotion should have created a crisis of faith for those who worshiped idols. Why sacrifice to the god of sailing when ships are destroyed? Why venerate the gods of fishing and grain harvest when seas are polluted and fields are burned up? Yet, even though it got worse when a horrible pandemic affected all humanity (except Christ's slaves, Rev 9:4)—where is the god Asclepius when you need him?—idol worshipers didn't learn their lesson. Despite the fact that their worst nightmare came true (the Romans feared an irrepressible army from the east would one day defeat them; Rev 9:14-17), such massive casualties of war didn't dissuade them from worshiping false gods and persisting in their immoralities (Rev 9:18-21).[25]

If not even disasters and death could convince idolaters to repent, what's a prophet to do? Is there anything left to say? If the purpose of the trumpet plagues was to convince pagans to question the sovereignty of their gods, but they stubbornly persist in their idolatrous ways, then giving witness to the world about the one true God would be a waste of time, wouldn't it? Indeed, some believers might be tempted to say, "Have the seventh angel blow the last trumpet and let's get this over with. Cue the Hallelujah chorus of Handel's *Messiah*" (Rev 11:15). But that's not what happens. Instead, once again, before the last trumpet sounds and "the mystery of God is finished" (Rev 10:7), there's a break in the action—a significant interlude that teaches us much about God's purposes for Christ's slaves who are his witnesses to the end of the world.

First, whether people want to hear it or not, the truth must be proclaimed. A strong angel gives the seer a book to eat, which tastes good but doesn't sit well in his stomach (Rev 10:8-11)—an apt description of what it feels like to tell the truth to the world. To us, the gospel truth is believable. Why don't nonbelievers "taste and see that the Lord is good"? We persist in our confession about Christ, a message of salvation and

---

[25]Stephen S. Smalley, *The Revelation to John: A Commentary on the Greek Text of the Apocalypse* (Downers Grove, IL: InterVarsity Press, 2005), 239-40, 408.

justice: "You must prophesy again to many people, nations, languages, and kings" (Rev 10:11). But we also know, in light of past experiences, our witness won't be received. What is good news to us will sound like bad news to them. When we tell the truth about the world—the idolatry, the immorality, that justice cannot happen until the unjust are judged by God—the world will hate us for it. They'll do everything they can to silence the messenger because they can't stand the message.[26] That's what happened to Christ. That's what happens to us. The bitter reality that we've swallowed the gospel whole, believing the Christ they've rejected is their only hope—well, even we recognize that what was sweet has turned sour for us too. Indeed, few things are more frustrating than trying to help the person you love—mother, father, sister, brother, wife, husband, daughter, son—who refuses to be helped. It makes me sick to my stomach, something I'll never get over. Until the people I love are saved from idols, I will be a restless witness.

But there's another lesson to learn. I, too, am tempted by idols, trusting in the gods of money and power rather than the one true God. I may gather with the saints as God's people worshiping in his temple (Rev 11:1)—even protected by the sacred work of Christ—but when I leave his courts of praise and go into the world, the lure of idolatry is all around me.[27] Celebrities (athletes, actors, musicians) are held up as gods, objects of desire and paragons of prosperity. They inspire dedicated followers on social media to jealously guard their image and shamelessly promote their fame. Why? Because everyone dreams of the good life, living like royalty, doing whatever we want whenever we want. We worship celebrity life, dreaming of how it would feel to be king for a day, venerating those who have made it big in the business. Politicians court financial backers and attract devoted workers, promising the masses that they'll make the world a better place. Yet, everyone knows that principled politicians don't last because everybody wants a piece of the action.

---

[26]So also Resseguie, *Revelation of John*, 156.

[27]Measuring the temple symbolized divine protection of the church "from spiritual danger," picturing the "ultimate salvation of the faithful" (Smalley, *Revelation*, 270).

There's a reason why big business bankrolls senators and representatives. They expect a return for their investment. It doesn't surprise us when politicians sell their influence to the highest bidder, and yet we still keep buying the promises they make.

It's especially evident when celebrities and politicians pack arenas and convention centers with the adoring masses who offer unreserved praise for their idols. Songs blare through the speakers, devotees raise their phones to record the moment when their idol takes the stage, fans scream for their hero, while the larger-than-life personality soaks up the adoration. This is modern-day worship. Every time I see it happen, I can't help but wonder whether Christians feel a little foolish joining in the veneration of our American idols—especially when supporting a celebrity such as the president is touted by his followers as the same as being devoted to God.

That's why God sends prophets to his people to wake us up, opening our eyes to the seductive power of our idols.[28] We don't want to see it, of course. When prophets point out our divided loyalties, we often dismiss their concerns as an overreaction—a dramatic ploy for attention. Indeed, prophets have been known to do some crazy things to arouse the sleepy masses. Isaiah walked around Jerusalem barefoot for three years with his backside exposed (Is 20:2-6). Jeremiah broke a pot (Jer 19:1-15). Hosea married a prostitute (Hos 1:2). Ezekiel recreated the siege of Jerusalem with bricks and ropes, then shaved his beard with a sword and disposed of the clippings during a bizarre ritual (Ezek 4:1–5:4). John the Baptizer wore an Elijah costume and ate locust (Mk 1:6; 2 Kings 1:8). Even Jesus acted like a prophet, clearing the temple to fulfill Malachi's prophecy (Mt 21:12-13; Mal 3:1-3). Prophets were God's way of giving Israel a heads-up. Even though the day of the Lord would take the nations by surprise, Israel should have known the day of judgment was near when a prophet showed up, preached against sin, called for repentance, and dramatized the message through bizarre, symbolic performances. There even seems

---

[28]Resseguie writes, "The church accomplishes what judgments alone were unable to accomplish. Where the plagues are ineffectual in moving humankind in the right direction, the testimony of faithful believers is effectual" (*Revelation of John*, 166).

to have been a Jewish eschatological expectation that two "prophetic witnesses" would reappear before the end of the world: Moses (Deut 18:18-22) and Elijah (Mal 4:5-6) redivivus.[29]

So, when two prophets appear in John's vision (Rev 11:3-10), acting like Moses (turning waters to blood, smiting the earth with plagues) and Elijah (fire destroying enemies, preventing rain), it's supposed to signal to God's people that the end of the world is near—something completely lost on nonbelievers. In fact, the fruit of their ministry as olive trees, the light of their witness as lampstands proves to be menacing to the people—so much so that when they are murdered, the people celebrate their deaths as if it were a holiday, exchanging gifts (Rev 11:10). The question, of course, is whether God's people join in the festivities.

PROPHETS ALWAYS SAY, "REPENT!"

To be sure, "Moses" and "Elijah" made it rough on everyone. The way the seer describes it, "these two prophets tormented those who live on the earth" (Rev 11:10). "Those from the people and tribes and tongues and nations" (a phrase that typically indicates the faithful) were part of the gawking crowds who didn't allow a proper burial for the two witnesses, their corpses left in the street for three and a half days (Rev 11:9). But what was intended as an act of ignominy ends up setting the stage for a divine act of rectification: God raised them from the dead for all the world to see (Rev 11:11-12). In an ironic twist to the Elijah story, where a remnant of seven thousand faithful men who had not worshiped Baal was supposed to encourage the prophet that he wasn't alone after the famous battle on Mount Carmel (1 Kings 19:18), this time seven thousand men are killed in an earthquake after the two prophets ascend to heaven (Rev 11:13). But the rest of the survivors "were terrified and gave glory to the God of heaven" (Rev 11:13). This is the only time it happens in the

---

[29]Deuteronomy Rabbah 3.17. According to the Apocalypse of Elijah 4.7-19 and the Apocalypse of Daniel 14.1-3, the two heavenly witnesses are Enoch and Elijah. For a detailed discussion of the two heavenly witnesses, see David E. Aune, *Revelation 1-5*, Word Biblical Commentary (Dallas: Word Books, 1997), 2:598-603.

Apocalypse: these people "give glory to the God of heaven" (the one true God!) after witnessing the work of God. The expression "give glory to God" probably indicates the survivors repented, especially when we see later that those who experienced the plague of the fourth bowl refuse to "repent to give glory to him" (Rev 16:9).[30] What was it about the scene that caused them to repent? That they survived the earthquake? Or was there something about the way the two prophets left this world that made them realize they shouldn't have acted like the world, contemptuous of these two prophets?

Since the seer reminds us that they were martyred in the same city "where their Lord was also crucified" (Rev 11:8), I think John believes we're supposed to hear echoes of the death, burial, resurrection, and ascension of Jesus in the ministry of the two prophets.[31] Imagine the emotional effect: one day you're celebrating that these troublemakers are dead and gone. Then three days later (what timing!), you connect the dots, "Wait a minute! There was an earthquake when Jesus was crucified. He was raised from the dead three days later. He ascended to heaven, disappearing in a cloud just like these two prophets. Oh no! I think we've made a terrible mistake. These men weren't false prophets. They were the two heavenly witnesses that are supposed to come just before the end of the world!" Indeed, they are, for the last trumpet sounds in the very next verse, announcing that the "kingdom of the world has become the kingdom of our Lord and his Christ" (Rev 11:15).

I wonder what God's last two prophets would look like today, two witnesses who are supposed to give us a heads-up that the end is near. Even though we don't know what "Moses" and "Elijah" preached in Revelation 11, since they were dressed in sackcloth (Rev 11:3) they probably started their sermons with "Repent!"—the same word that makes a lot of people angry today.[32] Today their words would be dismissed as

---

[30]Bauckham, *Theology of the Book*, 86; Aune, *Revelation*, 2:628-29; Smalley, *Revelation*, 286.

[31]According to deSilva, the two prophets are "the most focused appeal to emulation," the definitive Christlike witness that conquers through sacrifice (*Seeing Things John's Way*, 223-24).

[32]Bauckham, *Theology of the Book*, 86.

inflammatory because they have the gall to challenge the status quo (Rev 11:5). Pundits trying to prop up the ways of the world—"How dare you question what we believe!"—would try to destroy these prophets through ad hominem attacks. At first, God protects them, the truth of their message confirmed by their virtuous lives, lamps of God lighting up the darkness (Rev 11:4). But then, after God vindicates their message of judgment with plagues of drought and pollution that bring devastating economic loss (Rev 11:6), the political powers will step in and silence the voice of God (Rev 11:7). Like a beast from hell, the regime will crush the resistance, humiliating them in public for all the world to see. When it happens, we will *all* gawk at the spectacle—a video capturing their demise will go viral, the masses crowd-pounding the fools for daring to defy our way of life: "Look at these two idiots. They're getting what they deserve." The world will call it "justice," and the lesson will be learned once again: question the majority and we will crush you.

Then, a miracle will occur. God will raise these two prophets from the dead, and the church will finally wake up from our repose. Reminded of how the powers tried to silence the voice of God when they crucified our Lord, we will repent: "We have lived like the world long enough. Like these two heavenly witnesses, it's time to let our light shine and tell the truth: give up your idols. Christ is our Lord, we are his slaves, and nothing will separate us from his love. Defy the rulers of this world. Pray instead, 'His kingdom come, his will be done, on earth as it is in heaven.' Your nation cannot save you. Bend your knee to the Lord, swear allegiance to him alone, and believe this good news: the Lamb was slaughtered for you. He *alone* made the ultimate sacrifice. His blood covers a multitude of sins. Believe in him, follow the Lamb of God, and you will be saved from this wicked and perverse world." Indeed, if Moses and Elijah showed up today, they would prophesy against our idols when they preached the gospel. Since our world is filled with carefully crafted images, prophets who condemned our idolatry would be stoned to death because they dared to point out the obvious: we are a nation enslaved to the lust of our eyes.

I think I can hear their sermon now:

Stop watching your televisions. Stop watching your iPads. Stop watching your phones. Why do you spend all of your time looking at images that are fleeting—here one minute and gone the next? You waste hours, days, months, years because you always want to see more. And what do you see? You watch violence. You watch death. You watch sex. You watch hatred. You watch envy. You watch lust. All of it. You take it into your heart, into your soul, and you pretend like it doesn't affect you at all. You watch reality shows and you're quick to judge others. You watch pornography and it ruins your marriage. You watch your favorite sports team lose and it sours your mood. You watch slasher films and you can't sleep at night. You watch violent deaths and it numbs you to injustice. You watch political talk shows and you hate your enemies. It's time to look away. It's time to stop taking in all the madness. It's time to make a covenant with your eyes. Take a visual fast. No more idols, no more images, no more slavery to worldly masters. Just because they show it, doesn't mean you must see it. The next time you see the warning, "The following video may offend some viewers," don't take the bait. Shield your eyes. Look away. Don't give in to the lust of your eyes. Don't be suckered by marketers *always* trying to sell you something. Let the carnival barkers keep barking. You've got better things to see, better things to do. Let your eyes feast on what is noble, what is good, what is lovely, what is pure. Look on what God has made! Take a walk in the park. Feast on the trees, the flowers, the waters, the green grass. Consider the birds of the sky, the dogs sniffing for clues, the ducks on the pond. Look at the people—men and women are the true images of God! Take in their beauty, the miracle of their friendship, the restorative power of their good conversation. See the real world. The real world that God has made! O taste and *see* that the Lord is good, and throw away your idols. They are the bane of human existence, the death of human flourishing. Turn off your phones, tune into God, and drop out of the world's idolatry. For Christ's sake, turn off, tune in, and drop out. Then you will truly live.

Indeed, if a prophet showed up and started preaching a message like that, we would see the water we're all swimming in.

11

FOLLOW THE LAMB

Incarnating the Word

THE NUCLEAR-ARMS RACE between the United States and the Soviets during the Cold War forced us all to face the reality that the world might come to an end at any moment. Watching on television the devastating effects of a nuclear bomb while listening to experts talk about the number of nukes each country had in its possession ("We have the nuclear capability to destroy the world ten times over") brought home the sober reality that for the first time in human history we had the power to completely destroy ourselves and the entire world. All of a sudden, visions of total destruction in the Apocalypse seemed more real, more credible. A spate of films was quickly churned out by Hollywood, all following the same script: survivors of a nuclear holocaust try to stay alive in a postapocalyptic world. Convinced it could happen to them, doomsday preppers built private bomb shelters, stocking underground shelves with weapons, ammunition, and enough food to last for years. Schools added surprise drills to prepare students for a nuclear attack (as a boy growing up in Southern California in the 1960s, I remember huddling in the hallways with my classmates, all of us facing the wall, kneeling, heads bowed, hands clasped behind our heads, supposedly protecting the back of our necks, and thinking to myself, *This is going to keep us safe from Soviet bombs?*). Some towns buried time capsules, stocked with items from their world, hoping to preserve the past for future generations. Alarmed by the prospect of a nuclear holocaust,

television preachers claimed biblical prophecy was coming true. Dispen-
sationalists wrote bestselling books about the late, great planet Earth,
and the horrors of being "left behind." No matter where you looked or
what you heard during the fifties, sixties, and seventies, it was evident
that many of us had one thing on our minds: the end of the world is near.

That idea—the imminent apocalyptic end of all things—was foreign
to most people of the first-century Greco-Roman world. Jews and Christians were the only people who believed the world would come to an end
on the last day. Everyone else viewed time on earth as an endless cycle
of seasons, a never-ending wheel of life that would keep turning on earth.
Because they were in power, the Romans believed the gods had destined
them to rule the world forever, that the wheel of history would always
turn in their favor. Due to the success of his imperial rule, Caesar Augustus was hailed as the founder of a new world order, sent to establish
peace and justice on earth through law and order. As he was born on the
autumnal equinox, Caesar's birthday marked the beginning of a new
age—a proconsul in Asia Minor even changed the calendar to begin the
new year on September 23. Steven Friesen writes, "The birth of Augustus
could be reckoned as the beginning of time. Thus, in his own lifetime he
was becoming a mythic figure for the provinces."[1] Because he was worshiped as a god, the imperial cult promoted the myth that Augustus set
in perpetuity the glorious divine rule of the Romans over all the earth.
The last thing they could imagine, therefore, was that the world would
come to an end one day. The gods had established Rome as the eternal
city—"a city that will go up in flames and be laid desolate rather than live
up to its name," as David deSilva puts it.[2] Indeed, according to the
Apocalypse of John, Rome will fall prey to its own deception, instigated
by the one who is known by many names: the dragon, the serpent, the
devil, Satan, the one "who deceives the whole world" (Rev 12:9).

---

[1]See Steven Friesen, *Imperial Cults and the Apocalypse of John: Reading Revelation in the Ruins*
(Oxford: Oxford University Press, 2001), 123-24.
[2]David A. deSilva, *Seeing Things John's Way: The Rhetoric of the Book of Revelation* (Louisville, KY:
Westminster John Knox, 2009), 108.

THE GRAND DECEPTION

There was a time when Satan had the power to enter heaven and accuse believers of not truly fearing God (Job 1:9). That was his job; that is his name. The Hebrew word *satan* means "accuser." But Satan eventually lost his divinely endowed power, kicked out of heaven along with his minions. It happened when Jesus Christ came to earth, casting out demons by the Spirit of God, "binding the strong one" as proof that the reign of God had come to earth (Mt 12:28-29). That Satan was losing his grip was further evident when Jesus sent seventy disciples out "as lambs in the midst of wolves" (Lk 10:3). Not only did Jesus choose twelve disciples to reconstitute Israel, restoring the twelve tribes, but according to Luke's Gospel, he also sent seventy disciples (or seventy-two) ahead of his arrival to "every city and place" to warn them that "the kingdom of God has come near to you" (Lk 10:1, 9).[3] The numbers seventy and seventy-two are significant. According to Genesis 10, God divided the world into seventy nations (seventy-two according to the LXX and 3 Enoch 17.6, 8; 30.2), and set an angelic power (called "princes," Dan 10:13, 20) over each nation ("When the Most High divided the nations, as he divided the sons of Adam, he established boundaries for the nations according to the number of the angels of God," Deut 32:8 LXX). Michael was assigned by God to guard Israel (Dan 12:1; 1 Enoch 20.2). In Jewish apocalyptic literature, Satan (a.k.a. Belial, Azazel, Mastema, etc.) was the angelic power that taught humans how to make weapons, incited them to war, and led malevolent powers to wage war against Michael and God's people (1 Enoch 8.1-2; 1QM 15-19).[4]

Perhaps that's why Luke is keen on telling the story of Jesus sending seventy(-two) disciples to "every city and place." Here is the beginning of the good news of God's kingdom coming to all nations—a gospel

---

[3]The manuscript evidence about the number of disciples (seventy or seventy-two) is "almost evenly divided." See Bruce M. Metzger, *A Textual Commentary on the Greek New Testament* (Stuttgart: United Bible Societies, 1971), 150.
[4]See David E. Aune, *Revelation 1-5*, Word Biblical Commentary (Dallas: Word Books, 1997), 2:691-95.

invasion of the whole earth.[5] Indeed, when these seventy(-two) disciples preached the gospel, the demons lost their power (Lk 10:17). Christ saw a heavenly sign confirming the same: "I was watching Satan fall from heaven like lightning" (Lk 10:18). According to Paul, Christ fully "disarmed" the malevolent powers when he was crucified, making a "public display of them," having triumphed over them by canceling the debt against humanity (Col 2:13-15). Not only that, Christ suckered the malevolent powers into thinking they had defeated him when he gave himself up. The "rulers of this age" were ignorant of the mystery of the preexistent Wisdom of God, that evil would be defeated by the sacrifice of Jesus Christ (1 Cor 2:6-9). John emphasizes the same: "The Son of God appeared for this purpose: that he would destroy the works of the devil" (1 Jn 3:8). Through his life and death, Jesus stripped Satan of his power over us, evidenced when the accuser was kicked out of heaven.

That's what John saw when he witnessed the war against the dragon— a behind-the-scenes peek at what happened when Christ defeated Satan (Rev 12:1-10). Although we could quibble over the identity of the heavenly mother (whether Israel, the church, or Mary), it's quite obvious that the birth and ascension of her child is the story of Christmas and Easter rolled into one (Rev 12:1-5). Having recognized a significant threat (the child is destined "to shepherd all nations with an iron rod," Rev 12:5), the dragon incites an angelic rebellion: "He sweeps a third of the stars of heaven and threw them to earth" (Rev 12:4), to marshal forces against the vulnerable woman and child. But the child is whisked away to God's throne in heaven (Rev 12:5), while the woman finds refuge in the wilderness (Rev 12:6), eventually escaping the threat of treacherous waters that "the serpent spewed from his mouth at her" (Rev 12:15)—echoing Israel's exodus from Egypt. After the child ascends to God's throne (the Messiah reigns!) and the woman finds divine sanctuary on earth, a war breaks out in heaven. Since Michael and his forces overcome the dragon and his minions, kicking them out of heaven and exiling them to earth

---

[5]Joel B. Green, *The Gospel of Luke*, New International Commentary on the New Testament (Grand Rapids, MI: Eerdmans, 1997), 410-12.

(Rev 12:7-9), punctuated by the acclamation ("Now the salvation and the power of the kingdom of our God and the authority of his Christ have happened *because the accuser of our brothers has been thrown down*," Rev 12:10), it's easy to see the message of the vision: Christ stripped Satan of his power in heaven. No longer able to accuse believers before God ("they conquered him because of the blood of Christ and because of the word of their witness—to the extent that they didn't love their life even to death," Rev 12:11), Satan is imprisoned on earth, venting his wrath until the day of judgment, "knowing that he has only a little time" (Rev 12:12). Since he couldn't take out the woman and child, the dragon takes out his frustration on "the rest of her children, those who keep the commandments of God and hold to the testimony of Jesus" (Rev 12:17). The war on earth against believers is Satan's last-ditch effort to destroy the works of God.

Unsurprisingly, the dragon/Satan relies on deception to wage war against the saints. Rather than attack his enemies directly—one wonders what that would look like (Job?)—Satan gets others to do his dirty work. Like a general surveying the battlefield, the dragon launches an invasion by raising two beasts: one from water, the other from land (Rev 13:1-3, 11). Idolatry is their method; it's the way they find recruits on earth to "make war with the saints and overcome them" (Rev 13:7). The sea beast imitates a Christ miracle (resurrection) to get the masses to worship the dragon (Rev 13:3-4). When they boast about the beast and his sovereignty ("Who is like the beast, and who is able to wage war against him?" Rev 13:4), they sound like Israel praising God (Ex 15:11). The sea beast, however, blasphemes God, and everyone loves him for it—everyone except the Lamb's slaves, whose names are registered in his book (of property? Rev 13:6-8). If that weren't enough to convince the masses of idolatrous worship, the land beast imitates an Elijah miracle (fire from heaven) that compels the crowds to make an idol of the sea beast and worship it as well (Rev 13:13-15). Their allegiance is complete when the land beast convinces the masses to become slaves of the sea beast, his numerical, blasphemous name tattooed on their forehead or right hand (Rev 13:16-18). The beast owns them—so much so that they can't make a living without him. Those who refuse to worship the sea beast, on the other hand, are killed (Rev 13:15). Idolatry is a matter of life and death.

It is compelling to me that it takes deception to get people to worship false gods. The only way the dragon can get people to worship him is to imitate the works of the one true God. The sea beast overcoming a fatal blow to the head is a cheap imitation of the death and resurrection of the Lamb (Rev 13:3, 12, 14). A living, breathing, talking "image of the sea beast" is a counterfeit incarnation of God (Rev 13:15). The land beast "had two horns like a lamb" and talks like the dragon (Rev 13:11); the Lamb is the very Word of God (Rev 19:13). Slaves of the Lamb have his name written on their foreheads (Rev 9:4; 14:1); slaves of the sea beast have his numerical name on their foreheads and hands (Rev 13:17). Worshipers from every tribe, people, language, and nation were purchased by the blood of the Lamb (Rev 5:9). Having authority over every tribe, people, language, and nation, the sea beast kills the saints who don't worship his image (Rev 13:7, 15). Indeed, the dragon has to go to great lengths to trick people into worshiping him, having to hide the truth about him. Even he knows that, if we know the truth about idols, we won't be tempted to worship any god but the one true God. Given that people are drawn to worship deity when they see it, false worship can't happen without deception. According to the Apocalypse, the only way you can recognize false worship is when you are worshiping the one true God.

That's one of the major claims of the Revelation of John: we can only see the world for what it truly is when we are gathered to worship the Creator and the Lamb.[6] Since the Apocalypse was supposed to be read and heard when Christians gathered for worship on the Lord's day, it is telling that this vision, filled with idol imagery and false worship, was part of their worship experience. You would think a description of such blasphemous things would be banned from their meetings, that getting Christians to envision idols and false worship would be counter-productive. It is a bit odd, isn't it? Gathered for worship to focus your

---

[6]Some of the material in the remainder of this chapter I first shared on my blog at http://agenuinefaith .blogspot.com.

attention on the one true God, all of a sudden—as a part of your worship experience—you're picturing your neighbors worshiping the wrong god. It's one thing to see with your mind's eye Michael kick the dragon out of heaven, no longer able to accuse us because of the "blood of the Lamb." (Imagine the cheers coming from the crowd.) But encouraging these Christians to imagine idolatrous worship, perhaps even stirring up memories of their religious past as idol worshipers, seems out of place to us. Idolatry should be the last thing on your mind when you're worshiping God. But first-century worshipers couldn't afford to ignore the obvious. They lived in a world filled with idols.[7] In their day, you couldn't open your eyes without seeing one—not to mention the fact that idolatry was embedded in every facet of life: politics, economics, and religion. Shutting your eyes and refusing to think about idolatry wasn't an option. Instead, according to John's vision, what Christians needed to do was open their eyes to the lies, the deceit, the pretense of false worship— especially the worship of Caesar. They could only see the truth when they worshiped God.[8] The Revelation of John was a call to "first-commandment faithfulness," as Charles Talbert puts it.[9] Richard Bauckham writes, "Those who bear witness to the one true God, the only true absolute, to whom all political power is subject, expose Rome's idolatrous self-deification for what it is."[10]

That's what happens when we worship God: we not only see the truth about God but also recognize the pretense of self-deification—those competing for the honor due exclusively to God. During worship services, we often say our God is worthy of worship, which makes me think about who or what is *not* worthy of worship. Government is not worthy

---

[7]deSilva writes, "In effect, he causes them to inhabit the world of everyday experience and the world of the Scriptures simultaneously, knowing that this will lead them both to see and respond to the world in ways that John considers faithful to the Christian tradition" (*Seeing Things John's Way*, 311-12).

[8]Richard Bauckham writes, "These elemental forms of perception of God not only require expression in worship: they cannot be truly experienced except as worship." See Bauckham, *The Theology of the Book of Revelation* (Cambridge: Cambridge University Press, 1993), 33.

[9]Charles H. Talbert, *The Apocalypse: A Reading of the Revelation of John* (Louisville, KY: Westminster John Knox, 1994), 11.

[10]Bauckham, *Theology of the Book*, 39.

of worship. Wall Street is not worthy of worship. The military is not worthy of worship. Nature is not worthy of worship. Education is not worthy of worship. Lawyers are not worthy. Preachers are not worthy. Physicians are not worthy. Politicians are not worthy. Entrepreneurs are not worthy. Entertainers are not worthy. No one or no thing is worthy of worship but God. You would think, therefore, that we would be especially vigilant to protect God's honor, refusing to allow idolatry to creep into our worship services. Since all glory is supposed to go to God, we would be reticent to give glory to any person as part of our worshiping God. Yet, it happens all the time. We applaud musical performances. We create church celebrities through video. We pledge allegiance to governments. We sing songs about our native land. We exalt politicians when they visit our worship services. We praise soldiers for their military service. No one questions the legitimacy of these practices. It all happens automatically, as if it were a natural part of our worshiping God. Our adoration is impulsive, worshiping God one minute while venerating our heroes the next. Indeed, it's not much of a stretch to praise those we idolize even while we're praising God. And we thought idolatry was only a first-century problem.

This particular year, the Fourth of July fell on a Sunday. The auditorium was decked out in stars and stripes. An American flag was draped over the cross. The choir called us to worship with a hearty rendition of "God Bless America." Then we sang several patriotic songs: "O Beautiful for Spacious Skies," "You're a Grand Old Flag," and the "Battle Hymn of the Republic." The pastor stepped forward to lead us in the Pledge of Allegiance and offered a prayer for the leaders of our nation. Next, the music director invited the congregation to join in a medley of service anthems, asking members of the Army, Navy, Air Force, and Marines to stand while we all sang their fight songs:

> First to fight for the right and to build the nation's might . . .
> Roll out the TNT, anchors aweigh.
> Sail on to victory and sink their bones to Davy Jones, hooray . . .
> Off we go into the wild blue yonder, climbing high into the sun;

Here they come zooming to meet our thunder,

At 'em boys, give 'er the gun . . .

From the halls of Montezuma to the shores of Tripoli,

We fight our country's battles, in the air, on land and sea. . . .

With the words "roll out the TNT" and "give 'er the gun" still ringing in my ears, the choir sang "Statue of Liberty" while patriotic and religious images were projected on screens behind the choir. At one point, a picture of an American soldier appeared on the left screen while an image of the crucified Christ was projected on the right as the choir sang, "As the statue liberates the citizen, so the cross liberates the soul." Troubled by the vision and audition, I looked around to see whether anyone else was offended. The congregation was glowing with adoration, taking in the spectacle with pride and wonder. I kept thinking about the mixed message, unable to get out of my mind the images of a man who kills his enemies juxtaposed next to the man who died for his enemies. Throughout the sermon, while the preacher effortlessly blended freedom in Christ with the religious liberty protected by our nation, I imagined what a God-and-country worship service would look like in the first-century world.

That particular year, the autumnal equinox fell on a Sunday. Christians in Ephesus are gathered in the hall of Tyrannus for their special worship service.[11] The walls of the lecture hall are covered with murals depicting momentous events in the life of the Ephesians: citizens welcoming the victorious Mark Antony, the erection of the temple to Augustus, the birth of Artemis, scenes from the games held in Domitian's honor. In the corners, Roman standards decorate the hall—a Roman eagle perched on top of the flag at the front. A bust of Caesar stands in the pediment over the entrance, welcoming congregants as they gather for worship. As the service begins, a dignitary recites the inscription etched on the temple to Augustus, extolling his generous benefaction of the city. A chorus

---

[11]For an excellent description of life in Ephesus, see Paul Trebilco, *The Early Christians in Ephesus from Paul to Ignatius* (Grand Rapids, MI: Eerdmans, 2004), 11-52.

leads the congregants in singing selections from the Psalter, mixing in well-known anthems sung during the festival of Artemis—hymns of gratitude for the fertility of the land, the protection of their city, and the prosperity of their harbor.

After a few ex-soldiers are encouraged to stand and recite the sacramentum—their pledge of allegiance to the empire—the preacher offers a midrash on Isaiah 45:1, comparing Caesar to Cyrus, quoting lines from Paul's letter to the Romans: "Let every person submit to the governing authorities. For there is no authority unless it is given by God" (Rom 13:1). As he points to the bust of Caesar and the Roman standards, blending the *pax Romana* and the *pax Christi*, the staccato rhythm of his cadence accentuates Paul's words: "He who resists authority opposes the decrees of God. . . . It is a minister of God. . . . It does not bear the sword for nothing. . . . This is why you pay taxes, for the rulers are ministers of God. . . . So render to them what is due to them: taxes, customs, fear, honor" (Rom 13:2-7). After the homily, a patron invites everyone to his villa to celebrate the love feast as members embrace one another, passing the peace of Christ.

This is how easily idolatry sneaks into our worship of God.

What does God do when people worship false gods? He eventually lets them have the gods of their choosing. This is not the way he wants it. In fact, it makes him angry that people could be so dumb. But this is the lesson humanity needs to learn over and over again: the false gods we trust *will always* let us down. Yet, ironically, when things go terribly wrong—like bowls of wrath poured out on all creation—idolaters end up blaming *God* for the impotence of their gods (Rev 16:9). Strange, isn't it? We get mad at God when the idols we worship fail us. I've seen it happen too many times. We worship wealth, corporate greed cripples the economy, employees lose their jobs, and we get mad at God. We worship government, politicians lead us to war, innocent children are slaughtered, and we get mad at God. We worship luxury, industry pollutes the air and water, people get sick and die, and we get mad at God. One wonders how long God lets us pursue these false gods, holding back the deleterious effects of our ruinous idolatry until he decides to make us live with the results of our foolishness. Yes, this is God's doing; but we asked for it. He pours his wrath on all creation to unmask the pretense of self-deification (Rev 16:1-21), forcing us to look into the mirror of our idolatrous ways, knowing that we'll blame him for the mess. It's not like he hasn't tried to get our attention before it all hits the apocalyptic fan. God has been very patient, sending his servants into battle to restore his creation, hoping we'll take our eyes off our idols to see the true image of God incarnated in those who follow the Lamb, the only one who can lead us out of worldly bondage.[12]

The Song of Moses and the Lamb

When captive Israel watched the Lord plague Egypt ten times, they knew they were witnessing the battle of the gods: Yahweh versus the Egyptian pantheon (Ex 7:14–10:29). Like a sniper, the God of Israel picked off the various gods of Egypt—one by one—beginning with Osiris (the god of the Nile) and ending with Ra (the sun god). Pharaoh wasn't impressed when Moses turned the Nile into blood since the Egyptian magicians were able to do the same (Ex 7:20-23). But as God worked his way up the ladder of Egyptian deities, from the god of frogs to the lord of the flies, Pharaoh began to get the message. The God of Israel is stronger than all the gods of Egypt. You would think, therefore, that when God blotted out the sun for three days—killing Ra, the head of the Egyptian pantheon—it would have convinced Pharaoh to give up the fight and give in to Moses. But it took the tenth plague to convince the Egyptian king to "let my people go" (Ex 12:29-36)—the only plague Israel was required to partic-ipate in. For nine plagues Israel was a spectator. But for the last plague, the children of Israel had to get their hands dirty, smearing blood of the paschal lamb on their doorposts so that the death angel would "pass over" their homes and kill only the firstborn sons of the Egyptians, including Pharaoh. After the plagues, Israel escaped Egyptian slavery, having

---

[12]James L. Resseguie, *The Revelation of John: A Narrative Commentary* (Grand Rapids, MI: Baker Academic, 2009), 197.

crossed the Red Sea, singing songs of God's salvation as they began their exodus to the Promised Land—a generation that would die in the desert.

In the Apocalypse, the exodus of God's faithful slaves looks very different (Rev 14:1–16:21). This time, the plagues come *after* the exodus (Rev 15:2). God's people have already left the land of idols when he battles the false gods of the world, blighting the earth with seven bowls of wrath reminiscent of the plagues of Egypt (bloody rivers, frogs, skin disease). This time, the slaves of God participate in the *third* plague when *their* blood is poured into the rivers, forcing idolaters to drink the "blood of saints and prophets" (Rev 16:4-6). This time, God's people stand victorious *on* a "sea of glass mixed with *fire*," as they sing "the song of Moses the slave of God and the song of the Lamb" (Rev 15:2-3). This time, the people of the exodus are not guilty of immorality and idolatry (1 Cor 10:5-10) but are chaste, truthful, and blameless (Rev 14:4-5). This time, God's slaves die because they keep "the commandments of God and the faithfulness of Jesus"; they are the sacrificial "first fruits to God and the Lamb" (Rev 14:4, 12-13). This time, instead of a cloud by day and a pillar of fire by night, these slaves "follow the Lamb wherever he goes" (Rev 14:4).[13] Since the Lamb of God has overcome the world through his sacrifice, those who follow the Lamb will die—a paschal sacrifice that reveals the redemptive judgment of God. For just as the dragon marshaled forces to destroy the work of God by deception through idolatry (Rev 13:1-18), the Lamb gathers his army on Mount Zion to overcome the world by offering themselves as first fruits of the last harvest (Rev 14:1-20). That is the difference between false and true worship: the mark of the beast means survival for idolaters (Rev 13:16-17). The mark of the Lamb seals the slaves of God for sacrifice (Rev 14:1-4). Yet, both will reveal the judgment of God.

Even though the Lamb sends his army to wage war with the dragon's slaves, we never get to see the battle. Instead, what we get are brief vignettes picturing different stages of the war from a bird's-eye view. First, an angel

---

[13]Resseguie, *Revelation of John*, 196.

hovering over the scene announces the beginning of the campaign with a gospel message that essentially says: "It's time. Fear God. Worship the Creator" (Rev 14:6-7). Another angel declares Babylon is already doomed because the evil city is drunk with the wine of immorality (Rev 14:8)—later revealed as the blood of the slaves of the Lamb and other abominations (Rev 16:6; 17:4, 6). The third angel warns idolaters that they will be forced to drink the cup of God's wrath to the dregs, tormented in eternal fire (Rev 14:9-11). Then a heavenly voice rallies the Lamb's troops with written words (on a banner?): "Blessed are the dead who die in the Lord from now on!"—the Spirit adding that these soldiers will rest in peace because they were faithful to death (Rev 14:13).

Then comes the finale: a harvest of grain and grapes that looks like both redemption and judgment (Rev 14:14-19). Since a Christ figure ("like a son of man with a golden crown," Rev 14:14) harvests the grain, many interpret the first reaping as redemptive—the death of the righteous—while the vintage is punitive since the grapes are thrown into the "great winepress of God's wrath" (Rev 14:19).[14] However, in light of the negative imagery of a *sharp* sickle and prophets picturing threshing as judgment (Mt 3:12), some scholars think both the grain and grape harvest represent God's righteous judgment of the ungodly, echoing Joel 3:13 (4:13 Masoretic Text), "Put in the sickle, for the harvest is ripe. Come, tread, for the wine press is full; the vats overflow, for their wickedness is great" (NASB).[15] Since it is far past the time for the grain harvest (early May)—"the harvest of the earth has dried up [*exēranthē*]" (Rev 14:15)—when "ripe [*ēkmasan*]" grapes (Rev 14:18) are being harvested (early September), both harvests carry a negative connotation. The grain is dried up; the grapes of wrath are crushed.

To parse the vision in strictly binary terms—it must be either negative or positive—is to miss the irony of the beatitude, "Blessed are the dead

---

[14]Although the text never mentions what is reaped, a grain harvest is inferred from the line "the harvest of the earth has become dry" (Rev 14:15), referring to the stalks and husks.

[15]Aune, *Revelation*, 2:799-803; G. K. Beale, *The Book of Revelation*, New International Greek Testament Commentary (Grand Rapids, MI: Eerdmans, 1999), 770-76.

who die in the Lord from now on!" (Rev 14:13). Those who "die in the Lord" are the slaves who "follow the Lamb wherever he goes"—even to a cursed death. They are the "first fruits . . . who had been purchased from the earth" (Rev 14:3-4). Indeed, just as the Lamb has overcome his enemies via his sacrifice, his followers do the same. Consequently, their sacrificial deaths, as they are overcome by their enemies, will bring about both divine deliverance (symbolized by Christ's harvest and vintage) and divine judgment (symbolized by the plagues of seven bowls of God's wrath).[16] Besides, the vintage isn't a purely negative symbol, for the grape vine was a common image for not only Israel (Is 5:1-7; Ps 80:8-9) but also the Johannine community (Jn 15:1-6). Therefore, it shouldn't surprise us that the symbol of the harvest of grain and grapes embodies both positive and negative imagery mingled together—especially if the vision re-presents the Eucharist. By imitating Christ's death, the sacrifice of the faithful mimics the memorial meal of bread (grain) and wine (grapes).[17] This is why, having overcome the enemies of God by their faithful witness, the victors sing the song of Moses and the Lamb in heaven (Mt 26:30), and why the seven plagues re-create the liberation of Israel from Egyptian slavery. Both are deliberate echoes of Passover, when the righteous are delivered and the wicked are judged. Once the elements are served to the nations, the wicked drink judgment on themselves—something Paul warns the Corinthians about (1 Cor 11:27-31).

Notice how the blood of the righteous is given to the inhabitants of the earth to drink as the judgment of God (Rev 16:4-7), and ironically how they are described as worthy to drink the blood because they produced it. Likewise, the kings of the earth are made to drink of the wine of Babylon's immorality (Rev 17:2). Therefore, like the drunken kings, the

---

[16]G. B. Caird, *A Commentary on the Revelation of St. John the Divine* (New York: Harper & Row, 1966), 191-95; J. P. M. Sweet, *Revelation* (Philadelphia: Westminster, 1979), 229-33; N. T. Wright, *Revelation for Everyone* (Louisville, KY: Westminster John Knox, 2011), 132-35.

[17]The crushing of the grapes in the winepress of God's wrath happens "outside the city," echoing the crucifixion of Christ: "Therefore also Jesus, in order that he might sanctify the people through his own blood, suffered outside the city gate. Then let us go to him outside the camp, bearing his disgrace, for we do not have here a city that remains but we seek the city to come" (Heb 13:12-14).

queen/whore of Babylon is destined for destruction because she is also "drunk with the blood of the saints, and with the blood of the witnesses of Jesus," as she is paraded to her doom, holding her golden chalice of abominations (Rev 17:4-6). This is also why the wrath of God is finished with the pouring of the seven bowls on the earth: the eucharistic sacrifice of the faithful followers of the Lamb is evidence that God has finally answered the martyr's question, "How long, holy and true Lord, until you judge and avenge our blood on those who dwell on the earth?" (Rev 6:10). Earlier God told them, "when the number of their fellow servants and their brethren who were to be killed . . . [has] been completed" (Rev 6:11). Now it appears his promise has come true, when the bloody wine flows for two hundred miles, "up to the horses' bridles"—more than enough for the enemies of God to drink themselves to death.

That's what we tend to forget when we witness the violent deaths of Christians. One day, God will judge the wicked for murdering his people. It makes him angry when faithful believers endure such terrible injustices. That's why John can't picture redemption without envisioning scenes of the just punishment of God. Indeed, according to the Revelation of John, God's wrath will not be satisfied until the world he created is purged of all evil (Rev 15:1). That purging only happens because the blood of Christ is spilled—first his, then the blood of his martyrs. This is how God determined to restore his creation, through sacrifice. Loren Johns writes, "The Lamb is, in fact, the revelation of *how* God works in history. . . . Jesus' own suffering-reigning-resisting victory turns out to be *a way of being in the world*—a model for believers."[18]

That's something the Coptic Christians know full well. After several were publicly martyred in Libya, and many were killed and wounded when Islamic terrorists bombed several churches in Egypt in 2017, one of their bishops said, "Martyrdom is linked to the Christian life. To carry your cross and follow him. Since we are united to Christ, in this life we

[18]Loren L. Johns, *The Lamb Christology of the Apocalypse of John: An Investigation into Its Origins and Rhetorical Force* (Eugene, OR: Wipf & Stock, 2014), 163, 172, emphasis original.

are his image. As he forgave, so must we."[19] This is what Christians do because that's what Christ did. Since we follow Christ, like Christ, our faithful witness will challenge the ways of the world. Like Christ, the world will kill us for it. Like Christ, we will forgive them. And, as he did for Christ, God will raise us from the dead, and the wicked will be punished for what they have done. This is the way it has been. This is the way it is. This is the way it will always be because the work of Christ is eternal. It's why the Lamb is worthy to receive power, riches, wisdom, might, honor, glory, and blessing (Rev 5:12). His singular sacrifice effected the eternal work of God. The world crucified him, but he has overcome the world through his sacrifice. That's why Christians will *always* live in defiance of the ways of the world. The death of Christ exposes the counterfeit ways of the devil—his temporary power, empty riches, false wisdom, fleeting might, contrived honor, vainglory, and fake blessing. The slain-but-still-standing Lamb of God, on the other hand, is the incarnation of *true* power, riches, wisdom, might, honor, glory, and blessing. Those who follow the Lamb know the difference.

WHY THE DEVIL IS NOT WORTHY

Power. The devil grabs all the power he can get. The Lamb gave up his power. The devil uses his power to enslave the world. The Lamb empowers his slaves to be liberated from the world. Because he tried to save it, the devil will lose his power in the end. Because he lost it all, the Lamb receives power forever and ever. The next time you see someone trying to grab all the power they can get, manipulating people to their advantage, know that one day they will lose it all—just like the devil. For only those who lose their life like Christ will find it in the end: "I know your works. See! I have put before you an open door that no one can shut because you have a little power and you kept my word and did not deny my name" (Rev 3:8).

[19]Jayson Casper, "Forgiveness: Muslims Moved as Coptic Christians Do the Unimaginable," *Christianity Today*, April 20, 2017, www.christianitytoday.com/news/2017/april/forgiveness-muslims-moved-coptic-christians-egypt-isis.html.

Riches. The devil offers the riches of the world. The Lamb makes us rich through his sacrifice. The devil tempts us with idols of gold. The Lamb builds a city where we walk on streets of gold. The devil entices us to live for what we see. The Lamb inspires us to give our lives for what we hear. The next time you think about wasting your life on things that don't last, invest in the kingdom that lasts forever. Only those who lay up for themselves treasures in heaven, walking by faith and not by sight, will enjoy the good life: "I know your tribulation and your poverty (but you are rich). . . . Do not fear what you are about to suffer. See! The devil is about to throw some of you into prison to be tested, and you will be persecuted for ten days. Be faithful until death, and I will give you the crown of life" (Rev 2:9-10).

Wisdom. To the world, only a fool would die to save his enemies. To those of us who are being saved, the folly of the cross is the wisdom of God. According to conventional wisdom, you have to lose a little in order to gain more of what you want. According to the gospel, we lose it all because we see loss by cross as gain.[20] Many see rewards in this life as the only things worth living for. We see rewards in the next life as the only thing worth dying for. The next time you hear of a missionary willing to give up her American citizenship in order to live in a hostile land, remember what Jim Elliot said, "[She] is no fool who gives what [she] cannot keep to gain what [she] cannot lose." For Satan still tries to rule the earth by killing his enemies. But Jesus reigns on earth because his slaves are willing to die to love their enemies: "I know where you live, where Satan's throne is, and you hold tightly to my name and you did not deny my faith even when Antipas, my witness, was killed among you where Satan lives. . . . To the victorious one, I will give to her the hidden manna" (Rev 2:13, 17).

Might. A dragon standing on the seashore, acting like he rules the world, calling beasts from the sea and land to wage war against the righteous, appears ominous. But a slain Lamb standing in heaven, worshiped

---

[20]See Rodney Reeves, *Spirituality According to Paul: Imitating the Apostle of Christ* (Downers Grove, IL: IVP Academic, 2011), 27-31.

because he's worthy to effect the will of God on earth, having purchased a kingdom of priests who reign on earth through his sacrifice, is irrepressible. The finite masses cower in fear of the dragon who can take their life. The numberless multitude fears only God because the Lamb can make the dead live again. To spend the strength of your days for the things of this world and then die in vain is such a waste. To give our life for the Lamb who overcomes the world so that we might live in the kingdom forever is true strength. The dragon loses; the Lamb wins. No amount of evil in the world will change that. The devil's days are numbered. Our days, however, are eternal because, one day, the Lamb will raise us from the dead: "Hold on tight to what you have until I come. And the one who overcomes and keeps on doing my work until the end, to him I will give authority over the nations and he will shepherd them with the strength of an iron rod" (Rev 2:25-27).

Honor. The dragon and his beasts are cheap imitations of the real thing. They have to fool people into believing they are something special. They put on a big show. They love the spotlight. They're desperate for attention, always talking about themselves. They're loud braggarts, always clamoring for the approval of the masses. They use religious language to mask their evil ways. They demand unwavering loyalty of their blind followers. They act like they're gods so that the duped masses will boast about their superhuman abilities. They claim they're the only ones to make the world a better place so that their mindless devotees will place all their hope in them. When it comes to the dragon and his beasts, it's pay to play. Those who refuse to pay suffer the consequences, becoming targets of derision and scorn. But that's what followers of the Lamb expect. No surprise. Those who honor God are shamed by the world: "I know your deeds, your hard work and persistence, that you don't put up with evil men, and you examine those who claim to be emissaries of God (but they are not), for you found them to be liars" (Rev 2:2).

Glory. Creation reflects the glory of God because all things were created by him. That's why all creatures give glory to God when they worship him. He's worthy of their adoration because he created them.

The dragon has made nothing. Evil cannot create anything. That's why he's not worthy of worship. What does he do to steal the glory of God? He relies on false prophets to convince the people to worship what is created (idol) instead of the Creator (God). Since God's glory is embedded in everything he's created, the dragon is able to sucker fools into worshiping what is seen: the glory of gold, the glory of sunsets, the glory of good food, the glory of fine wine, the glory of children, the glory of ancestry, the glory of cities, the glory of lakes, the glory of music, the glory of sculpture, the glory of man, the glory of woman. We are mesmerized by glory, and we'll do anything to get it. That's how the devil so easily deceives people to worship *anything* but the unseen God. We are dazzled by all that glitters. But the Lamb would have us live for something more—to *be* like him, the glorious image of God: "I advise you to buy from me gold that is refined by fire so that you might become rich, and white clothes so that you be dressed and not be naked and ashamed, and eye drops to wash your eyes so that you might see clearly" (Rev 3:18).

Blessing. This is the acclamation that always confused me. The other six make sense: the Lamb is worthy to receive power because he gave it away; he's worthy to receive riches because he became poor; he's worthy to receive wisdom because he was crucified as a fool, and so on. But when did the Lamb lose the blessing of his heavenly Father? Some might think the death of Christ reveals the loss of divine blessing. God said twice, "This is my beloved Son! I'm very pleased with him"—once at his baptism, the other time during the transfiguration. Shouldn't God have said the same thing when his Son was crucified?[21] Should we take the silence of heaven as the only time the Lamb lost favor with God? But that doesn't make sense. Christ obeyed the Father, offering his life for the sins of the whole world. That certainly pleased God. Besides, don't we speak of Christ's sacrifice as God's blessing, his gift? So, if the Lamb that was slain is the blessing of God, what blessing could we offer? Our lives? That can't be right. We don't bless him with our lives. He blessed us with his. He bought us with

---

[21]See Rodney Reeves, *Matthew*, Story of God Bible Commentary (Grand Rapids, MI: Zondervan, 2017), 343, 546.

his blood. We are his slaves, nothing more—unworthy slaves who have been redeemed from a messed-up, broken world. What blessing do we have to give the one who is the very incarnation of God's blessing?

It helps to know the word translated "blessing" (*eulogia*) means "good word." *Eulogia* can be used to refer to a gift, a thing that is given. But it is also the word that is used for "praise," that is, to speak well of someone. That makes more sense to me, especially since the Lamb never says a word in the Revelation of John. He is silent, never claiming anything for himself with words. Instead, his actions speak for him: "Worthy is the Lamb *who was slain*." That's why all creation is compelled to speak well of him. The Lamb is worthy of our praise—good words—because he stood silent like a lamb before his shearers, and now we can't help but fill the silence with good words about him. That must drive the dragon crazy, because he never says a word in the Apocalypse either. He may trick idolaters into worshiping him, but their words of praise are for the beast—what they can see: "Who is like the beast, and who is able to wage war with him?" (Rev 13:4). How desperate he must be to hear words of praise about him. But no one says, "Worthy is the dragon." He's never done anything for us—another reason why idolatrous worship looks so foolish. Why worship a dead idol that can do nothing for you? False gods can only take what you give. Why worship the devil, who can't create anything? All he can do is muck up what God has made. It's no wonder no one praises the devil. He has no temple. He has no book of life. Earth is his prison. Hell is his destiny. His nameless slaves are nothing more than dead men walking toward destruction: "I know your deeds, that you have a name that you are alive but you are dead. Wake up and strengthen the things that remain that are about to die. . . . He who is victorious will be dressed in white clothes, and I will not erase his name from the book of life" (Rev 3:1-2, 5).

> "See! I'm coming like a thief. Blessed is the one who stays awake and keeps his garments ready so that he doesn't walk around naked and everyone sees his shame." And they gathered them together at the place that is called "Har Magedon" in Hebrew. And the seventh angel poured his bowl

in the air, and a loud voice came out of the temple from the throne saying, "It's done." (Rev 16:15-17)

The end of the world is near. No time capsule, no safety drill, no bomb shelter will save you from the Apocalypse. Only the Lamb's slaves—those whose names are written in his book of life—are going to make it.

12

HEAVEN ON EARTH

Abiding in the Word

CHRISTIANS ARE NOT THE ONLY ONES to claim the end of the world is coming. Astronomers predict the sun will burn out in about five billion years, making the earth uninhabitable in one billion years—the sun becoming so hot it will dry up all the oceans on earth. Novelists envision a postapocalyptic world, convinced that we will nearly destroy ourselves with nuclear weapons, leaving a scorched earth for a handful of stragglers trying to survive the holocaust. A few recent films attribute the coming apocalypse to a comet crashing into earth, compelling characters to embrace their fate by seeking a friend for the end of the world. The one thing all of these apocalyptic scenarios have in common is that, in the end, the earth will be uninhabitable for humans. It's no wonder that a mission to colonize Mars is on the minds of entrepreneurs and astrophysicists. For, even though the sun will get so hot it will burn up the earth in a billion years, that could put Mars in the "goldilocks zone"— not too hot, not too cold—the perfect distance from the sun for life to thrive on the red planet like it once did on earth.

According to John's Revelation, the only way the earth will be inhabitable for humans after the apocalypse is if God renews it. To be sure, like scientists, novelists, and filmmakers, John sees the earth being destroyed in the end—a rather unsettling image since this is our home. But unlike modern flights of fancy or dreamy acts of nihilistic fatalism, John claims the only way we're going to get out of the mess we've made is if God saves us. We're going to need a Savior from above, the man on the white horse, to defeat the destructive forces of evil below to make room for the full reign of God on earth. That's one of the main themes of the Apocalypse. According to Richard Bauckham, "Babylon must fall so that the New Jerusalem may replace her. Her satanic parody of the ideal of the city must give way to the divine reality."[1] The earth is the Lord's; it's supposed to be a hospitable place of grace. He made it; he must take it back—every inch of it. That's why the strong man's house must be sacked (Mt 12:29), the slumlord thrown in jail (Rev 20:1-3). John sees the rightful owner coming back to his old neighborhood to clean up the place, giving squatters a tongue-lashing with words that kill like a knife (Rev 19:11-21).

THE QUEEN IS DEAD

During the Revelation, John saw the end of the world several times: both the faithful rewarded (Rev 7:13-17; 11:15-18; 15:2-4; 20:4-6; 21:9–22:5) and the wicked punished (Rev 6:12-17; 16:17-21; 18:2-3, 21; 19:19-21; 20:14-15). The rhetorical effect on John's hearers gathered for worship, hearing the same thing over and over again, would have inspired a certain clarity about the future.[2] It may have looked like Rome was running the place, conducting business at will and at the pleasure of their gods, but deeply embedded in their rule was their own ruin. Those who live by the sword will die by the sword (Rev 13:10). Rome may have claimed to be the eternal city on earth, like a queen boasting that her royal line will never die (Rev 18:7), but anyone with ears to hear the Revelation of John knew that her days were numbered. Babylon would be destroyed. The ironic twist of her demise comes when the queen, who beds all the kings of the earth (Rev 17:2) and brags, "I am not a widow, I will never see mourning" (Rev 18:7), is stripped naked and devoured by her lovers (Rev 17:9-10, 16).

---

[1]Richard Bauckham, *The Theology of the Book of Revelation* (Cambridge: Cambridge University Press, 1993), 130.

[2]Charles H. Talbert, *The Apocalypse: A Reading of the Revelation of John* (Louisville, KY: Westminster John Knox, 1994), 8.

The end of Babylon comes with two big surprises: how it happens (Rev 17:1-18) and how quickly it happens (Rev 18:1-24). Since the Apocalypse tells the story of how sin city will one day be replaced by the holy city— knowing that we've reached the climax of the prophecy—one would expect God to take a more active role in defeating his nemesis.[3] After all, Babylon and Rome were the two cities that destroyed his temple (586 BC and AD 70), so "Babylon" is a nickname for Rome. If God's righteous anger has been burning for centuries against Babylon and decades against Rome, shouldn't we expect him to roll up his sleeves and get his hands dirty (Is 59:16-20), annihilating the wicked city that destroyed his temple and murdered his people? To be sure, Christ eventually appears on a white horse, charging down from heaven to war against the kings of the earth arrayed for battle (Rev 19:11-21). But that's after Babylon has already fallen. And it didn't take a heavenly invasion of angelic forces to destroy the city. That's what we might expect, especially after seeing the plagues of seals, trumpets, and bowls unleashed on the earth by divine design. Instead, a coup d'état brings down mighty Babylon. Powers once loyal to the wicked queen end up betraying her when they assassinate her (echoes of Julius Caesar?). One moment they're carrying her on their shoulders to a banquet celebrating her dominion; the next minute we see her courtiers devouring her like she's the main course (Rev 17:3-16). God never has to lift a finger to destroy Babylon. He simply gives his enemies the idea, and the queen's lovers turn on her (Rev 17:17). In the end, the treachery em- bedded in evil ensures its demise. Evil will be undone by evil. Regardless of what the emperor claimed, Rome, the eternal city, would never last.

Steven Friesen claims, "Revelation does not envision a gradual trans- formation of this world into the kingdom of God."[4] This is not a story about how the world gets better every day. The Apocalypse isn't a pro- gressive work. There are no benchmarks of improvement, no evidence

[3]Richard Bauckham, *The Climax of Prophecy: Studies on the Book of Revelation* (Edinburgh: T&T Clark, 1993), 5-7.

[4]Steven Friesen, *Imperial Cults and the Apocalypse of John: Reading Revelation in the Ruins* (Oxford: Oxford University Press, 2001), 182.

that good is slowly overcoming evil. Instead, the end comes quickly, and everyone is amazed—from the greatest to the smallest. No one saw this coming. How could they? The queen was so strong, so beautiful, so vibrant (Rev 18:10, 16, 19). Everyone wanted her; everyone needed her. But then she was gone. At her funeral, mourners marvel over how quickly things fell apart, repeating their woes three times: "In one hour your judgment came. . . . In one hour such great wealth turned into a wasteland. . . . In one hour she became a wasteland" (Rev 18:10, 17, 19). But they're not just mourning for her. They have suffered loss because of her death. Having lost their power, kings fear they will suffer the same fate (Rev 18:9-10). Having lost their buyer, merchants weep over the end of their business (Rev 18:11-17). Having lost their investor, ship owners and sailors throw dust on their heads, lamenting their imminent bankruptcy (Rev 18:17-19). For them, her death is the end of the world, the omen of their own demise. Like parasites clinging to their host, the death of one means the end of many. Since this Roman queen promised to reign forever, her sudden death takes everyone by surprise—everyone except those who have ears to hear the Revelation of John.

What a difference a day makes (Rev 18:8). One minute you're ruling the world; the next minute you're being carried to your grave. For those of us who follow the Lamb who was slain, this comes as no surprise. In one day, Jesus went from celebrating Passover to hanging on a cross. But, unlike his twelve disciples, that day didn't take him by surprise. He saw it coming and tried to prepare his disciples for his sudden departure—not only telling them in advance what would happen to him but also what would happen to them (Jn 13:1–16:33). They too would be hated by the world (Jn 15:18). They too would suffer persecution (Jn 15:20). They too would be killed by those convinced that they were doing the work of God (Jn 16:2). They too would follow him to God's house (Jn 14:1-3). Since he told them in advance, he hoped that they would find peace in a world filled with trouble because "I have overcome the world" (Jn 16:33). It's surprising, therefore, to see God's people in the funeral procession mourning the destruction of Babylon, especially since the wicked city had become "the home of demons and a prison of every unclean spirit" (Rev 18:2). Living there must have been a living hell for the faithful. But they still joined the procession of mourners lamenting their losses, as if the end of her immorality were a reason to grieve (Rev 18:3). Rather than rejoicing, God's people act like they are suffering distress too, until a voice cries out from heaven: "Come out of her, my people!" (Rev 18:4). It's as if God looks down from heaven at the funeral procession and shouts to his people: "Get out of line! Why are you grieving? You should be celebrating —everyone in heaven is rejoicing. Why aren't you?" (Rev 18:20).

That's a good question. Why wouldn't God's people celebrate the destruction of Babylon? He did this for them (Rev 18:20). Why would they grieve the loss of the harlot queen who got drunk on the blood of the saints (Rev 17:6)? Did they "participate in her sins" (Rev 18:4)? Like the waters on which she sat, did they keep her afloat (Rev 17:1, 15)? Since there's a high probability that some of the merchants and sailors were Christians who also benefited from her royal enterprise, did they join their comrades in the funeral march? Had they already justified the injustices and idolatry of imperial economics to the point that grieving the end of their economic prosperity seemed natural to them?[5] In other words, did God's people have to be told to stop grieving the destruction of Babylon because they had enjoyed their life in Babylon? What about us? If our Babylon were thrown in the sea like a millstone—sinking so quickly into oblivion—would some Christians mourn the loss? Heaven expects us to celebrate the end of the world because that means the city of God is coming. But are we too comfortable living in Babylon to no longer yearn for the city of God? Is that why the earliest prayer of the church, *Maranatha*, is no longer on the lips of American Christians? Have we convinced ourselves that Jesus was wrong, that we *can* serve God and Mammon? Do we really believe it's necessary for the city of man to be taken out of the way so that the city of God may come? Being so

---

[5]See the discussion "Merchants in Bed with a Whore," in J. Nelson Kraybill, *Apocalypse and Allegiance: Worship, Politics, and Devotion in the Book of Revelation* (Grand Rapids, MI: Brazos, 2010), 144-45.

comfortable here, are we more inclined to pray, "Lord, we know you're coming one day. But you don't need to come right away. We've got plans. Weddings. New businesses. Children. Careers. Graduate school. Dream homes. Retirement." Do we really want the strong angel to throw Babylon in the sea? Because when that happens,

> The sound of harpists and musicians and flutists and trumpeters will not be heard among you anymore; and no craftsman of any craft will be found among you anymore; and the sound of the mill will not be heard among you anymore; and the light of the lamp will not shine among you anymore; and the voice of the groom and bride will not be heard among you anymore; because your merchants were the great men on earth, and all the nations were deceived by your magic. (Rev 18:22-23)

Of course, the reason God expects us to celebrate the end of Babylon is that, while taking in the ruins, we would remember the victims of injustice—that all worldly gains come at a cost: "For the blood of the prophets and saints was discovered in her, as well as all who had been slaughtered [like lambs] on the earth" (Rev 18:24).[6] That's why the first word of the "Hallelujah" song is *salvation* (Rev 19:1). The primary reason God judged Babylon, bringing an end to her ruinous reign, was to save the victims of her injustice (Rev 18:2). Friesen writes,

> In John's system, then, there was no legitimate place for earthly empire. His religious criticism was specifically aimed at Roman imperialism, but the character of the critique had broader implications. John was not just anti-Roman; he was anti-empire. The violence required to establish hegemony is not the prerogative of humans; Rome's use of military force was a blasphemous usurpation of God's right and ability to judge justly. The economic inequities of empire were the result of corporate and personal immorality; they merited the condemnation of God. So in John's text, imperial cults are not an aberration; they are the fitting manifestation of imperialism. They take us to the heart of the confrontation over who is king of kings.[7]

---

[6]The same word, translated "slaughtered"—even the same form, perfect participle (*esphagmenon*)—is used for the "slain" Lamb (Rev 5:6).

[7]Friesen, *Imperial Cults*, 208-9.

That's the reality the Revelation is trying to get us to envision: whether we are ready to admit that Jesus is the King of kings, reigning over *every* empire—even our own.

It's hard for citizens of the United States to imagine America as modern-day Babylon. We're more likely to cast Russia, Iran, or China in that role. After all, in all three countries Christians are persecuted for their faith, just like the Apocalypse. We often thank God during worship services that we have the freedom to worship God in our country—and rightly so. Christians are not killed in America for our faith; the whore of Babylon's chalice won't be filled with the blood of faithful Christians living in the United States. But, when we remember that Roman rule extended way beyond Italy, that the blood of faithful Christians filling the harlot's cup came from innocent victims who lived in "foreign" cities such as Smyrna and Philadelphia, having suffered the violence of imperial power—well, that's when the promise of God's judgment against the harlot can be unsettling to American Christians. When American jets dropped bombs on the Iraqi people during the Gulf War, did we even consider the fact that Christians—our brothers and sisters—would die as a result of our aggression? When economic sanctions were imposed on Iraq in our effort to depose Saddam Hussein, and malnutrition sky-rocketed, leading to the deaths of thousands of children, did we even think twice about the hundreds of children of our brothers and sisters who starved to death due to American national interests? When they buried their dead, did they wonder why God didn't save them from American cruelty? When they lamented the starvation of their children, did they pray to God to avenge their deaths? When they read the Apoca-lypse, did they find hope in the promise that one day God would judge the harlot for killing faithful Christians over their economic need for oil— that shippers of oil tankers would one day mourn the end of America? Did they wonder why Christians in America stood back and watched the horror of their hell on earth without protest? And, most disturbingly, when Iraqi Christians read the part about those mourning the end of the whore and the voice from heaven having to cry out, "Come out of her, my people," did they have any doubts that God would scold American Christians for grieving the end of their life of luxury? Indeed, when I try to read the Apocalypse with Iraqi eyes, it's easy to identify the whore of Babylon. Ironically, it's not where ancient Babylon used to be: Iraq.

During the Covid-19 pandemic, it felt like the plagues of Revelation were coming true right before our eyes. The virus spread so quickly, killing the most vulnerable among us. At first, we talked optimistically about flattening the curve while complaining about the loss of sporting events. But then we saw how shortages of masks and protective equipment jeopardized the welfare of health care workers. Panic set in as we watched hospitals overrun with patients, temporary morgues set up in parking lots, and thousands of burial plots quickly dug out for the dead. Trapped in our homes during the quarantine, we all wondered, *When will it be over?* Businesses shut down, employees were furloughed, and panic spread through Wall Street. On the verge of economic collapse, the US government tried to keep families and businesses afloat with stimulus checks. The Trump administration downplayed the threat; many joined in the chorus, claiming it was a hoax—a political ploy—to exaggerate the danger during an election year. Experts, on the other hand, predicted it would only get worse. The experts were right. Things got much worse. Despite dire predictions, some people disregarded the warnings not to join large gatherings. Numbers of infected people soared. Fatalities in the United States exceeded wartime statistics. A new vaccine looked promising. But new strains of the virus made us wonder whether we were fighting a losing battle. Through it all, some of us couldn't help but ask, "Are we watching the end of Babylon?" I noticed how public personalities used apocalyptic language in an apparent attempt to sway the noncompliant to wear masks. Then the Capitol was stormed by insurrectionists, our democracy teetered on the edge of destruction, and we all wondered, *What is happening to us?* It seemed like the end of the world.

During the darkest days of the pandemic, as we grieved the loss of our American way of life, lamenting that our best days might be over, I wondered what it would feel like to hear a heavenly voice cry out, "Come out of her, my people!" How hard would it be to join the hallelujah chorus in heaven, convinced that God was finally bringing his righteous judgment against our nation, the whore of Babylon? Deprived of first-world comforts, many were upset over having to wear masks and observe social distancing. Can you imagine Christians in the United States refusing to lament our losses, singing praises to the Lamb instead because we long for the city of God to come to earth? In the middle of such heart-rending loss, should we expect believers to praise God for bringing about the end of the world?

Yet, according to John's Revelation, that's exactly what God expects: while all hell is breaking loose on earth, we see the faithful singing hallelujahs in heaven. It's because they know that, before heaven comes to earth, the earth must be purified of evil. It's only after the bride has remained pure during the betrothal that the groom comes to carry her away to the home of his Father. The end is finally here. And it will be glorious: heaven on earth.

BEAUTY AND THE FEAST

Like a bride who has dreamed of her wedding day ever since she was a little girl, or an architect who has taken the ideas of a married couple and drawn up plans for their dream home, John has a vision of what heaven will look like on earth: a jeweled bride and a crystal city (Rev 21:9–22:5). With the harlot out of the way—no more temptation—invitations are sent out announcing the imminent marriage of the Lamb and his bride. A heavenly voice gives two reasons why it's time: (1) because God reigns and (2) because "his bride has prepared herself, and her wedding dress—bright and clean— was given to her, for her wedding dress is the righteous deeds of the saints" (Rev 19:6-8). That idea—that the bride has kept herself pure during the betrothal, symbolized by white garments—not only echoes throughout the Apocalypse (Rev 3:4-5; 6:11; 7:9, 13-14; 14:4) but also contrasts with those who have "soiled their garments" and fornicated with the harlot, symbolized by drinking the "wine of her immorality" (Rev 3:4; 14:8; 17:2, 4; 18:3, 9).[8] Sex

---

[8]David E. Aune, *Revelation 1–5*, Word Biblical Commentary (Dallas: Word Books, 1997), 3:1029.

and wine go together like money and prostitution—murals on the walls of bathhouses commonly depicted the same scenes of drunken debauchery and sexual immorality. But this woman has kept herself pure for her husband; dressed in righteousness, the bride is ready for the wedding. So, according to traditional wedding practices, the second invitation is sent (Rev 19:9) because the food is ready (Mt 22:4) and the groom is about to arrive with his entourage.[9] But the feast John sees being prepared is like no other wedding banquet (Rev 19:17-21). The way the groom and his entourage come to collect his bride looks more like a military invasion than a peaceful community celebration (Rev 19:11-16).[10]

When the groom appears on a white horse, ready to take his bride to his father's house, it's a bit of a jolt to hear that he comes ready for war (Rev 19:11). At first, it looks like this might be a rescue mission: the groom charges down with an army from heaven to steal his bride away from his enemies on earth. But after his enemies are defeated, and the wedding feast is made ready (vultures dining on the flesh of kings!), there is no sight of the bride. It's as if the wedding has been put on hold, that the man on the white horse has other matters to attend to before he marries. The vision of combat quickly morphs into a trial scene (Rev 19:11–20:15), and then the wedding is resumed (Rev 21:2-9). Even though this brief interlude—war and trial—interrupts the wedding, we're not surprised by it. Yes, Babylon has fallen. But the enemies of God—the powers behind the queen's throne—are still standing, arrayed for battle, ready to fight to the bitter end. We know this day is coming. Lasting peace will come to earth only when the Word of God defeats evil and suffering once and for all: on the battlefield and in the courtroom. Then there will be time for a wedding.

---

[9]See Kenneth E. Bailey's description of the typical Middle Eastern wedding in *Jesus Through Middle Eastern Eyes: Cultural Studies in the Gospels* (Downers Grove, IL: IVP Academic, 2008), 271-73.
[10]See the brief description of wedding details in David W. Chapman, "Marriage and Family in Second Temple Judaism," in *Marriage and Family in the Biblical World*, ed. Ken M. Campbell (Downers Grove, IL: InterVarsity Press, 2003), 206. First, the bride prepares herself by bathing, wearing perfume, and putting on her wedding dress; second, she is carried to the groom's house while her friends and family sing and dance; third, the groom and his entourage come to receive her in his house; and fourth, the wedding festival, including blessings and feasting, lasts for a week.

The Revelation has been building to this moment: the last battle between God and Satan, Christ and the beasts, good and evil. It's been called
"the great day of their [God and the Lamb's] wrath," "the war of the great
day of God Almighty," and "Har-Magedon," when the last trumpet sounds
and "the kingdom of this world has become the kingdom of our Lord and
his Christ" (Rev 6:17; 11:15; 16:14, 16). When the beast and the kings of the
earth marshal forces to do battle against Christ and his army from heaven
(Rev 19:19), we expect to see a bloodbath—the war to end all wars. We
anticipate, like a scene from Lord of the Rings, long battle scenes, mon-
sters warring against the righteous, the forces of darkness using every evil
ploy to try to overcome the army of light. But that's not what happens.
When Christ shows up, he simply seizes the beasts and throws them in
the lake of fire (Rev 19:20). That's it. No fight. No war. Then Christ slays
the kings with the sword of his mouth (Rev 19:21). There's no lengthy
battle. No protracted campaign. The entire "battle" lasts two verses. The
Word of God simply defeats his enemies with the power of his tongue. A
line from Martin Luther's hymn captures it well: "One little word shall fell
him."[11] For some people, then, the great battle popularly called Arma-
geddon is a letdown in the Apocalypse. Christ needs nothing more than
his word to destroy evil forces that tried to battle him on earth. But what
about the dragon? The accuser kicked out of heaven, the evil one who
empowered the beasts, the troublemaker on earth—evidently, he wasn't
foolish enough to stand with his stoolies and fight against Christ on earth.
Where can he go? What can he do? How will Satan meet his end?

At first, it looks like a trial will bring divine judgment against Satan. An
angel binds him in chains and throws him in prison, "the abyss," for a
thousand years, after which he is released (Rev 20:1-3). That used to bother
me—that Satan would be released after doing time for his crime. Even
though a thousand years is a long time, it didn't seem long enough to my
American-justice ears. For all the evil Satan has done, I would expect God
to lock up Satan for much longer, even forever. That's why it didn't make

[11]Martin Luther, "A Mighty Fortress is Our God," c. 1529.

sense to me that Satan was released "for a short time." Why? Wouldn't God know that a thousand years wouldn't be enough to rehabilitate him? That's one of the reasons we incarcerate criminals in America; we hope they will be rehabilitated. But right after Satan gets out of prison, he gathers an army to attack the city of God (Rev 20:7-9). No surprise. Satan has become evil to the core. Why would God let him out of prison?

Unlike the American judicial system, prison wasn't considered a legal form of punishment for the Romans.[12] Instead, prisons were used to incarcerate the accused until it was time for the trial. There were different kinds of incarceration, depending on the status of the defendant and the crime. High-status defendants and those accused of less serious crimes would be placed under house arrest, where rented quarters were used to detain the accused, sometimes chained to a guard or a soldier. Low-status defendants and those accused of a capital offense (crimes against Rome) were thrown into harsh prison conditions, called the *carcer*. Once the magistrate was ready to hear the case, the prisoner was released from jail and brought to trial. Criminals convicted of serious offenses would be punished (depending on the status of the defendant) by execution or exile. That may explain why Satan is released from jail. It is time for his trial. The judges are assembled (Rev 20:4). The books are opened (Rev 20:12). It's judgment day.

If the Roman judicial system provides the background for Revelation 20, then why isn't there a trial for Satan? A crucial part of a Roman trial was receiving testimony from character witnesses. In fact, some think that's what determined the outcome of the trial, even more than the evaluation of evidence.[13] If a high-status defendant could deliver dozens of character witnesses, then the judge was more likely to rule in his favor. Perhaps that's why Satan travels to the ends of the earth (Rev 20:7-8): to gather witnesses for his trial. By Satan's deception, though, the mob turns

---

[12]For further discussion, see Rodney R. Reeves, "To Be or Not to Be? That Is Not the Question: Paul's Choice in Philippians 1:22," *Perspectives in Religious Studies* 19 (1992): 275-81.

[13]See Ramsay MacMullen, *Corruption and the Decline of Rome* (New Haven, CT: Yale University Press, 1988), 60-88.

into an army ready for war: the last coup d'état. They lay siege to the city
of God, surrounding the saints with an endless army—as many as the
sand of the seashore (Satan's pseudo-Israel, Rev 20:8). Of course, it appears as though Satan has deceived himself as well. Did he really expect
to starve them out? That was the purpose of laying siege to a city; the army
would surround their captives so that no water or food could come into
the city. Weakened by hunger and thirst, the people wouldn't put up much
of a fight in the end. But the story doesn't get that far, for as soon as Satan's
army surrounds the city, fire falls from heaven and destroys them (Rev
20:9). Then Satan is thrown into the lake of fire, the eternal punishment
for his crimes (Rev 20:10). Like a war without a battle (Rev 19:19-21), here
we see a verdict without a trial. The last rebellion has made the trial moot.
Satan's army of witnesses already testified to his true character: the de-
ceiver deceives to the very end, leaving nothing to be decided but the just
punishment of God—not only for Satan and the beasts, but for everyone
whose name is not written in the Lamb's book of life (Rev 20:11-15).

HERE COMES THE BRIDE

With all of the enemies of God defeated and the dead judged unworthy
to attend (see Mt 22:11-13), the wedding can resume. But when the bride
appears, it's a city that "comes down out of heaven from God," the new
Jerusalem (Rev 21:2)—the converse of the prostitute Babylon. When the
Bride's presence is announced, a voice from heaven introduces her as the
"tabernacle [skēnē] of God," the way God will dwell (skēnōsei) among
humanity (Rev 21:3). The same language shows up in John 1:14: "And the
Word became flesh and dwelt [eskēnōsen] among us." Just as the heavenly
Word of God tabernacled on earth, the bride of Christ will be the tabernacle of God when heaven comes to earth. This bride/new Jerusalem/
tabernacle of God will be the complete opposite of the whore/Babylon/
prison of demons—seen clearly in the list of what is "no longer." After
Babylon is judged by God like a millstone thrown in the sea, there is "no
longer" music, craft, milling, light, or weddings in the wicked city (Rev
18:22-23). After the new Jerusalem descends from heaven to earth like a

bride ready to be wed to her husband, there is "no longer" tears, death, mourning, crying, or pain in the city of God (Rev 21:4). The "first things have passed away," so it's time for the last things. Thus, God says, "Look! I am making everything new" (Rev 21:5). He's the only one who can make everything new because he's "the Alpha and the Omega, the beginning and the end" (Rev 21:6). The one who spoke the first word, "Let there be light," will have the last word, "It is done"—spoken words that must be written down because they "are faithful and true" (Rev 21:5-6).

It is ironic that one of the angels who spilled the bowls of God's plagues on the earth introduces the bride of the Lamb to the seer (Rev 21:9), once again contrasting the two women: the whore of Babylon and the bride of Christ. The agent that brings about such destruction now helps the seer envision the beauty of heaven on earth. Once again, John hears one thing, "Here comes the bride," and sees something else, "the holy city, Jerusalem" (Rev 21:9-10). By now we're used to the abrupt transition from audition to vision, able to make sense of how a Lion can be a slaughtered Lamb (Rev 5:5-6) or how the bride of the Lamb can be a holy city. Like a jeweled bride dressed in a dazzling, white wedding gown, the faithful followers of the Lamb process from heaven as a perfectly dimensioned, brilliantly shiny, heavenly city planted on earth (Rev 21:10-11). All of the gems and precious metals worn by the whore (gold, precious stones, and pearls, Rev 17:4) are refashioned into the material used to construct the city of God: pearly gates, walls adorned with "every kind of precious stone," and streets of gold (Rev 21:19-21). While the whore of Babylon tried to camouflage her ugly life with the glory of earthly jewelry, the bride of the Lamb *embodies* the heavenly glory of God (Rev 21:11). The whore wore what is beautiful; the bride embodies beauty. As the bridal city, the church doesn't wear pearls; she is the pearl. She doesn't wear gems; she is a gem. She doesn't wear gold; she is golden. The city is a temple; Christ abides in her (Rev 21:22). The earth without the sun, God is her light (Rev 21:23).

It makes sense that the church is depicted in the Apocalypse as both a bride and a city, a people and a place. That's the way we talk about the church today. We describe our gathering as a fellowship, a people of

common purpose and identity. We also talk about "going to church" on
Sundays, a place where we gather for worship. Yet, most of us don't think
of the church as the bride of Christ or the city of God. For some of us, it's
difficult to identify with the hope of becoming Christ's bride—especially
if marriage was never a desirable goal. The motivation for being faithful
to Christ, seeing our reward as getting to wear a beautiful dress on our
wedding day, just doesn't inspire a lot of us (especially men). Besides,
weddings are overhyped these days. As we all know, it's the marriage that
really matters. Yet, despite some of our hang-ups about the bridal imagery that dominates John's vision of heaven on earth, I think it's even
more difficult for many of us to envision the church as the city of God,
regardless of what Augustine had to say.

Some of us can identify with the church as a bride keeping herself pure
for her wedding, envisioning our life in the resurrection as marital bliss.
But to picture the church as a walled city, especially for those of us who
enjoy living in rural environs—well, that doesn't seem appealing at all.
The big city is heaven on earth? Really? Give me the country life: fishing
in beautiful streams, hiking glorious mountain trails, traversing flowery
meadows, basking in sun-drenched beaches, hearing the surf crashing on
the sandy shore, taking in all of the color, the smells, the textures, the
beauty of creation. Now that sounds like heaven on earth! Even big-city
people know it, working hard all year to take a vacation in the country.
The idea of being crammed into a walled city (even one that is fifteen
hundred miles wide, deep, and high)—regardless of how well it's decked
out with jewels and precious metals—doesn't sound very appealing at first.
Then again, a city without fear, without crime, without violence, without
palaces, without a temple, where God lives with everyone, where the gates
are always open, where pearls and gems are not possessions but building
material, where streets are made of gold, where everyone drinks from the
fountain of youth and eats from the tree life for free, where the one who
created us and saved us abides with us, where the curse is no more (Rev
21:1–22:5)—where beauty is not only seen on the outside but experienced
on the inside—that might sound like heaven on earth to everyone.

Some might say, "It's nice to dream of heaven on earth. But, visions are nothing more than words," which is why, I think, the angel has to repeat the same claim several times to John: "These are the true words of God. . . . Write, for these words are faithful and true. . . . These words are faithful and true" (Rev 19:9; 21:5; 22:6). This vision doesn't rest on the fanciful hopes of men and women. These dreams are not born of wishful thinking. This vision of heaven on earth is built on the words of the One who said in the beginning, "Let there be light." And it was so. Therefore, just as we live in the world created by the Word of God, John expects his hearers to abide in the Word of God that enables us to envision the end of the world. It helps to know how it's all going to end, to understand where we're all headed, to see what lies ahead, to picture what heaven on earth looks like. One day, after he destroys all of his enemies, God will say, "It is done," and the great expanse between heaven and earth will collapse. Heaven will crash into earth. Earth will be raised to heaven's purpose. Faithful followers of the Lamb will be the tabernacle of God's presence. We will abide with Christ the Word forever. That is our destiny. That is our purpose, which is why the angel says, "Blessed is the one who *keeps* the words of the prophecy of this book" (Rev 22:7). We are not only meant to hear the words in order to see the vision; we are supposed to keep it. But what does that mean? What would it look like for the church to keep the vision, as if it were a commandment?

The Apocalypse is not only a revelation of the *end* of the world; it is a revelation of the *church* at the end of the world. God knew that, as we watched the world fall apart around us, we would need to see our place in a crumbling world. When the earth quakes at the weight of glory, when heaven shakes the earth to its core, when idols are destroyed and the kingdoms of men fall, when pandemics threaten humanity, when all creation is purified of evil and all that is left is what God has made, where will the church abide?

We will abide in words—God's words that tell us no matter how messed up the church can be on earth, we are still heavenly lampstands that shine the light of Christ. No matter how hellish it can get on earth, we are still a kingdom of priests who serve God. As the Lamb's slaves, we follow him to the end of the world. As God's numberless army, we keep marching into battle with the weapon of our sacrifice. Like John the seer, we can't help but tell the good news one more time to people who don't want to hear it. Like two heavenly witnesses, we can see how the world would celebrate our demise, convinced they would be better off without us. We know Satan can no longer accuse us. We know idolatry when we see it. We are the sacrificed first fruits. We are the bride of Christ. Therefore, we do not grieve the end of Babylon. We long for the city of God. For we believe one day God will have the last word. Christ will come. Evil will be destroyed. Heaven will come to earth. We will abide forever with the one we love more than our own lives because we abide in the Word of life. That's what believers do: we abide in the words of God because we abide in the Word of God, all the way to the end of the world.

Makes me want to hear every word of the Revelation of John, again and again.

CONCLUSION

The Last Word

WORDS ARE POWERFUL THINGS. Writers use them to create literary worlds. Politicians use them to promise future worlds. God used them to create the world. Since John believed our spirituality depended on abiding in words—words written, words read aloud, words heard—then the words ringing in the ears of the first Christians who gathered to hear John's Gospel, letters, and Revelation should help them imagine a world redeemed by the Word. Of course, they had heard from John's books that the Alpha who spoke the first word in the beginning, "Let there be light," was also the Omega who will have the last word in the end, "It is done." But I wonder whether the first words they heard from Christ, "What are you looking for?" (Jn 1:38) were a question that haunted them during the week as they tried to remain faithful to him, being encouraged by his last words, "Yes, I am coming quickly" (Rev 22:20). It's not difficult to abide in his words on the Lord's Day when we're gathered together to hear his word. But after we go our separate ways, that's when it gets hard—abiding in him alone.

That's one of the reasons why John wrote his Gospel: to help us see what it looks like to follow Jesus individually. I imagine a member of John's community, facing the challenge of being a faithful witness in a world filled with idols, deriving a lot of comfort and wisdom from the story of the man born blind. His enemies may accuse him of betraying the gods due to his blind devotion to Christ. But as far as he's concerned, they are the ones who can't see truth in the light of day. When they call him a fool for believing such nonsense, he can't help but repeat what he's heard: "I know one thing: once I was blind, but now I see" (Jn 9:25). Or, when a childless wife has to bury her husband, facing the grave circumstances of living alone in a hostile world, she hears the Lord say to her, "I am the resurrection and the life; the one who believes in me shall live even if he dies. . . . Do you believe this?" Remembering the story of Lazarus, she whispers Martha's confession at her husband's tomb, "Yes, Lord. I have believed that you are the Christ, the Son of God, the one who is coming to the world" (Jn 11:27). Then, when she gathers with the faithful on the Lord's Day to hear the brand-new book that some people are calling a "Revelation of John," and the reader gets to the part when Christ returns and raises the dead, she shouts, "Hallelujah!" That's when she realizes she's not alone. For she belongs to the community of faith, where the Spirit (*pneuma*) who helped John remember the words of Christ (Jn 14:26) and inspired these visions (Rev 2:7) also breathes life into the words she hears (1 Jn 2:27)—which makes perfect sense to the faithful. Without breath (*pneuma*), words are never spoken.

That's what it takes to abide in Christ: words from John, the anointing of the Spirit, and a community of faithful believers. Without John's words, we would never hear Christ—the Word who created all things and will resurrect all things—say, "I am coming quickly" or the Spirit say, "Come" or the ones who hear say, "Come" (Rev 22:17, 20). These are the words we hear. These are the words we confess. These are the words we incarnate. These are the words in which we abide. According to John, that means we are the last word of Christ until he comes again. That was true for the first believers who heard the words of John, and it will be true for the last believers to hear his Gospel, letters, and Revelation. Since we live in a cacophonous world of mixed messages and loudmouths, where theology is ignored and everyone extols the virtue of love, John's spirituality couldn't be more crucial than it is for us today. If there ever were a time for the church to be the word of God incarnate—for nonbelievers *and* believers to see the Word as well as hear the word—it is now. We need someone to teach us how to live what we say we believe, to abide in the Word, to be faithful to the end. We need to hear the words of Christ. We need one another to obey the new commandment. We need a vision of what it looks like to be faithful to the Lamb until the last word is spoken. We need the last prayer of the Bible, *Maranatha*. We need to listen to John.

If we have ears to hear the words of John, confessing what is true, incarnating the Word of God, abiding in Christ till he comes again, then the last verse of the Scriptures will abide in us as well: "The grace of our Lord Jesus be with you all." Amen.

Imagine that.

FOR FURTHER READING

Below are some resources that make scholarship on the Johannine literature more accessible to the church. Included are introductory works to John's theology and writings as well as a few commentaries written primarily for teachers and preachers.

INTRODUCTION TO THE JOHANNINE LITERATURE

Pate, C. Marvin. *The Writings of John: A Survey of the Gospel, Epistles, and Apocalypse.* Grand Rapids, MI: Zondervan, 2011.

Rainbow, Paul A. *Johannine Theology: The Gospel, the Epistles and the Apocalypse.* Downers Grove, IL: IVP Academic, 2014.

JOHN'S GOSPEL

Bauckham, Richard. *The Gospel of Glory: Major Themes in Johannine Theology.* Grand Rapids, MI: Baker Academic, 2015.

Burge, Gary M. *Interpreting the Gospel of John: A Practical Guide.* 2nd ed. Grand Rapids, MI: Baker Academic, 2013.

———. *John.* The NIV Application Commentary. Grand Rapids, MI: Zondervan Academic, 2000.

Card, Michael. *John: The Gospel of Wisdom.* Downers Grove, IL: InterVarsity Press, 2014.

Clark-Soles, Jamie. *Reading John for Dear Life: A Spiritual Walk with the Fourth Gospel.* Louisville, KY: Westminster John Knox Press, 2016.

Culpepper, R. Alan. *The Gospel and Letters of John.* Nashville: Abingdon Press, 1998.

Gorman, Michael J. *Abide and Go: Missional Theosis in the Gospel of John.* Eugene, OR: Cascade Books, 2018.

Koester, Craig. *The Word of Life: A Theology of John's Gospel.* Grand Rapids, MI: William B. Eerdmans Publishing, 2008.

Metzger, Paul Louis. *The Gospel of John: When Love Comes to Town.* Downers Grove, IL: InterVarsity Press, 2010.

Wright, N. T. *John for Everyone.* 2nd ed., parts 1 and 2. Louisville, KY: Westminster John Knox Press, 2004.

John's Letters

Burge, Gary M. *The Letters of John*. The NIV Application Commentary. Grand Rapids, MI: Zondervan Academic, 1996.

Campbell, Constantine R. *1, 2 & 3 John*. The Story of God Bible Commentary. Grand Rapids, MI: Zondervan, 2017.

Kruse, Colin G. *The Letters of John*. The Pillar New Testament Commentary. Grand Rapids, MI: William B. Eerdmans Publishing, 2000.

Thompson, Marianne Meye. *1-3 John*. The IVP New Testament Commentary Series. Downers Grove, IL: InterVarsity Press, 1992.

John's Revelation

Bauckham, Richard. *The Theology of the Book of Revelation*. New Testament Theology. Cambridge: Cambridge University Press, 1993.

Duvall, J. Scott. *The Heart of Revelation: Understanding the 10 Essential Themes of the Bible's Final Book*. 2nd ed. Nashville: B&H Academic, 2019.

———. *Revelation*. Teach the Text Commentary Series. Grand Rapids, MI: Baker Books, 2014.

Gorman, Michael J. *Reading Revelation Responsibly: Uncivil Worship and Witness—Following the Lamb into the New Creation*. Eugene, OR: Cascade Books, 2010.

Peterson, Eugene H. *Reversed Thunder: The Revelation of John and the Praying Imagination*. San Francisco: Harper Collins, 1991.

Resseguie, James L. *The Revelation of John: A Narrative Commentary*. Grand Rapids, MI: Baker Academic, 2009.

Talbert, Charles H. *The Apocalypse: A Reading of the Revelation of John*. Louisville, KY: Westminster John Knox Press, 1994.

SCRIPTURE INDEX

John
1–4, *27*
1:1, *2, 3*
1:2, *27*
1:3-4, *61*
1:5, *79, 148*
1:5-11, *26*
1:9, *61*
1:10-13, *61*
1:11, *107*
1:13, *28*
1:14, *3, 61, 88, 109, 125,*
    138, 168, 254
1:14-18, *61*
1:19-22, *14*
1:20, *14*
1:22-23, *15*
1:29, *14*
1:29-34, *15*
1:30-34, *14*
1:36, *14, 15*
1:37, *14*
1:38, *14, 259*
1:38-39, *13*
1:39, *6, 89*
1:40-42, *16*
1:41, *15, 16*
1:42, *16, 21*
1:43-51, *16*
1:45, *15*
2:4, *63*
2:7-8, *61*
2:11, *61*
2:13-22, *85*
2:18-20, *27*
2:19, *89*
2:22, *21, 82, 93*
2:23, *62*
2:23-25, *26*
3:1-2, *26*
3:1-15, *29*
3:2, *26*
3:3, *126*
3:3-13, *28*
3:7-8, *32*
3:8, *89*
3:9, *30*
3:10, *27*
3:12, *27*
3:14, *28, 54*
3:14-15, *29*
3:16, *80, 163*

3:19-21, *112*
3:29, *85*
4:4, *85*
4:7, *83*
4:8, *6*
4:10, *84*
4:13-14, *84*
4:14, *90*
4:15, *84*
4:18, *87*
4:19, *84*
4:20, *87*
4:21, *88*
4:21-24, *89*
4:22, *89*
4:23-24, *126*
4:25, *84, 90*
4:26, *90*
4:27, *82, 83*
4:28, *90*
4:29, *84, 89, 90*
4:30, *83*
4:31-33, *82, 83*
4:32, *83*
4:34, *83*
4:34-38, *83*
4:35, *83*
4:36, *83*
4:37, *84*
4:38, *83, 84*
4:39, *84, 90*
4:41, *90*
4:41-42, *84*
4:42, *89, 90, 93*
4:45, *62, 63*
4:46-47, *62*
4:47, *62*
4:48, *62, 63, 65*
4:49, *63*
4:50, *61, 64, 79*
4:51, *62*
4:52, *62, 64, 65*
4:53, *65*
5:1-18, *29*
5:8, *61*
5:16-18, *27*
5:24, *60*
6, *18, 132*
6:5, *18*
6:14-15, *63*
6:22-40, *63*
6:26-40, *81*

6:35, *72*
6:38, *81*
6:48, *127*
6:52, *29, 127*
6:53, *17*
6:60-66, *17*
6:63, *18, 60, 126, 127*
6:64, *127*
6:66, *17, 127*
6:66-69, *17*
6:67-69, *132*
6:68, *18, 26, 60*
6:69, *17*
7:1-32, *27*
7:26, *27*
7:31, *27*
7:37-39, *107*
7:41, *27*
7:41-42, *27*
7:50-52, *27, 29*
7:51, *29*
7:52, *27*
8:24, *81*
8:28, *54*
8:31-32, *60*
8:38, *60*
8:43, *60*
8:47, *60*
8:58, *80*
9:1-7, *59*
9:1-34, *29*
9:2, *59, 70, 71, 77*
9:3, *59, 73, 79*
9:4, *73*
9:4-7, *73*
9:5-6, *72*
9:6, *72*
9:7, *61, 72*
9:8, *71, 79*
9:11, *74*
9:13-15, *73*
9:16-17, *75*
9:16-18, *73*
9:17, *75*
9:19, *71, 73*
9:24, *73*
9:24-33, *74*
9:25, *74, 76, 260*
9:26, *71*
9:26-27, *73*
9:27, *74*
9:28, *74*

9:29, *73*
9:30, *74*
9:30-33, *75*
9:31, *74*
9:32, *74*
9:33, *74*
9:34, *74, 75*
9:35, *71, 75*
9:38, *79*
9:39-41, *73*
9:41, *114*
10:16, *21*
10:17-18, *151*
11:1, *15*
11:3, *38, 39, 99*
11:4, *38, 39, 44*
11:5, *99*
11:6, *38*
11:8, *38*
11:11, *38*
11:12, *38*
11:14, *38*
11:15, *38*
11:16, *38, 48, 49, 51,*
    53
11:20, *40*
11:21, *39, 40*
11:22, *40*
11:24, *40*
11:25, *39, 54, 72*
11:27, *41, 260*
11:32, *39*
11:33, *44*
11:35, *44*
11:36, *44, 99*
11:37, *44*
11:39, *38, 40, 42, 43*
11:41, *43*
11:43, *61*
11:49-50, *30*
11:53, *38*
11:55-57, *91*
12:1-2, *91*
12:3, *91*
12:3-7, *31*
12:5, *92*
12:7, *92*
12:8, *81, 92*
12:9, *91*
12:9-11, *39*
12:11, *91*
12:12-13, *92*

ALSO BY RODNEY REEVES

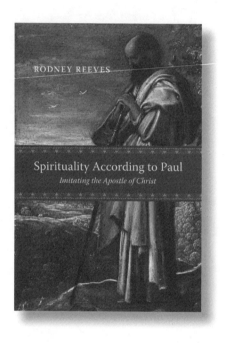

RODNEY REEVES

Spirituality According to Paul
Imitating the Apostle of Christ